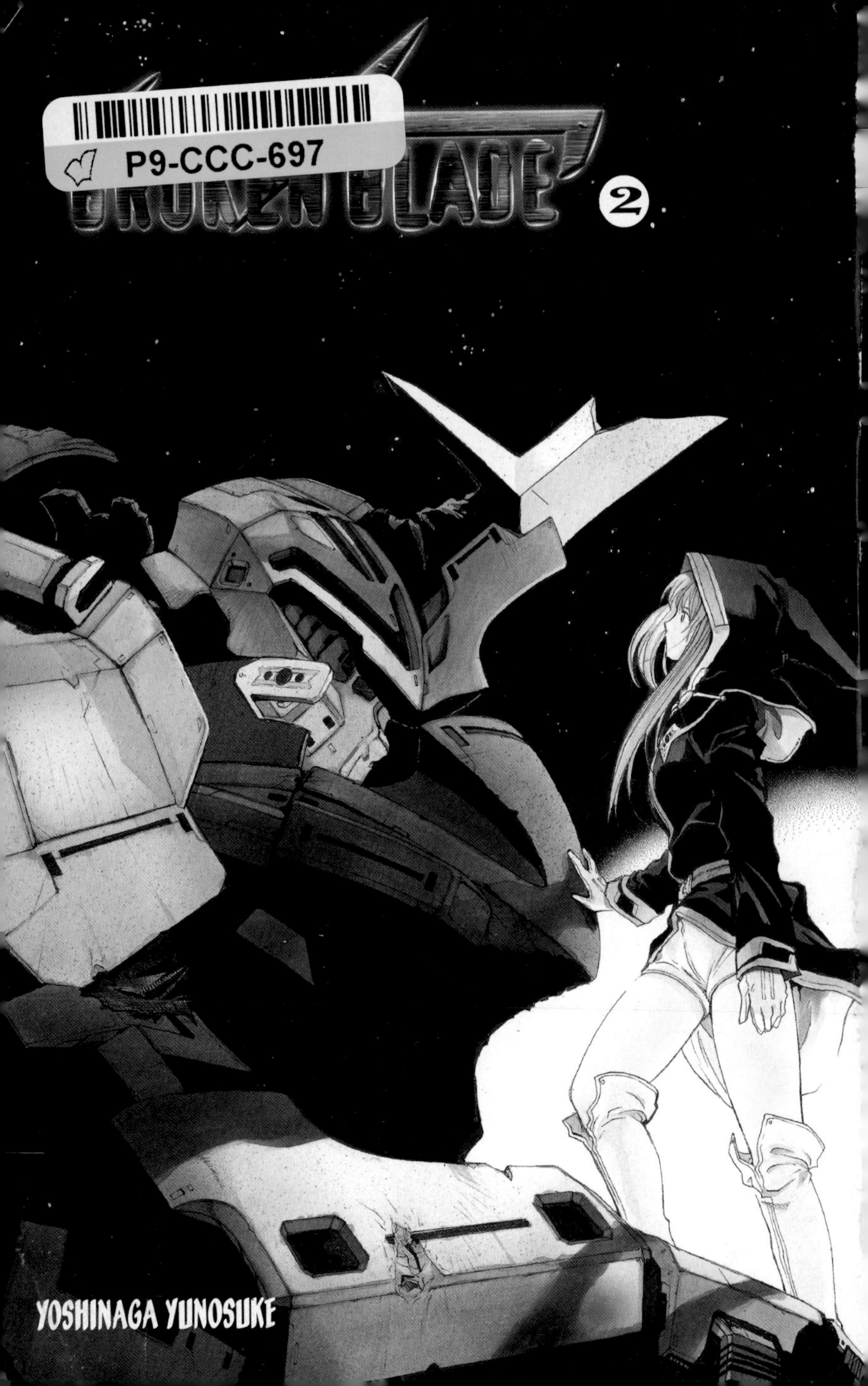
BLADE
2
YOSHINAGA YUNOSUKE

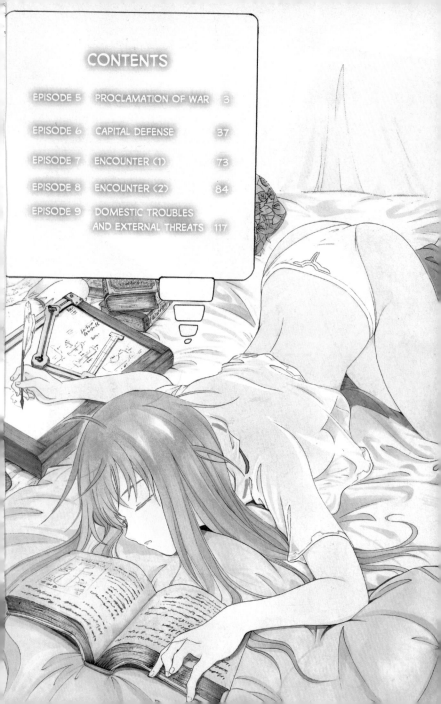

CONTENTS

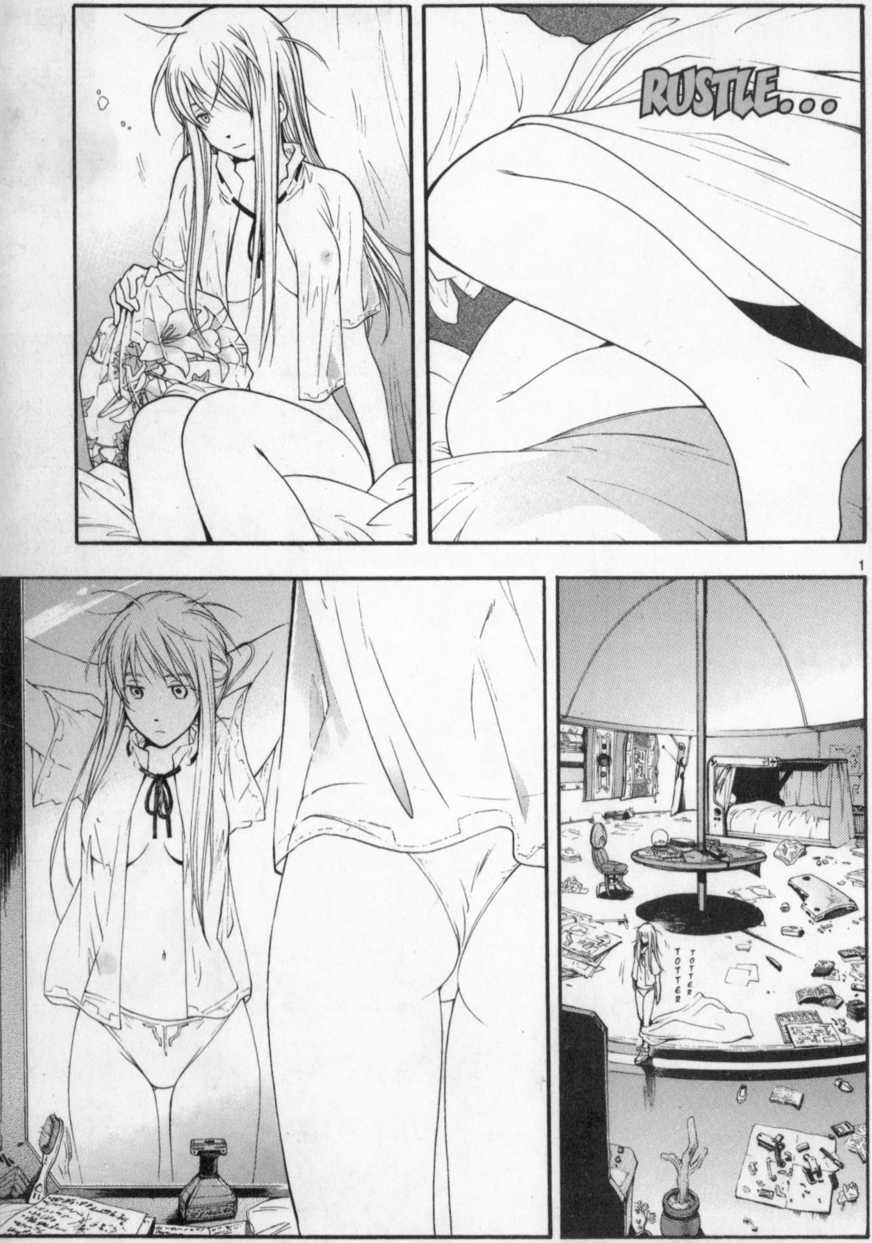
RUSTLE...
TOTTER
TOTTER

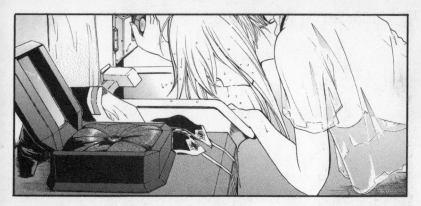

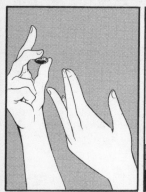

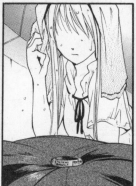

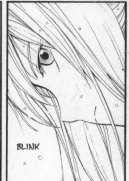

BLINK

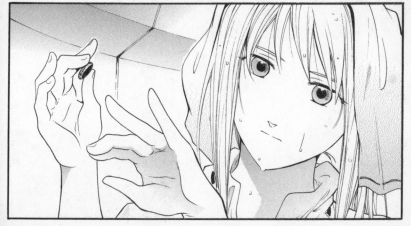

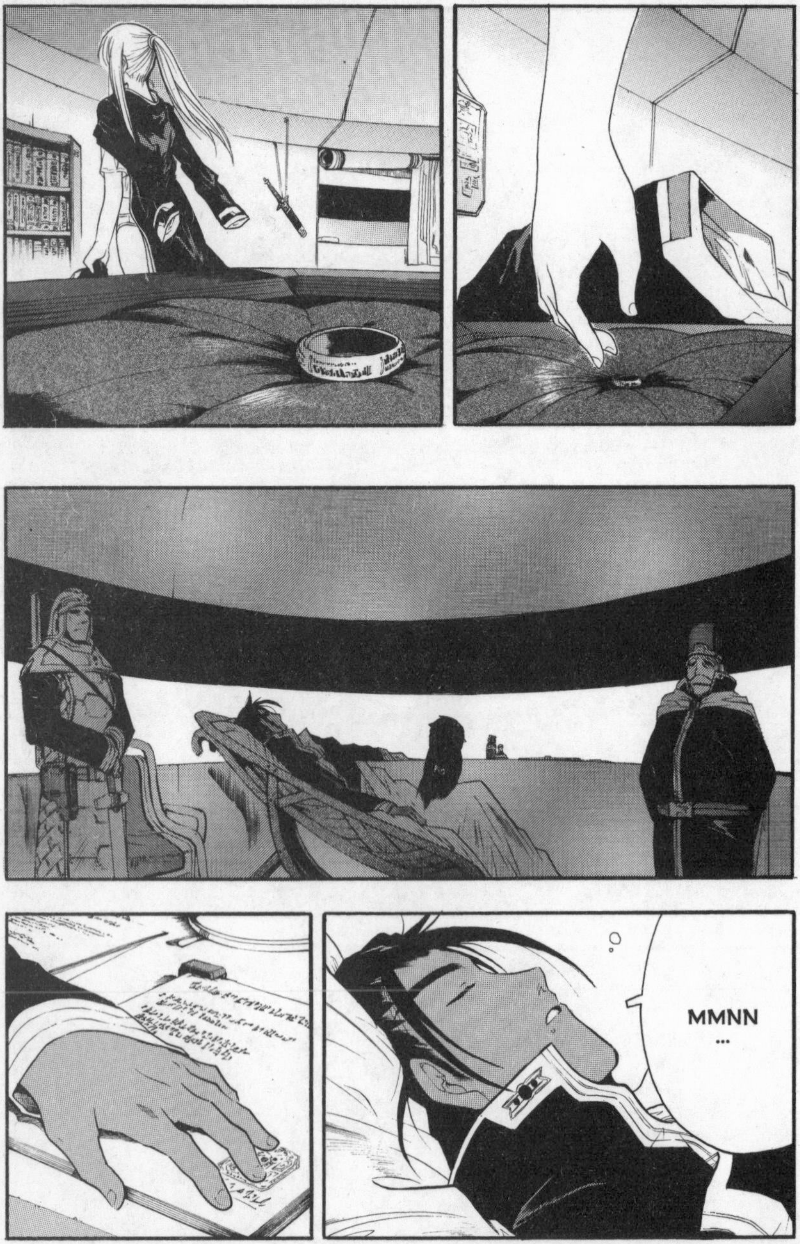
MMNN
...

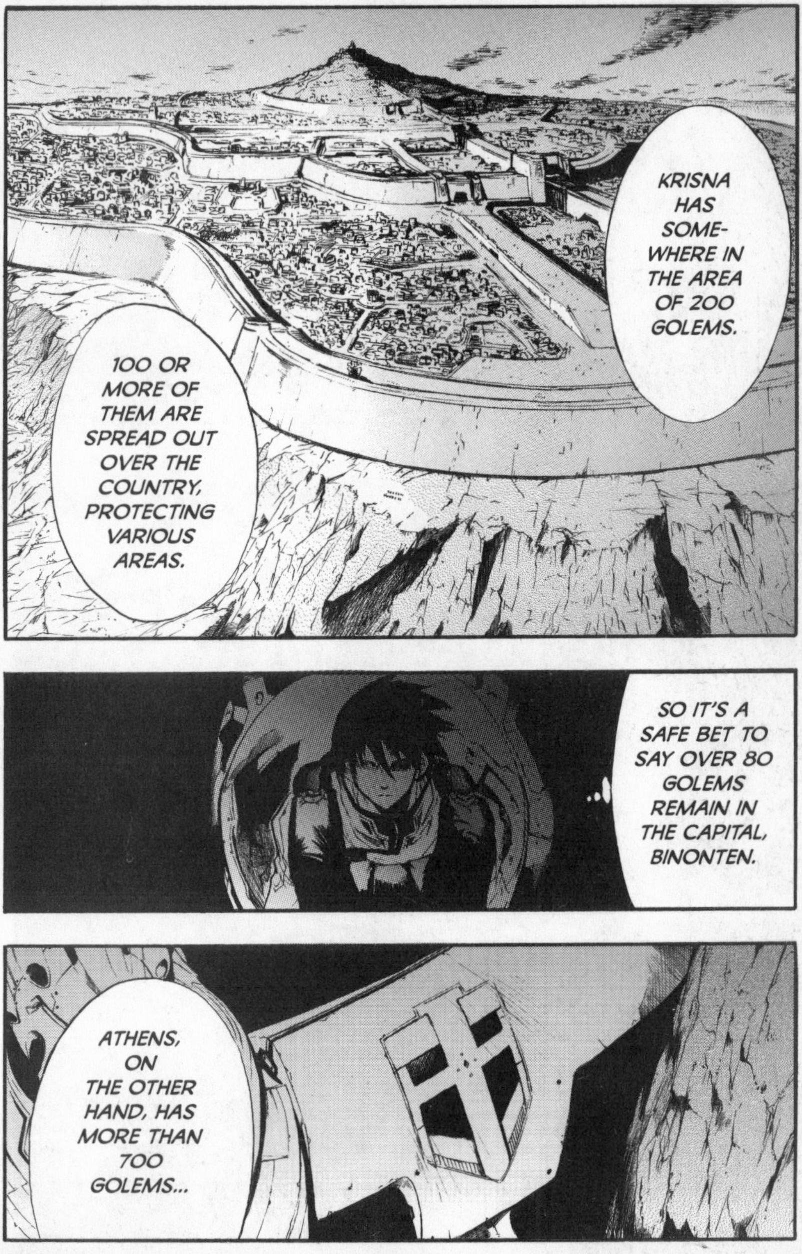
KRISNA HAS SOME-WHERE IN THE AREA OF 200 GOLEMS.
100 OR MORE OF THEM ARE SPREAD OUT OVER THE COUNTRY, PROTECTING VARIOUS AREAS.
SO IT'S A SAFE BET TO SAY OVER 80 GOLEMS REMAIN IN THE CAPITAL, BINONTEN.
ATHENS, ON THE OTHER HAND, HAS MORE THAN 700 GOLEMS...

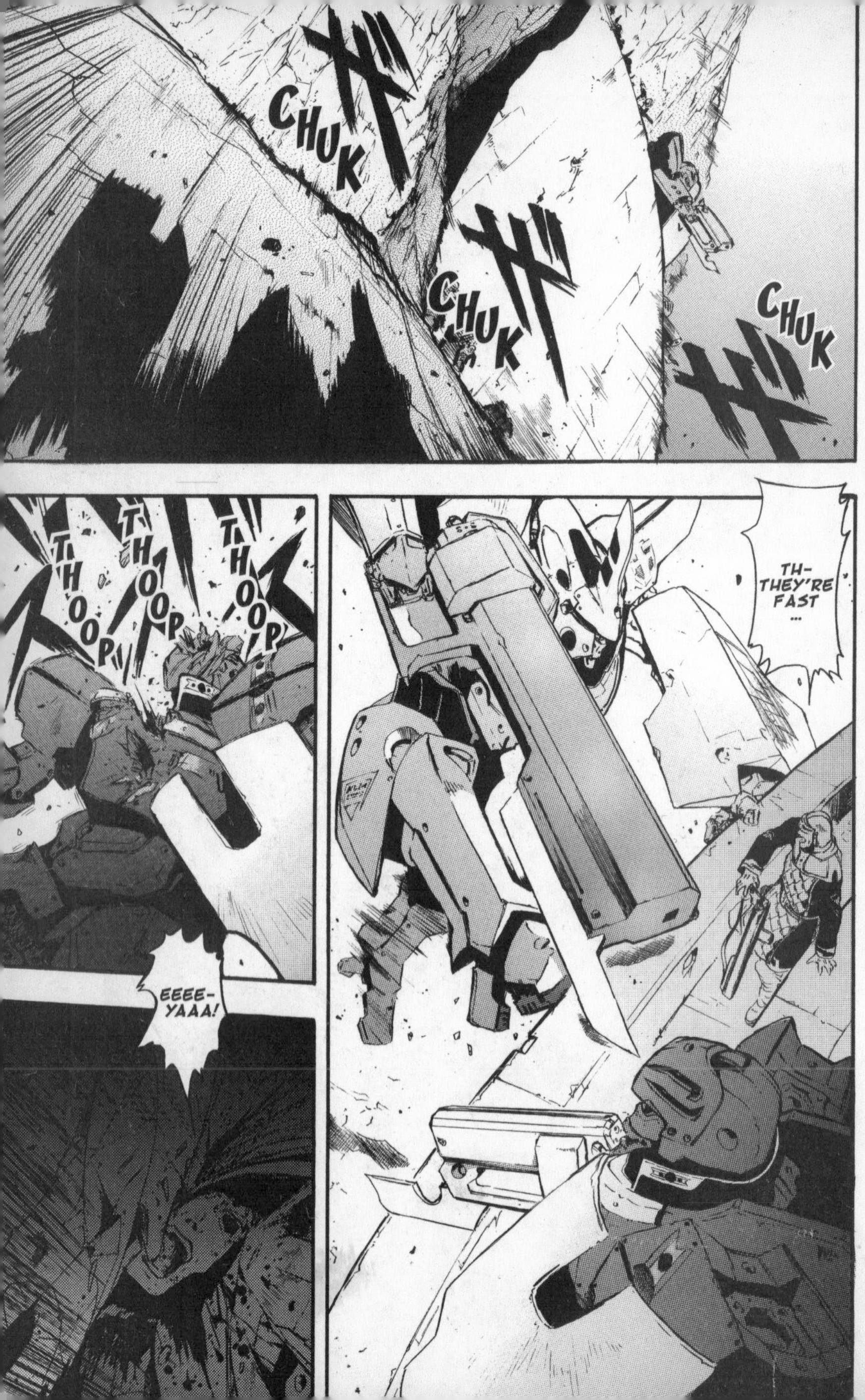
CHUK
CHUK
CHUK
TH-THEY'RE FAST ...
THOOP
THOOP
THOOP
EEEE-YAAA!

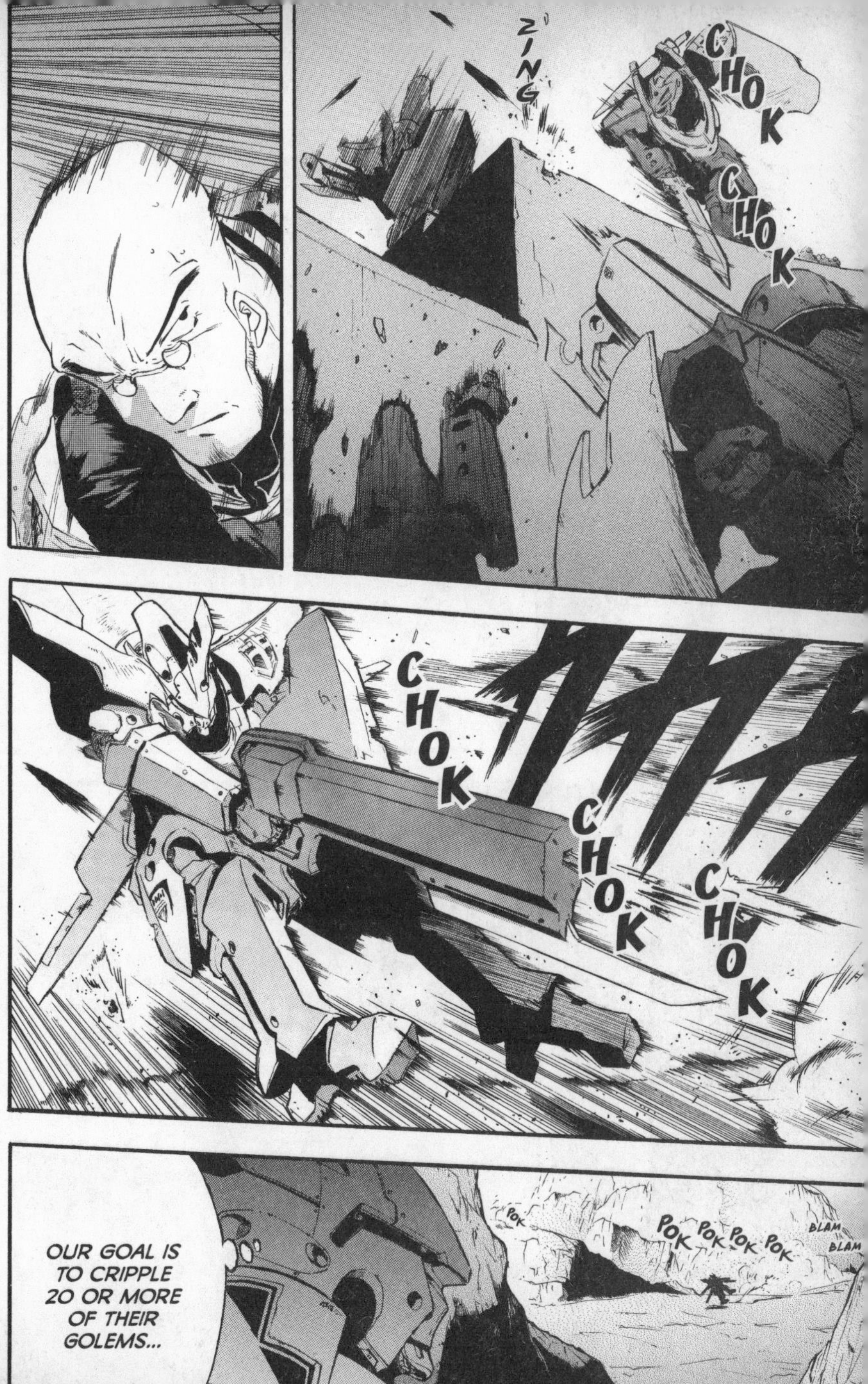
CHOK
CHOK
ZING
CHOK
CHOK
CHOK
BLAM
BLAM
POK POK POK POK
POK
OUR GOAL IS TO CRIPPLE 20 OR MORE OF THEIR GOLEMS...

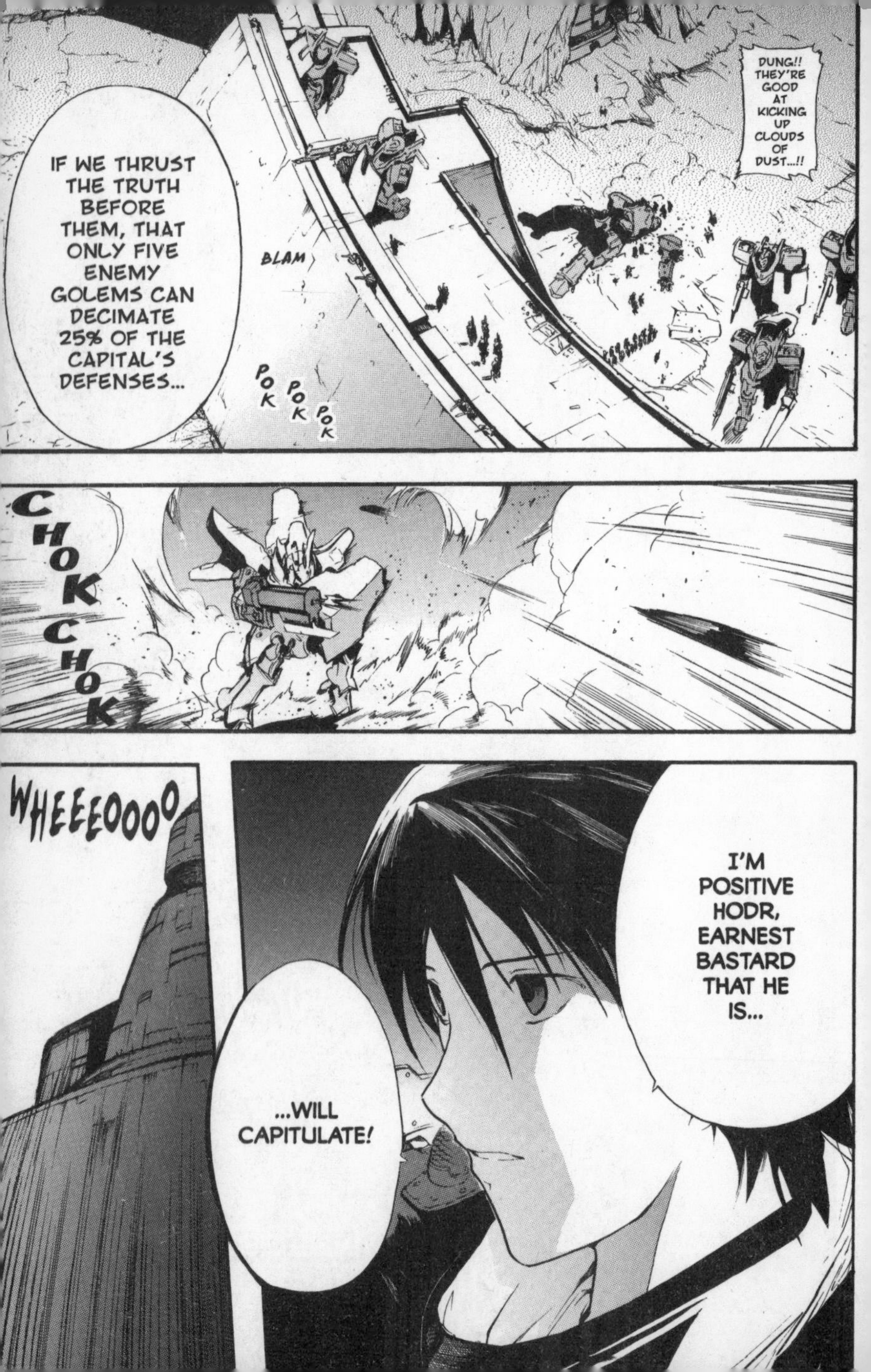
DUNG!! THEY'RE GOOD AT KICKING UP CLOUDS OF DUST...!!
IF WE THRUST THE TRUTH BEFORE THEM, THAT ONLY FIVE ENEMY GOLEMS CAN DECIMATE 25% OF THE CAPITAL'S DEFENSES...
BLAM
POK POK POK
CHOK CHOK
I'M POSITIVE HODR, EARNEST BASTARD THAT HE IS...
...WILL CAPITULATE!
WHEEEOOOO

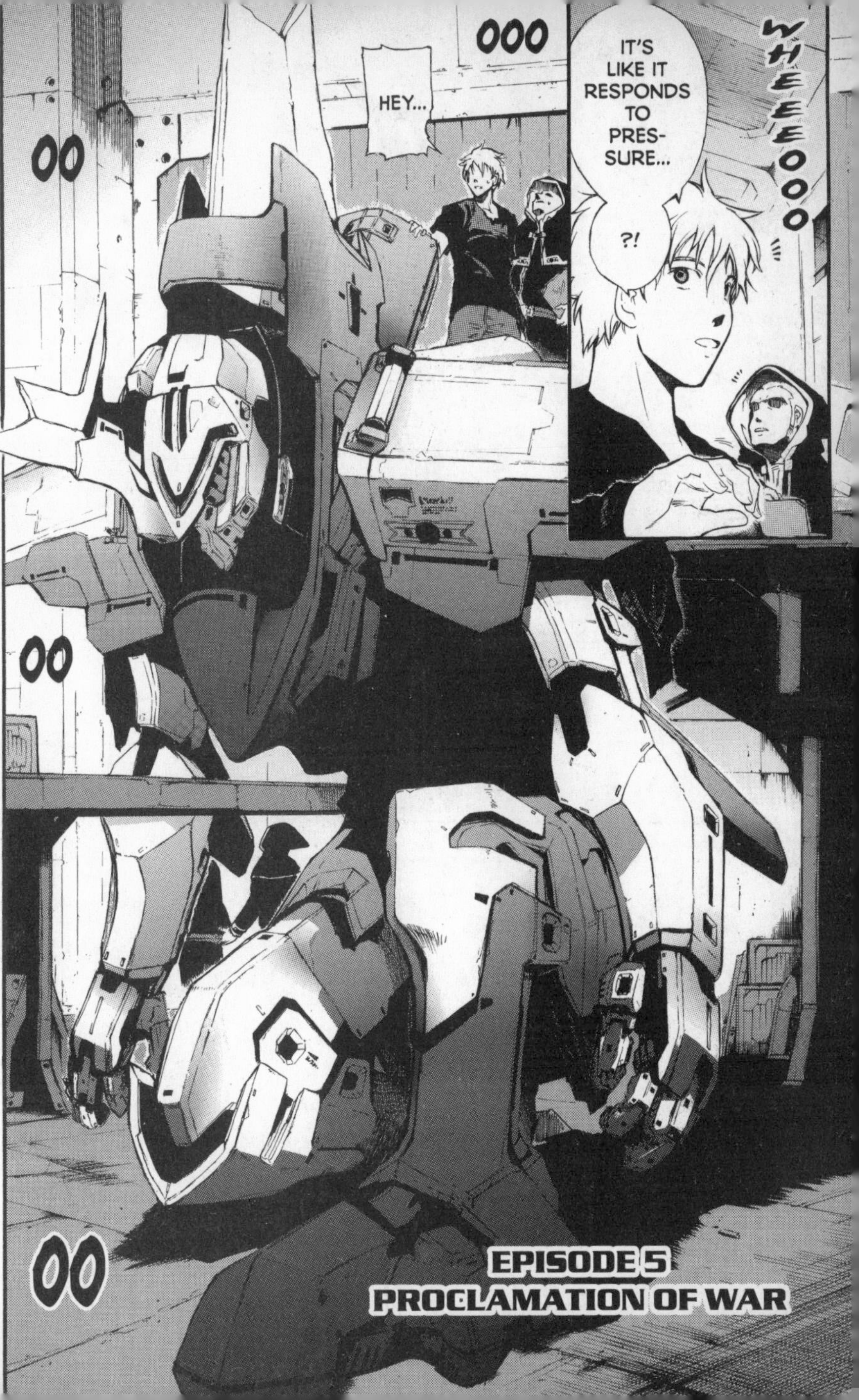
WHEEEEOOO
IT'S LIKE IT RESPONDS TO PRES-SURE...
?!
OOO
HEY...
OO
OO
EPISODE 5
PROCLAMATION OF WAR
OO

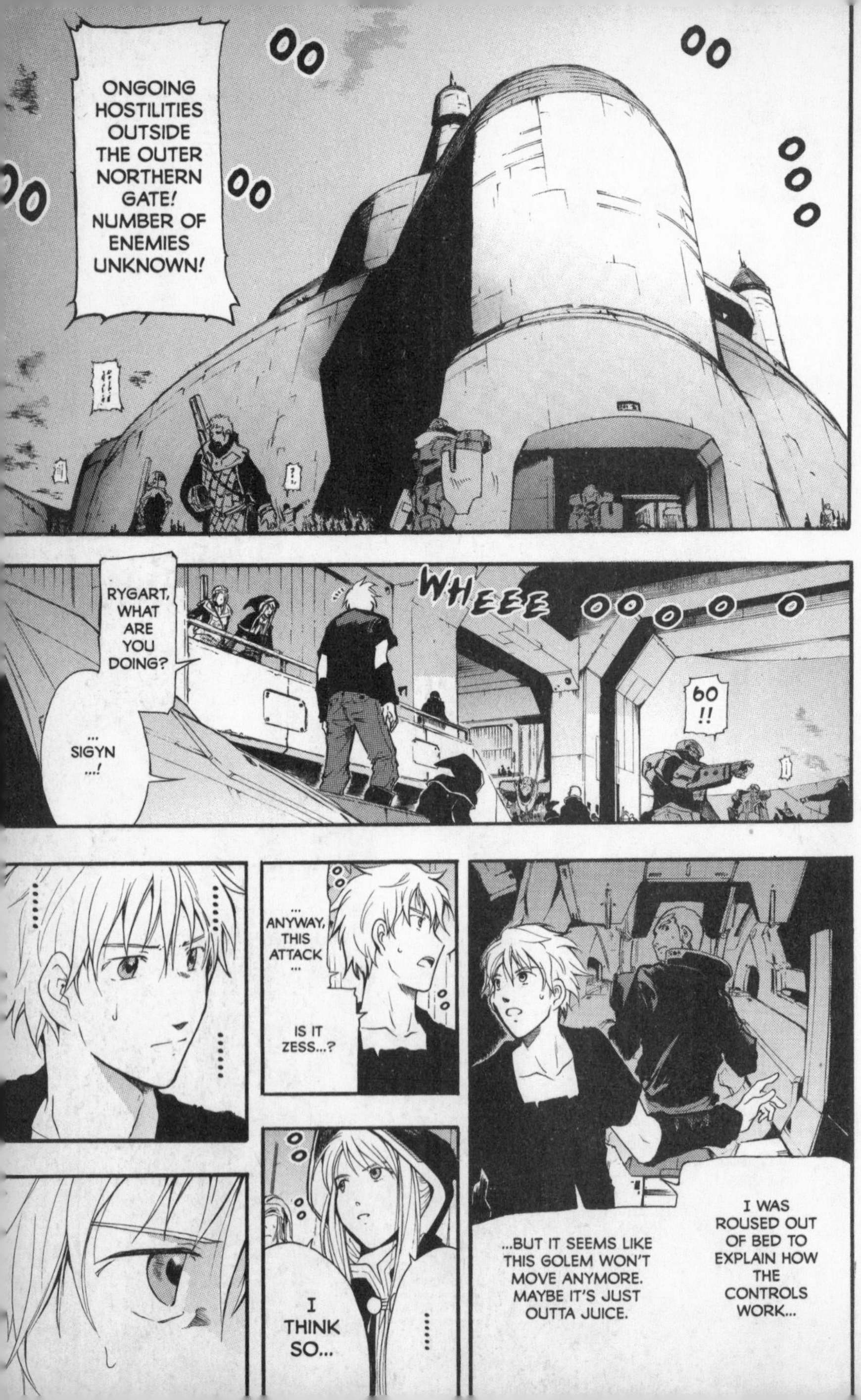
ONGOING HOSTILITIES OUTSIDE THE OUTER NORTHERN GATE! NUMBER OF ENEMIES UNKNOWN!
WHEEE OOOOO
GO!!
RYGART, WHAT ARE YOU DOING?
...SIGYN...!
I WAS ROUSED OUT OF BED TO EXPLAIN HOW THE CONTROLS WORK...
...BUT IT SEEMS LIKE THIS GOLEM WON'T MOVE ANYMORE. MAYBE IT'S JUST OUTTA JUICE.
...ANYWAY, THIS ATTACK...
IS IT ZESS...?
......
......
I THINK SO...
......

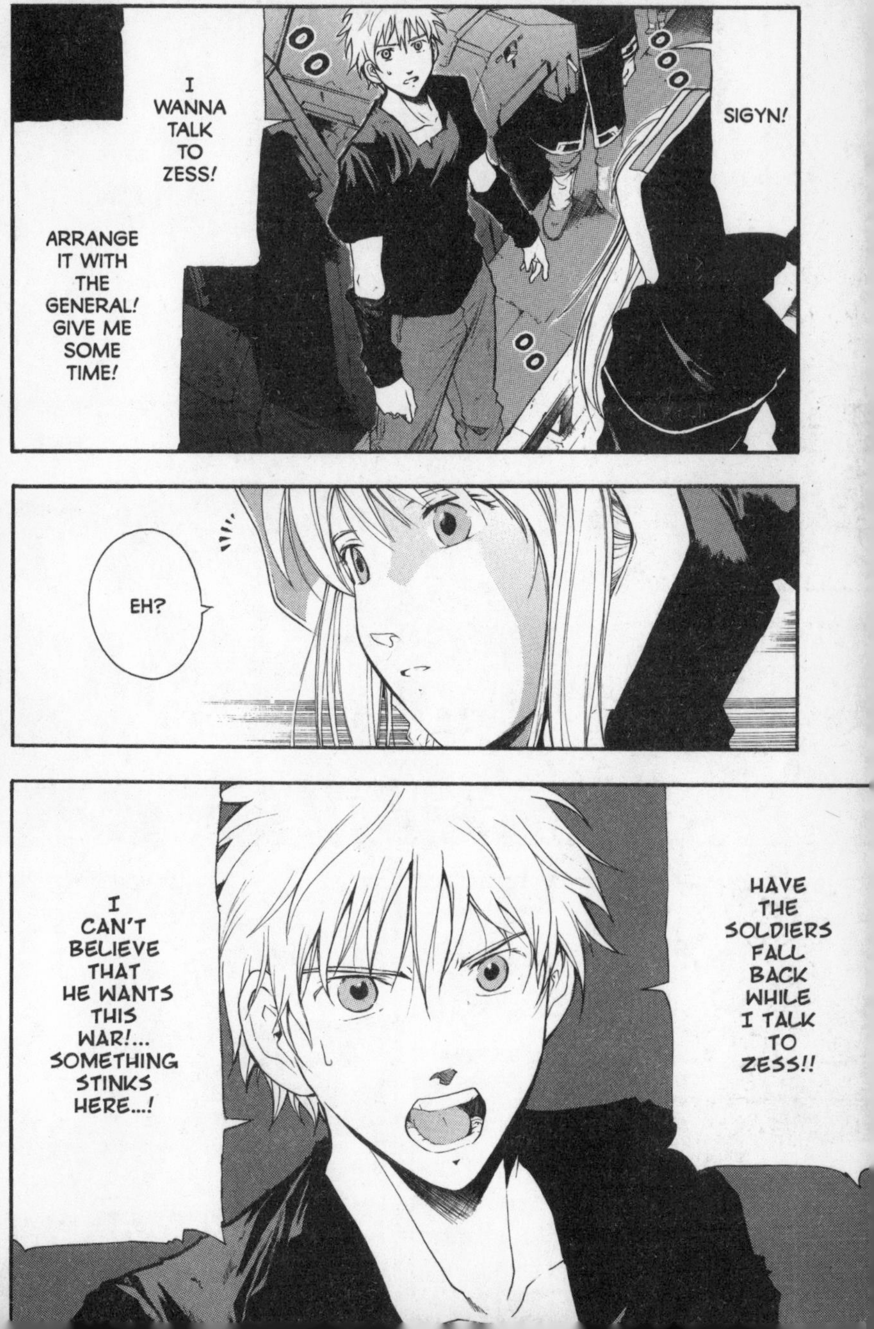
SIGYN!
I WANNA TALK TO ZESS!
ARRANGE IT WITH THE GENERAL! GIVE ME SOME TIME!
EH?
HAVE THE SOLDIERS FALL BACK WHILE I TALK TO ZESS!!
I CAN'T BELIEVE THAT HE WANTS THIS WAR!... SOMETHING STINKS HERE...!

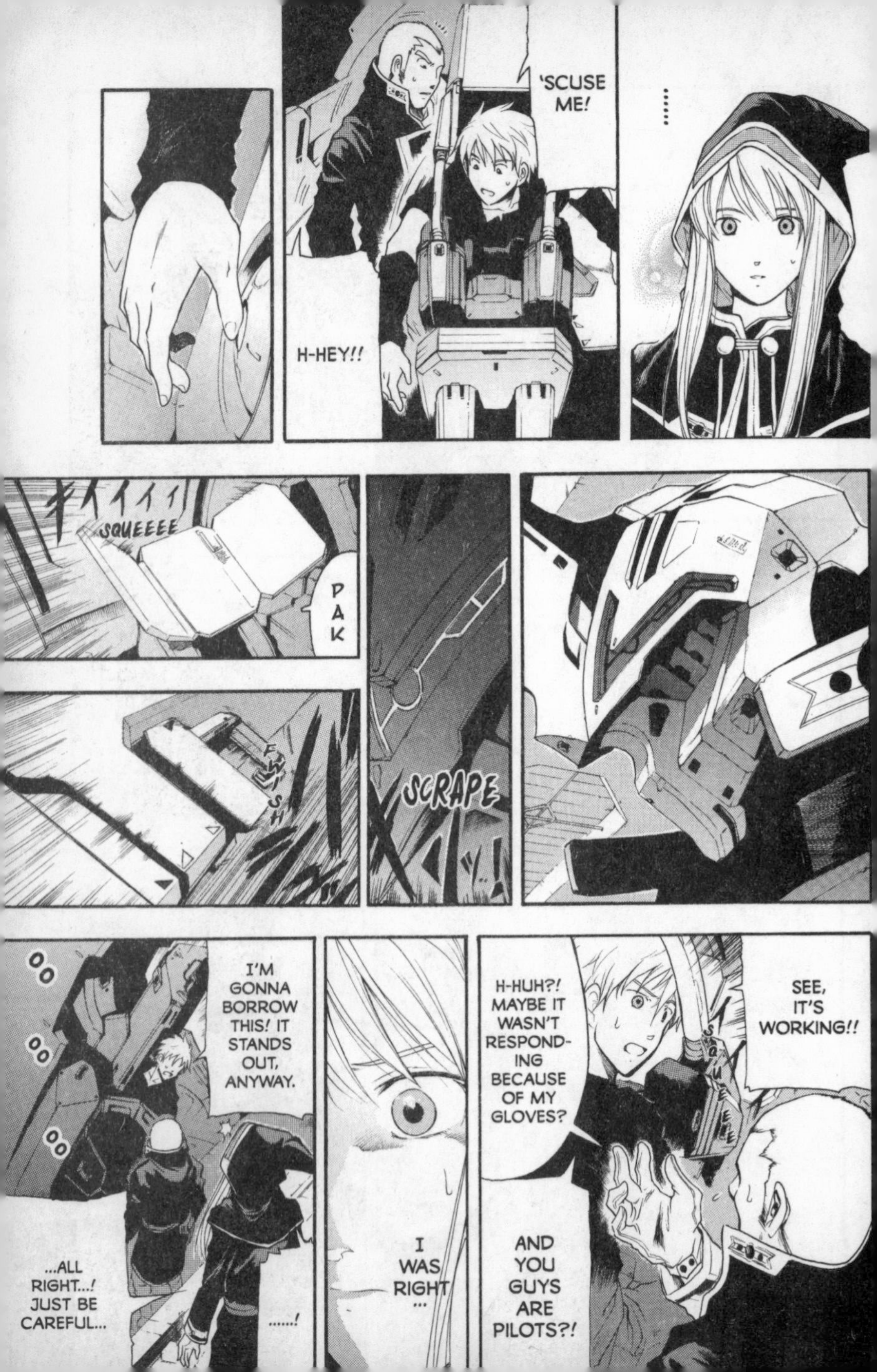
......
'SCUSE ME!
H-HEY!!
SCRAPE
SQUEEEEE
PAK
FWISH
SEE, IT'S WORKING!!
SQUEEEE
H-HUH?! MAYBE IT WASN'T RESPOND-ING BECAUSE OF MY GLOVES?
AND YOU GUYS ARE PILOTS?!
I WAS RIGHT...
I'M GONNA BORROW THIS! IT STANDS OUT, ANYWAY.
OO
OO
OO
...ALL RIGHT...! JUST BE CAREFUL...
......!

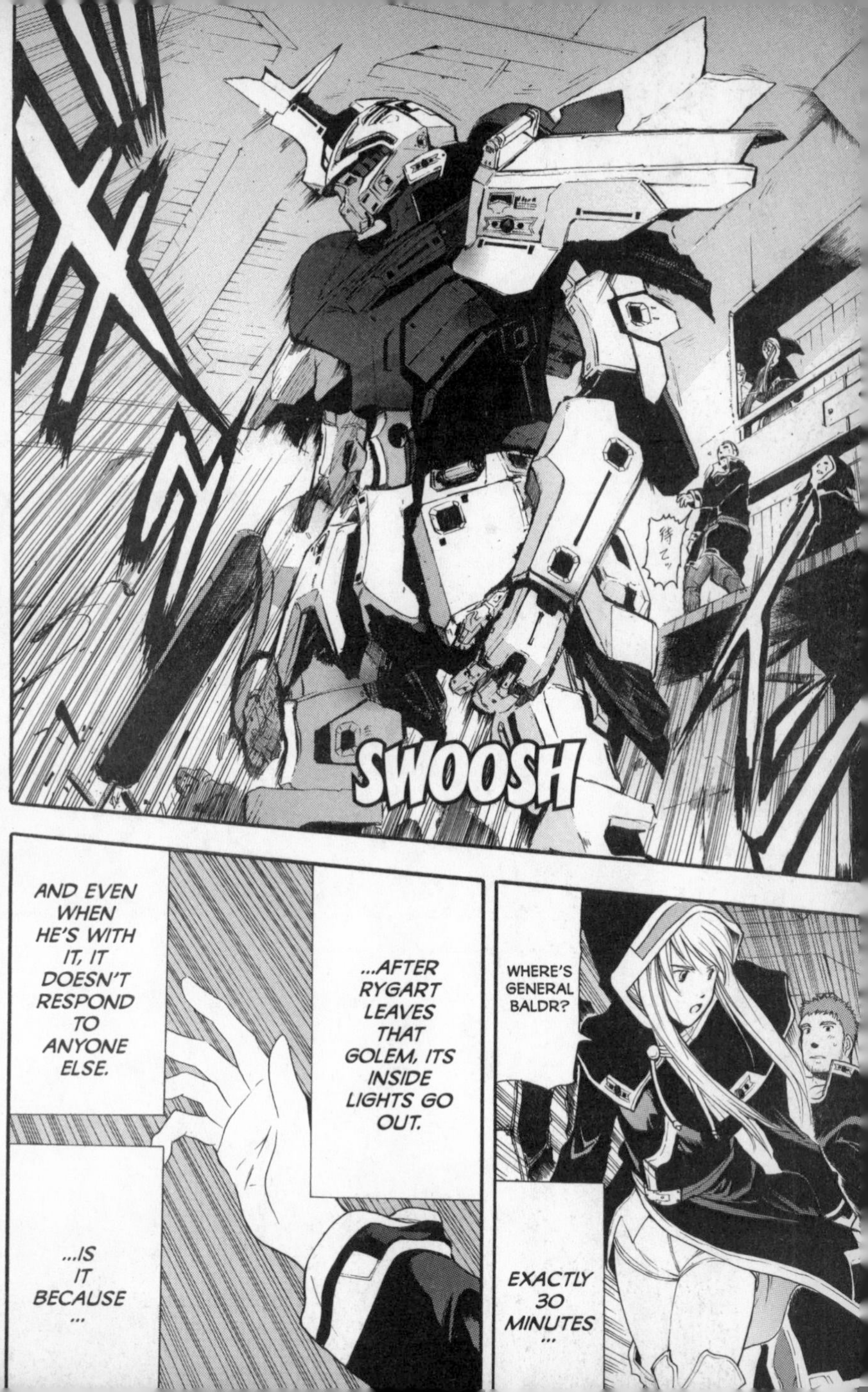
待てッ
SWOOSH
WHERE'S GENERAL BALDR?
EXACTLY 30 MINUTES ...
...AFTER RYGART LEAVES THAT GOLEM, ITS INSIDE LIGHTS GO OUT.
AND EVEN WHEN HE'S WITH IT, IT DOESN'T RESPOND TO ANYONE ELSE.
...IS IT BECAUSE ...

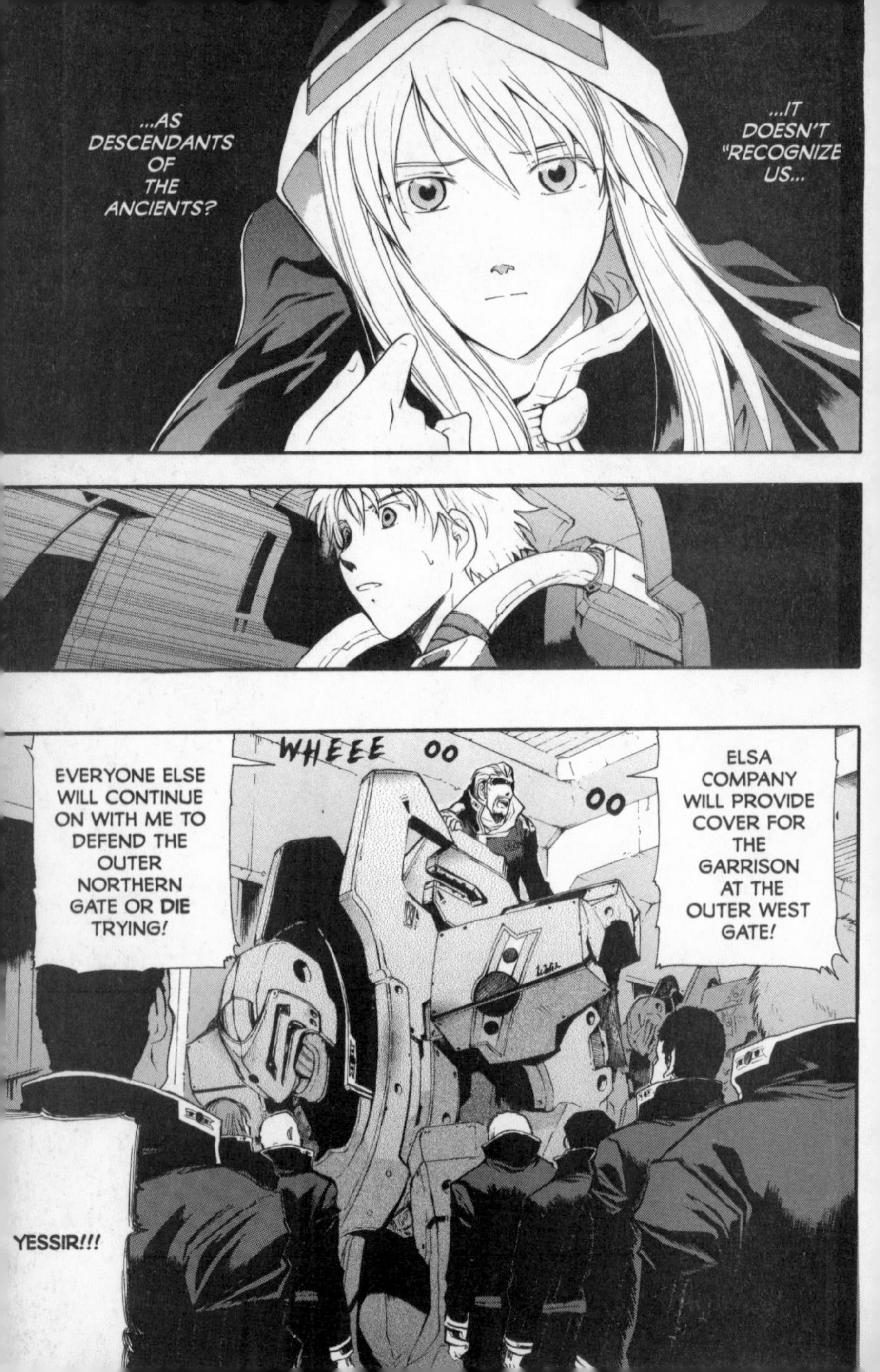
...IT DOESN'T "RECOGNIZE US...
...AS DESCENDANTS OF THE ANCIENTS?
WHEEE OO OO
ELSA COMPANY WILL PROVIDE COVER FOR THE GARRISON AT THE OUTER WEST GATE!
EVERYONE ELSE WILL CONTINUE ON WITH ME TO DEFEND THE OUTER NORTHERN GATE OR DIE TRYING!
YESSIR!!!

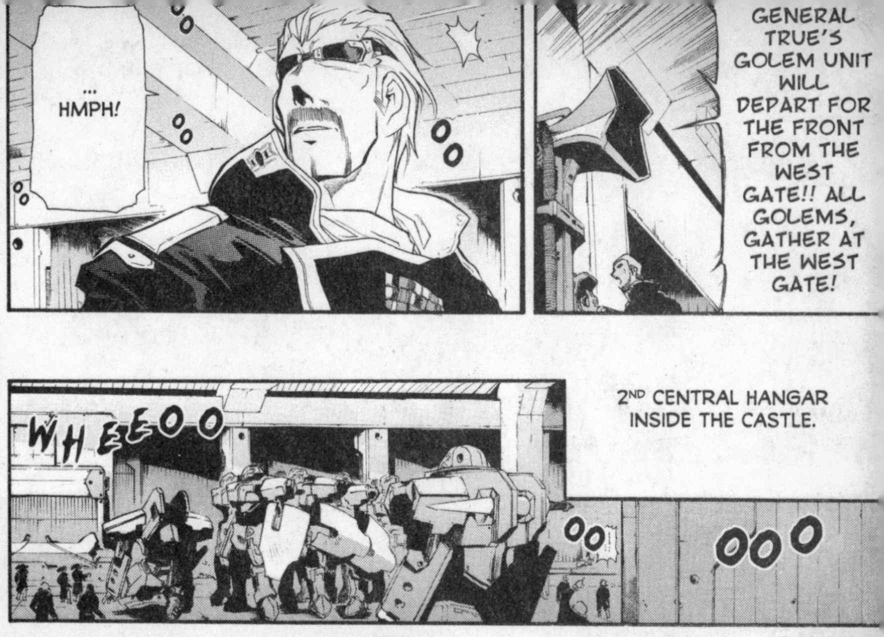
GENERAL TRUE'S GOLEM UNIT WILL DEPART FOR THE FRONT FROM THE WEST GATE!! ALL GOLEMS, GATHER AT THE WEST GATE!
... HMPH!
2ND CENTRAL HANGAR INSIDE THE CASTLE.
WHEEOO

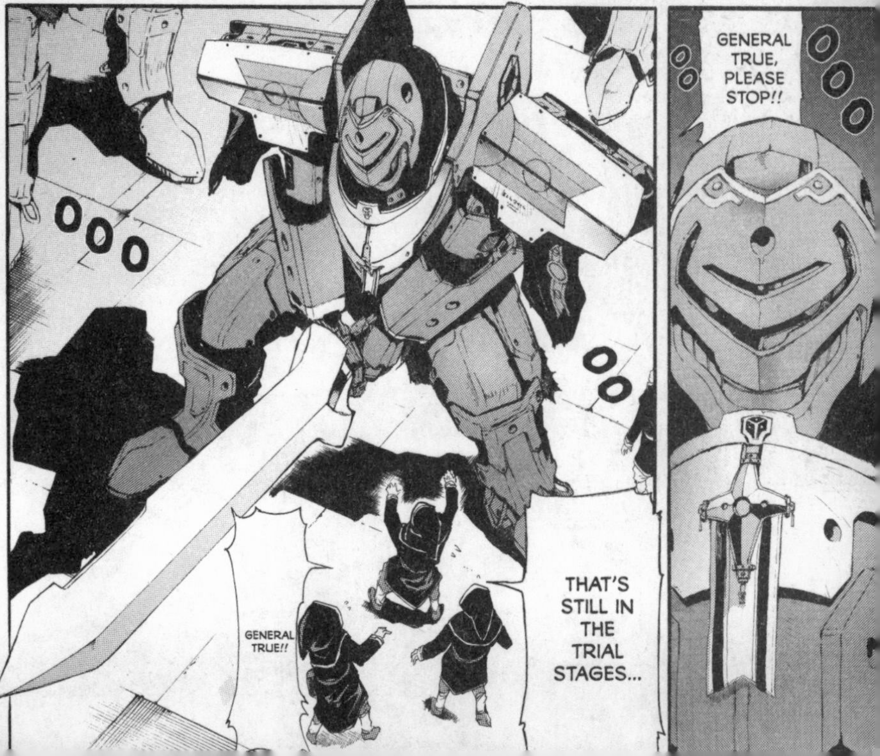
GENERAL TRUE, PLEASE STOP!!
THAT'S STILL IN THE TRIAL STAGES...
GENERAL TRUE!!

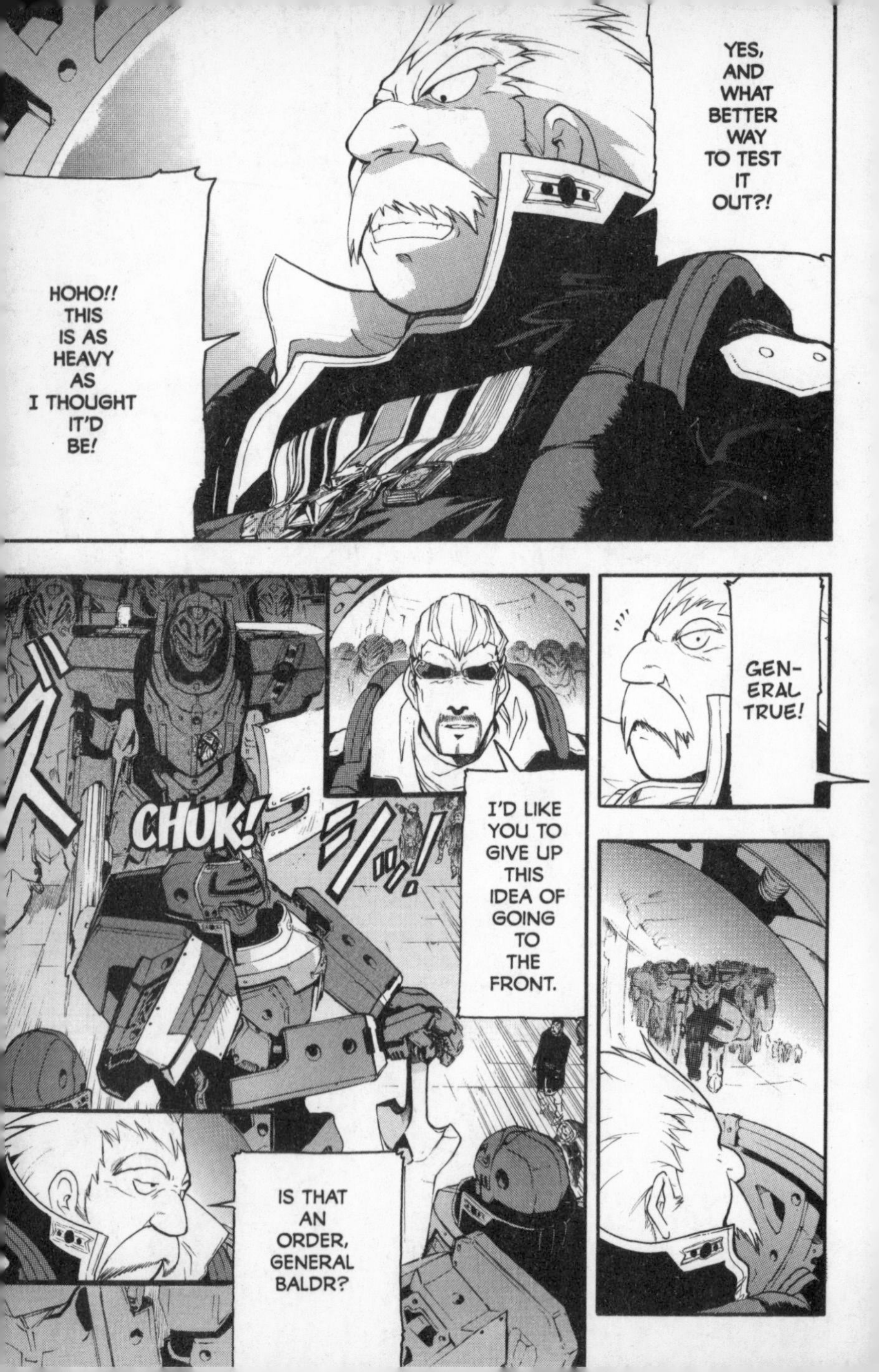
YES, AND WHAT BETTER WAY TO TEST IT OUT?!
HOHO!! THIS IS AS HEAVY AS I THOUGHT IT'D BE!
GEN- ERAL TRUE!
I'D LIKE YOU TO GIVE UP THIS IDEA OF GOING TO THE FRONT.
CHUK!
IS THAT AN ORDER, GENERAL BALDR?

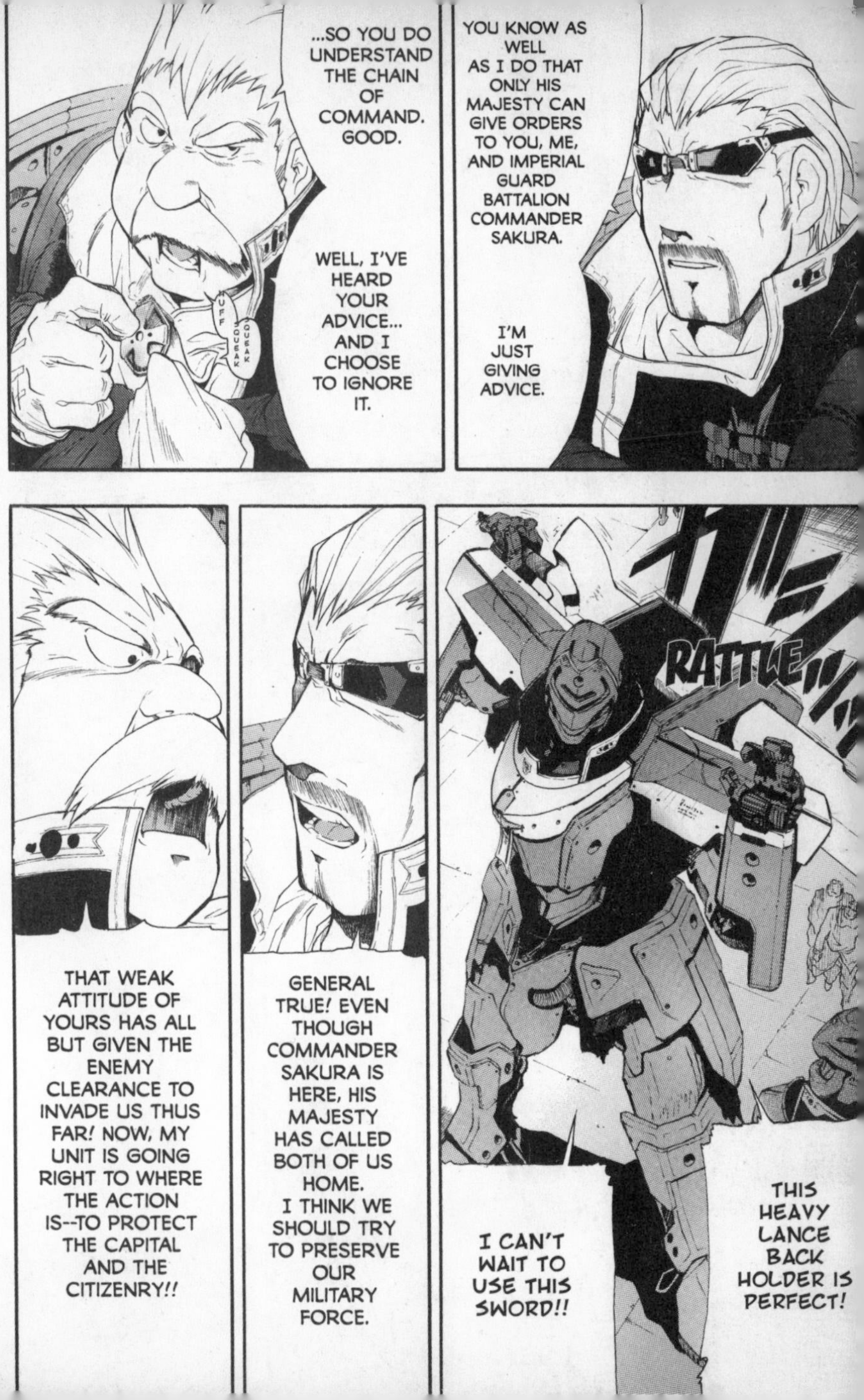
YOU KNOW AS WELL AS I DO THAT ONLY HIS MAJESTY CAN GIVE ORDERS TO YOU, ME, AND IMPERIAL GUARD BATTALION COMMANDER SAKURA.
I'M JUST GIVING ADVICE.
...SO YOU DO UNDERSTAND THE CHAIN OF COMMAND. GOOD.
WELL, I'VE HEARD YOUR ADVICE... AND I CHOOSE TO IGNORE IT.
UFF
SQUEAK SQUEAK
RATTLE!!!
THIS HEAVY LANCE BACK HOLDER IS PERFECT!
I CAN'T WAIT TO USE THIS SWORD!!
GENERAL TRUE! EVEN THOUGH COMMANDER SAKURA IS HERE, HIS MAJESTY HAS CALLED BOTH OF US HOME. I THINK WE SHOULD TRY TO PRESERVE OUR MILITARY FORCE.
THAT WEAK ATTITUDE OF YOURS HAS ALL BUT GIVEN THE ENEMY CLEARANCE TO INVADE US THUS FAR! NOW, MY UNIT IS GOING RIGHT TO WHERE THE ACTION IS--TO PROTECT THE CAPITAL AND THE CITIZENRY!!

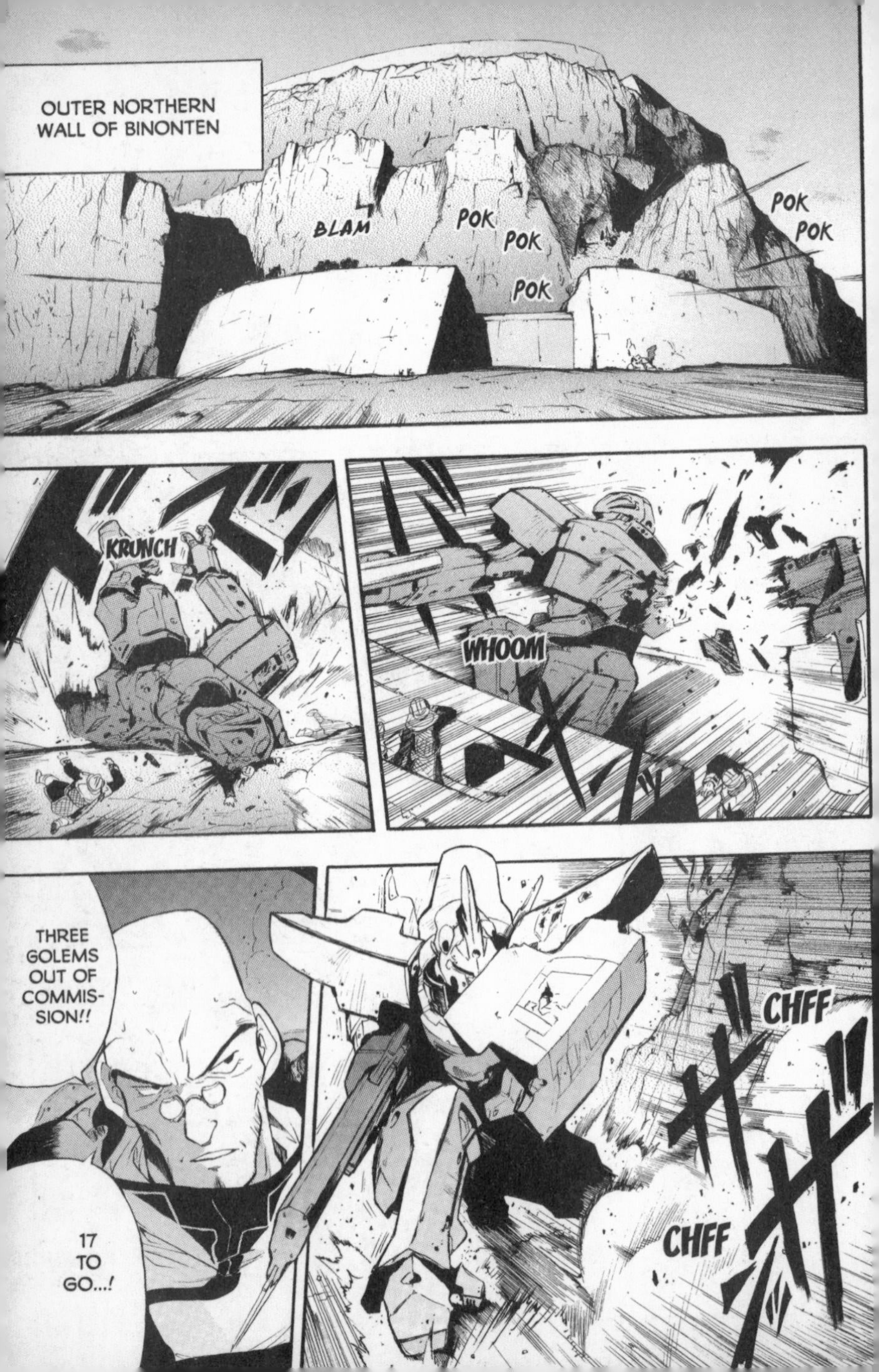
OUTER NORTHERN WALL OF BINONTEN
POK POK
POK POK POK
BLAM
WHOOM
KRUNCH
CHFF
CHFF
THREE GOLEMS OUT OF COMMIS-SION!!
17 TO GO...!

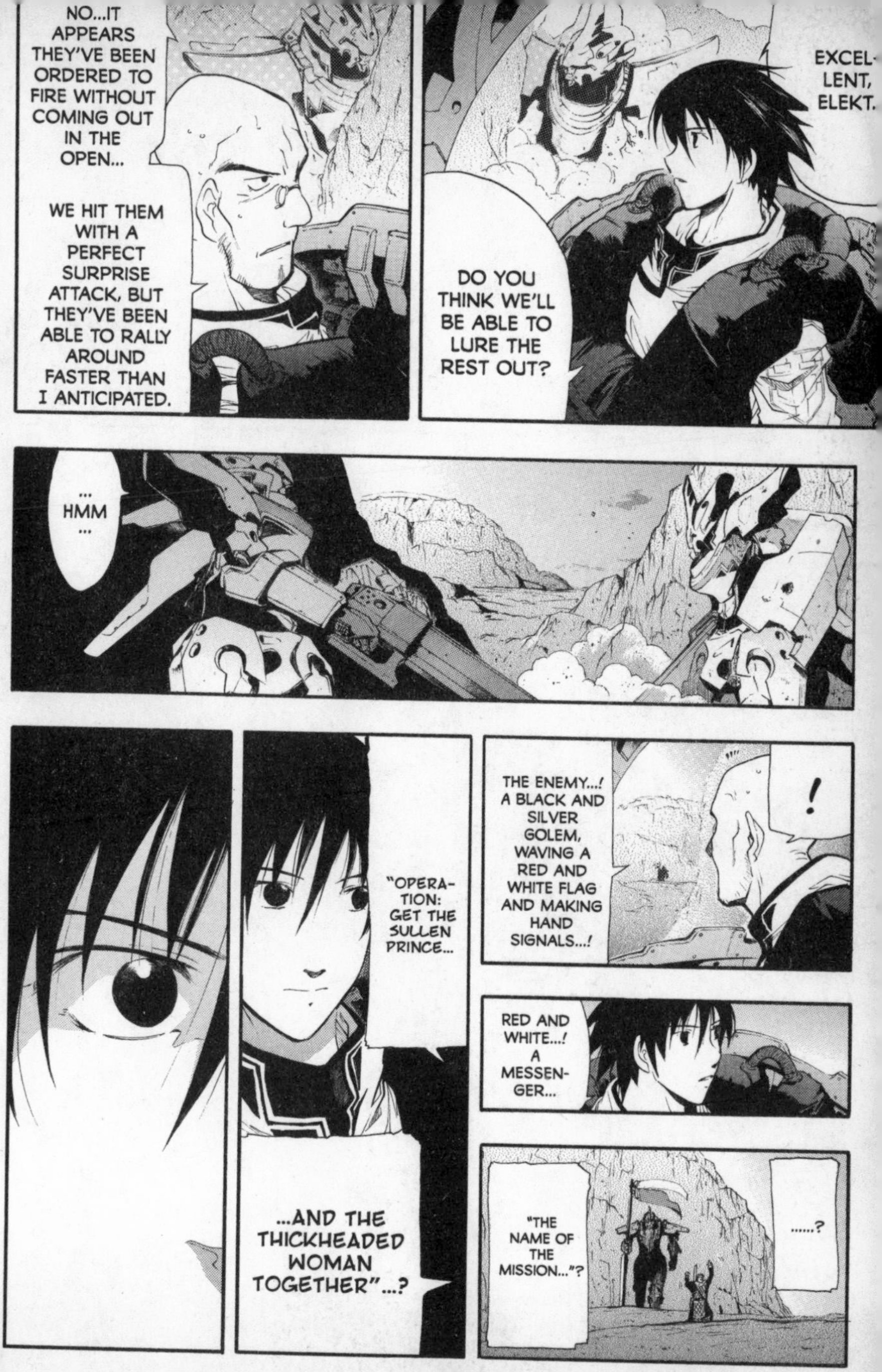
EXCEL-LENT, ELEKT.
DO YOU THINK WE'LL BE ABLE TO LURE THE REST OUT?
NO...IT APPEARS THEY'VE BEEN ORDERED TO FIRE WITHOUT COMING OUT IN THE OPEN...
WE HIT THEM WITH A PERFECT SURPRISE ATTACK, BUT THEY'VE BEEN ABLE TO RALLY AROUND FASTER THAN I ANTICIPATED.
...HMM...
!
THE ENEMY...! A BLACK AND SILVER GOLEM, WAVING A RED AND WHITE FLAG AND MAKING HAND SIGNALS...!
RED AND WHITE...! A MESSEN-GER...
......?
"THE NAME OF THE MISSION..."?
"OPERA-TION: GET THE SULLEN PRINCE...
...AND THE THICKHEADED WOMAN TOGETHER"...?

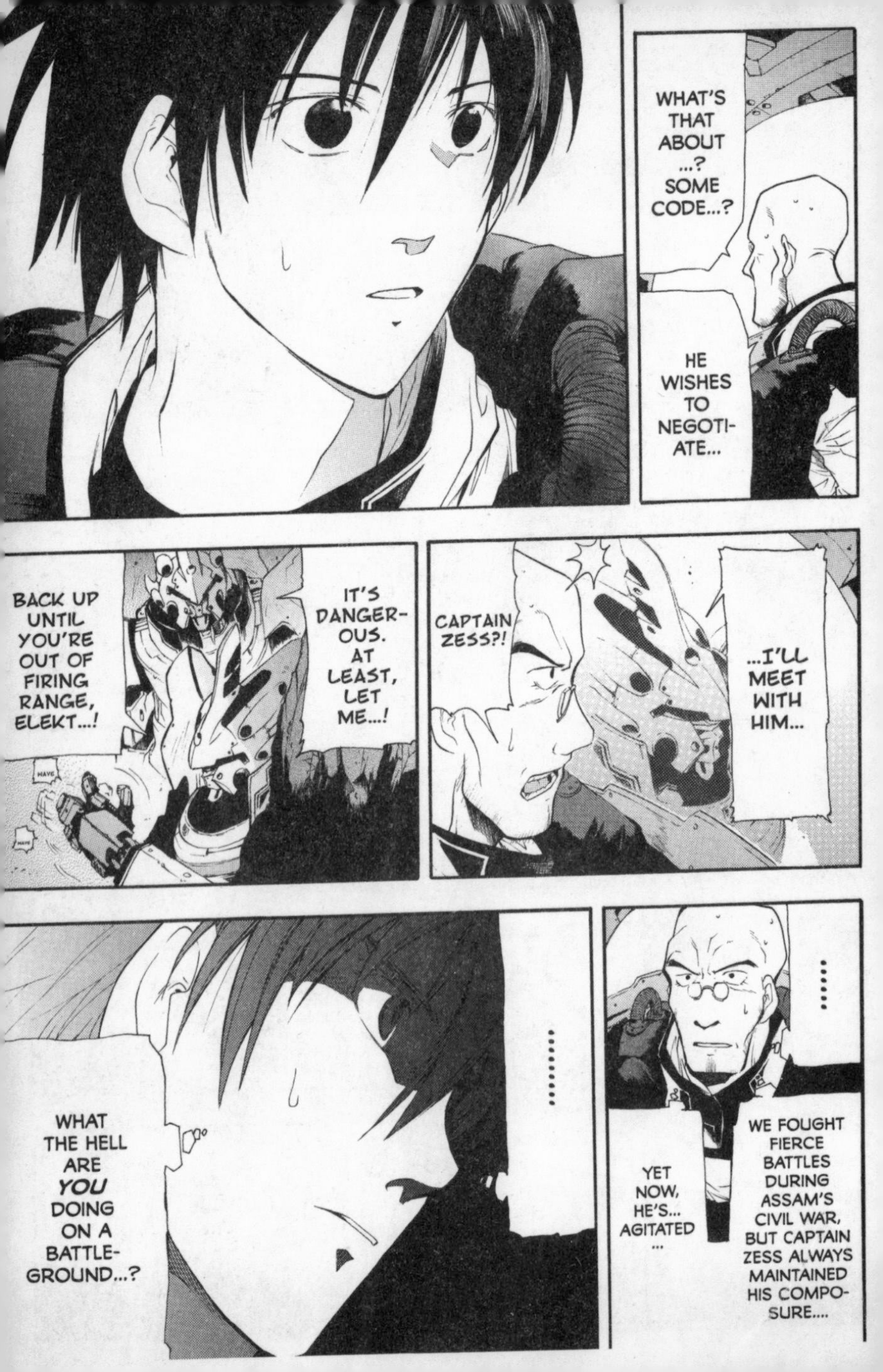
WHAT'S THAT ABOUT ...? SOME CODE...?
HE WISHES TO NEGOTIATE...
...I'LL MEET WITH HIM...
CAPTAIN ZESS?!
IT'S DANGEROUS. AT LEAST, LET ME...!
BACK UP UNTIL YOU'RE OUT OF FIRING RANGE, ELEKT...!
......
WE FOUGHT FIERCE BATTLES DURING ASSAM'S CIVIL WAR, BUT CAPTAIN ZESS ALWAYS MAINTAINED HIS COMPOSURE....
YET NOW, HE'S... AGITATED ...
....
WHAT THE HELL ARE *YOU* DOING ON A BATTLEGROUND...?

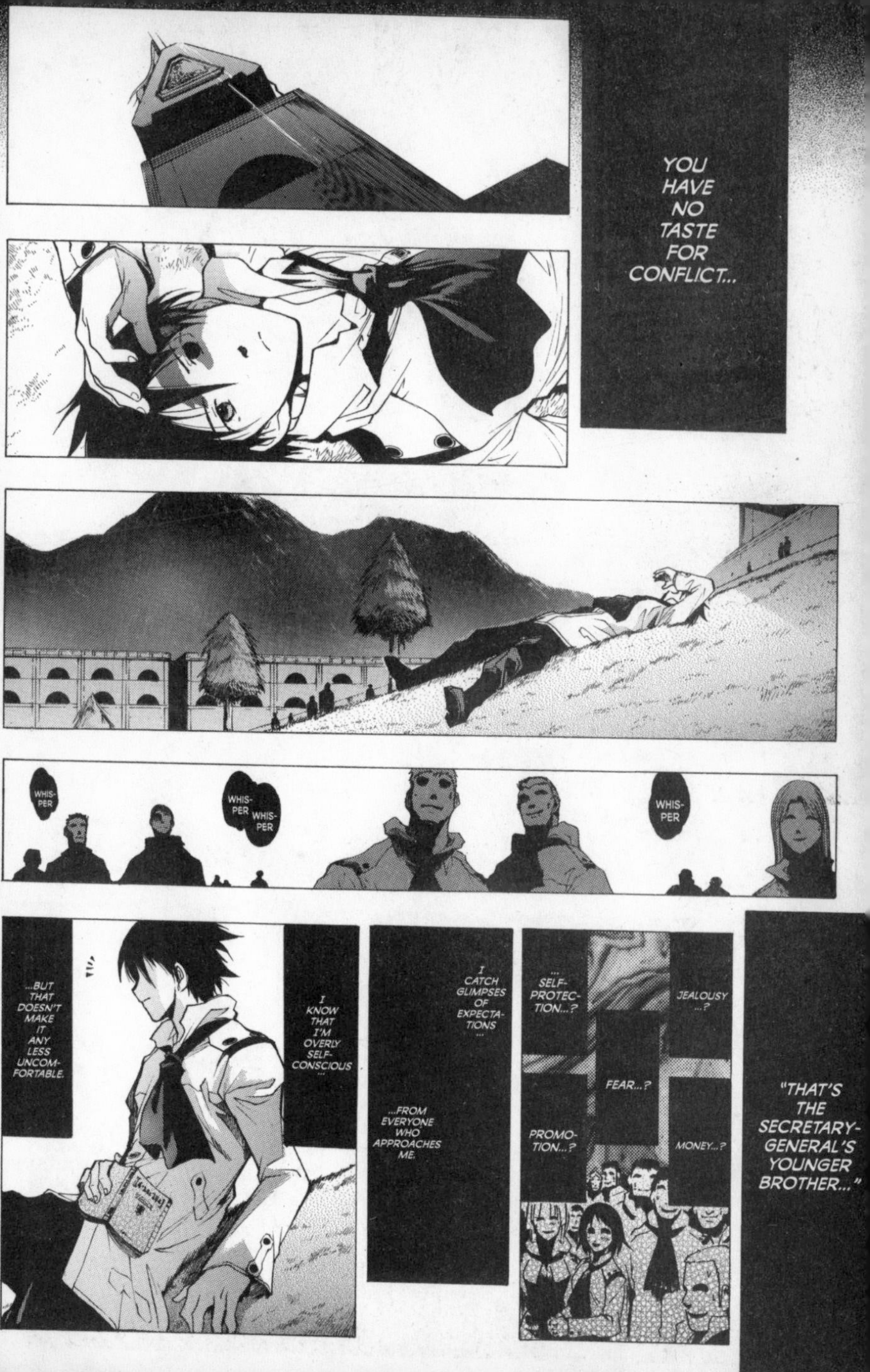
YOU HAVE NO TASTE FOR CONFLICT...
WHISPER
WHISPER WHISPER
WHISPER
"THAT'S THE SECRETARY-GENERAL'S YOUNGER BROTHER..."
JEALOUSY...?
...SELF-PROTECTION...?
FEAR...?
MONEY...?
PROMOTION...?
I CATCH GLIMPSES OF EXPECTATIONS...
...FROM EVERYONE WHO APPROACHES ME.
I KNOW THAT I'M OVERLY SELF-CONSCIOUS...
...BUT THAT DOESN'T MAKE IT ANY LESS UNCOMFORTABLE.

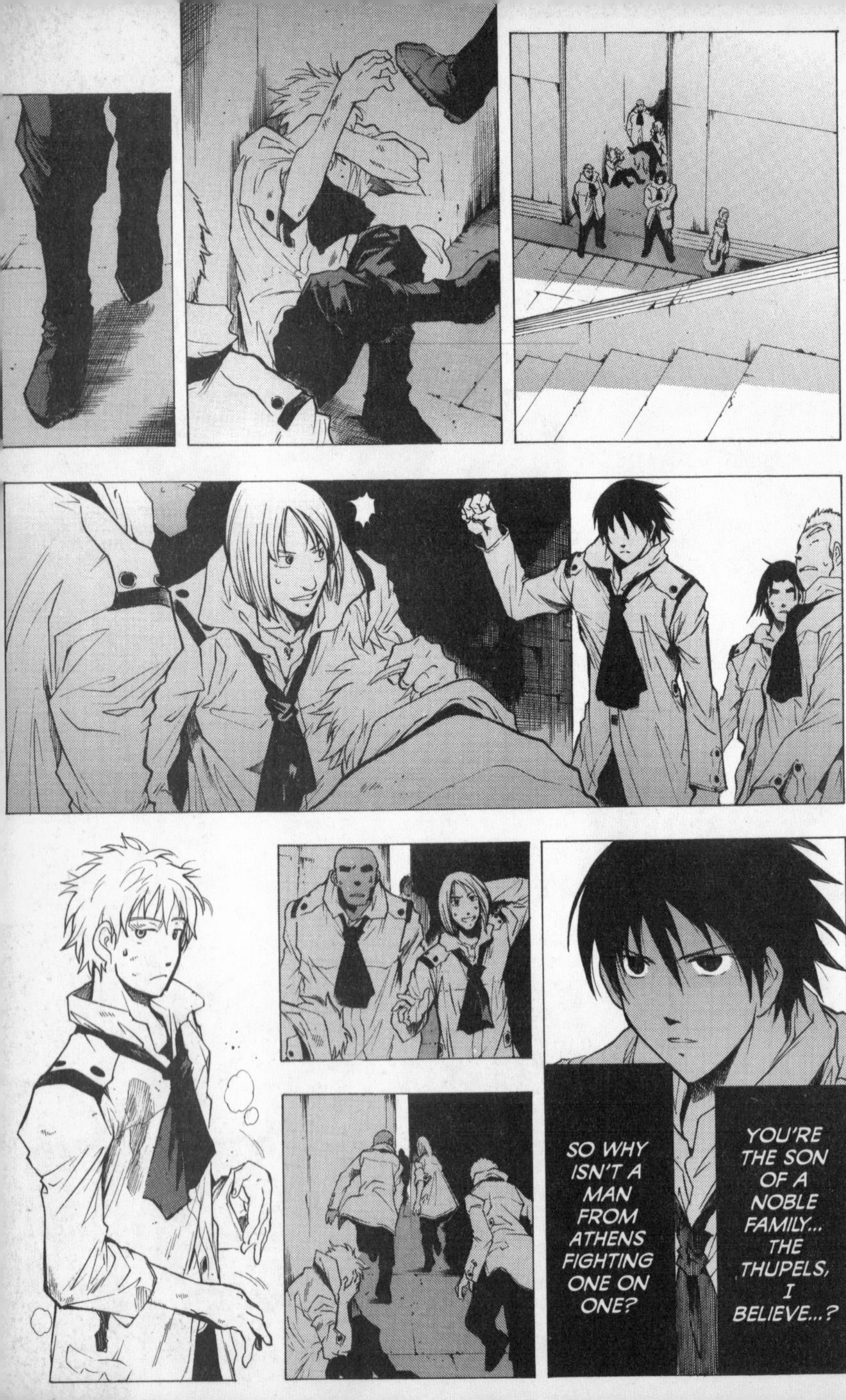
YOU'RE THE SON OF A NOBLE FAMILY... THE THUPELS, I BELIEVE...?
SO WHY ISN'T A MAN FROM ATHENS FIGHTING ONE ON ONE?

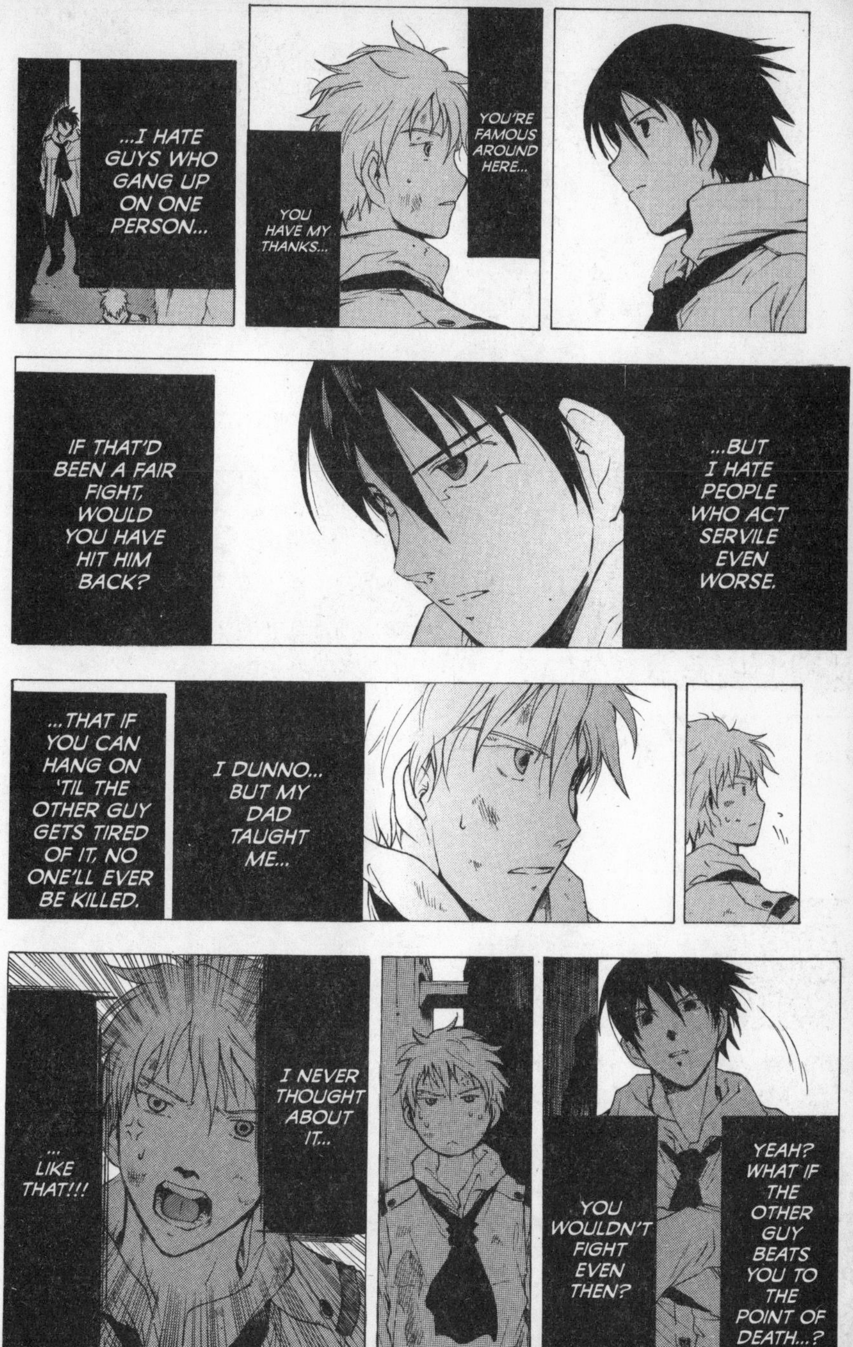
YOU'RE FAMOUS AROUND HERE...
YOU HAVE MY THANKS...
...I HATE GUYS WHO GANG UP ON ONE PERSON...
...BUT I HATE PEOPLE WHO ACT SERVILE EVEN WORSE.
IF THAT'D BEEN A FAIR FIGHT, WOULD YOU HAVE HIT HIM BACK?
I DUNNO... BUT MY DAD TAUGHT ME...
...THAT IF YOU CAN HANG ON 'TIL THE OTHER GUY GETS TIRED OF IT, NO ONE'LL EVER BE KILLED.
YEAH? WHAT IF THE OTHER GUY BEATS YOU TO THE POINT OF DEATH...?
YOU WOULDN'T FIGHT EVEN THEN?
I NEVER THOUGHT ABOUT IT...
...LIKE THAT!!!

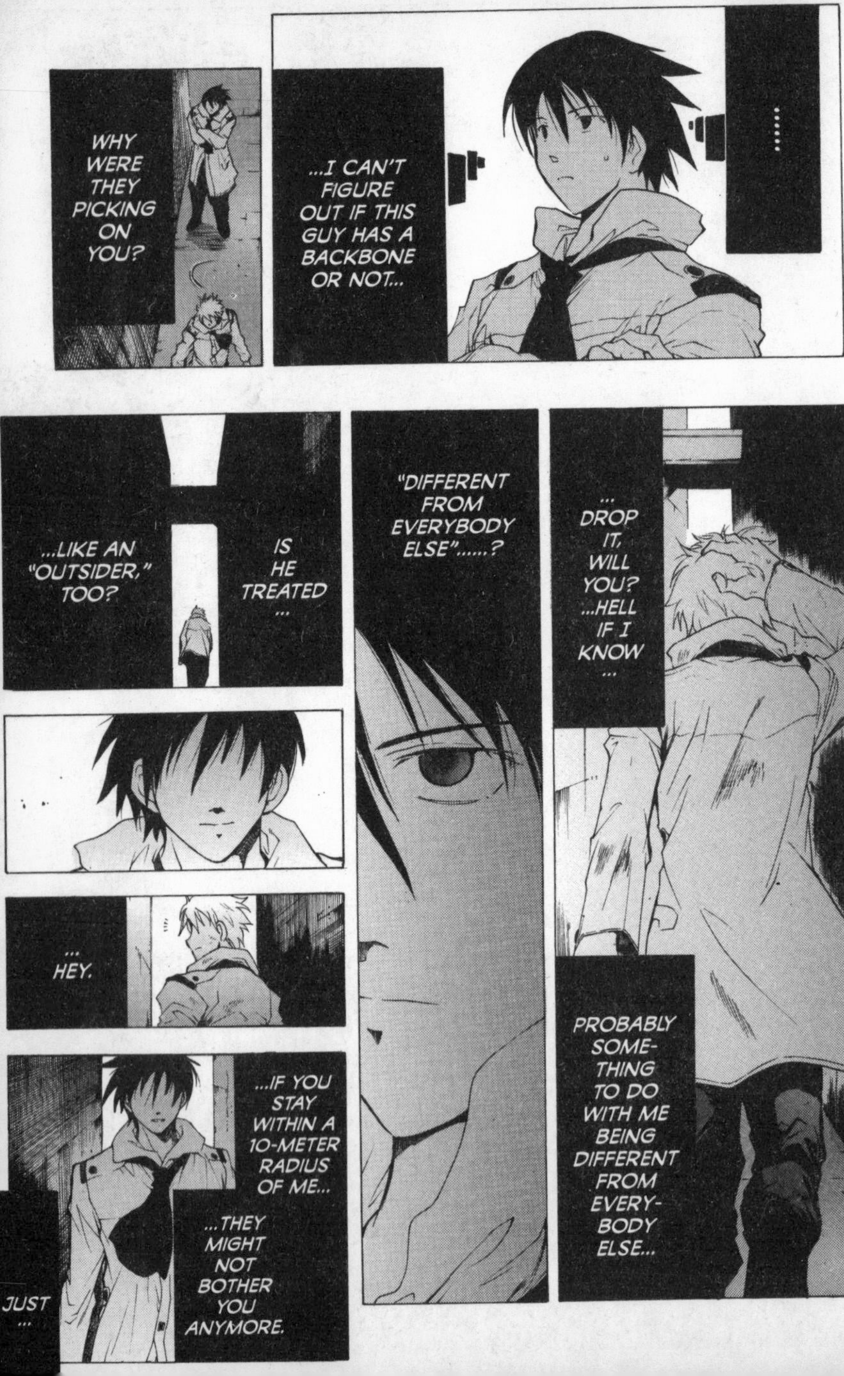
......
...I CAN'T FIGURE OUT IF THIS GUY HAS A BACKBONE OR NOT...
WHY WERE THEY PICKING ON YOU?
...DROP IT, WILL YOU? ...HELL IF I KNOW...
PROBABLY SOME-THING TO DO WITH ME BEING DIFFERENT FROM EVERY-BODY ELSE...
"DIFFERENT FROM EVERYBODY ELSE"......?
IS HE TREATED...
...LIKE AN "OUTSIDER," TOO?
...HEY.
...IF YOU STAY WITHIN A 10-METER RADIUS OF ME...
...THEY MIGHT NOT BOTHER YOU ANYMORE.
JUST...

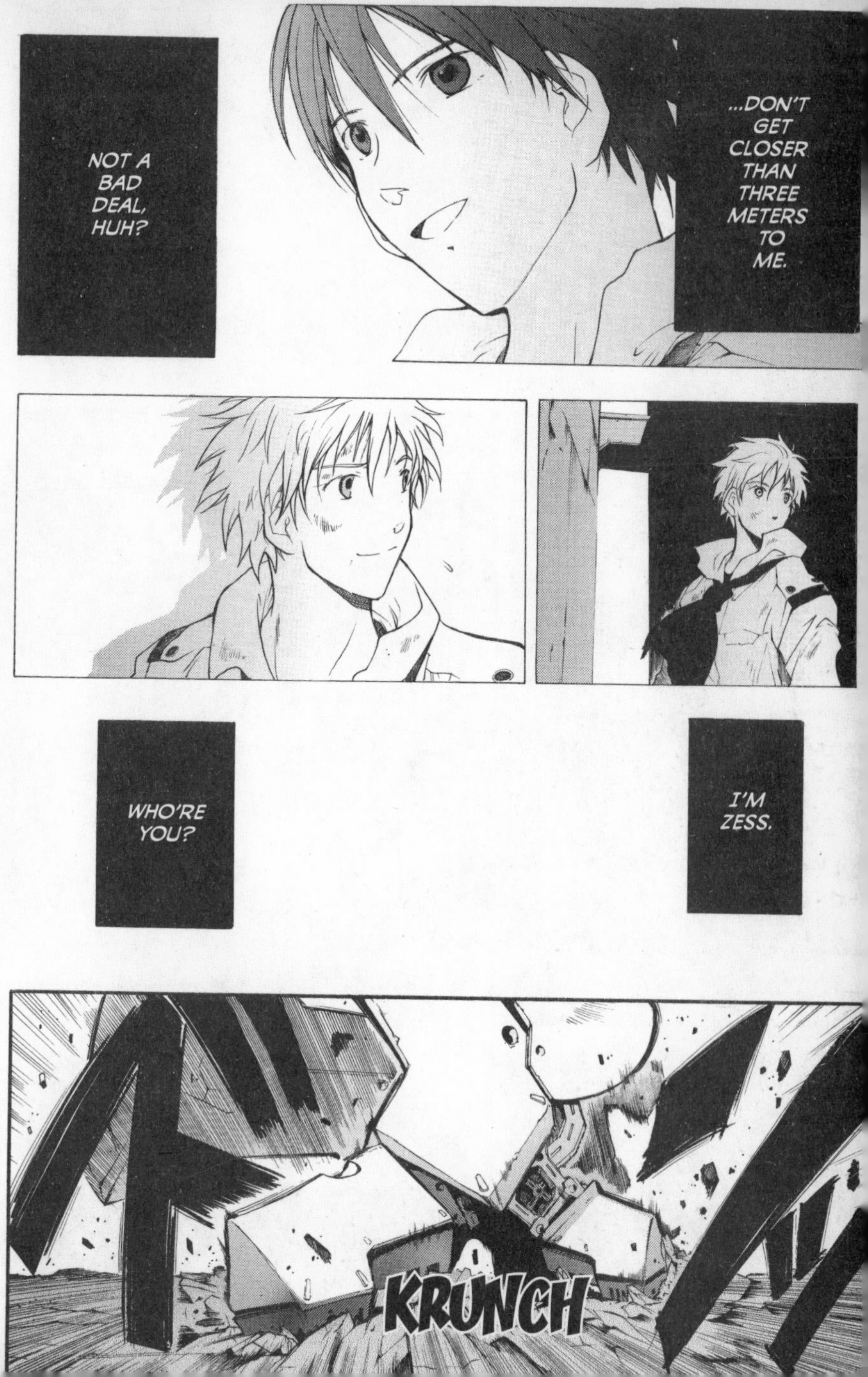
...DON'T GET CLOSER THAN THREE METERS TO ME.
NOT A BAD DEAL, HUH?
I'M ZESS.
WHO'RE YOU?
KRUNCH

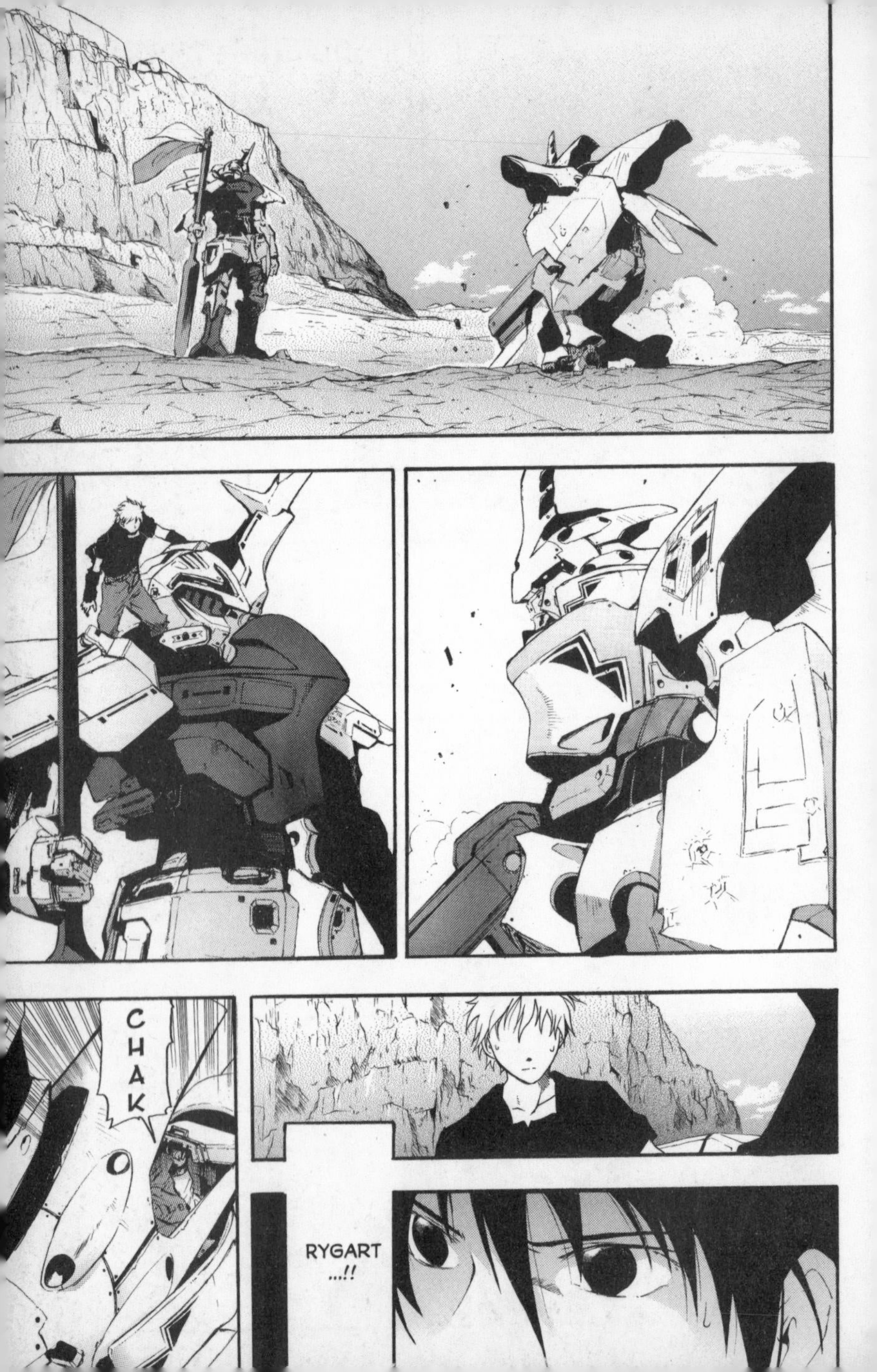
CHAK
RYGART ...!!

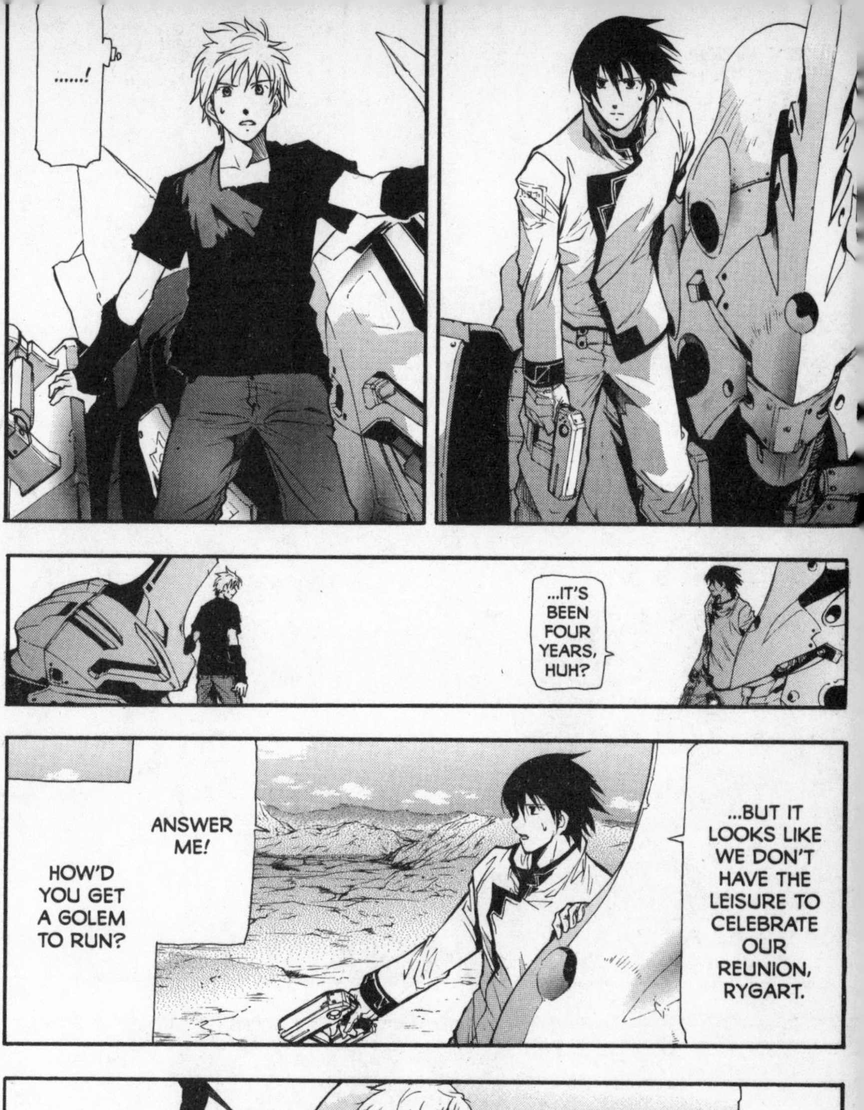
......!
...IT'S BEEN FOUR YEARS, HUH?
...BUT IT LOOKS LIKE WE DON'T HAVE THE LEISURE TO CELEBRATE OUR REUNION, RYGART.
ANSWER ME!
HOW'D YOU GET A GOLEM TO RUN?
ZESS...!
LET ME ASK THE FIRST QUESTION!
WHY THE HELL ARE YOU ATTACKING HODR'S COUNTRY?!

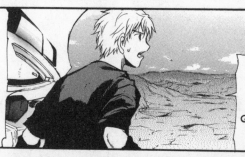

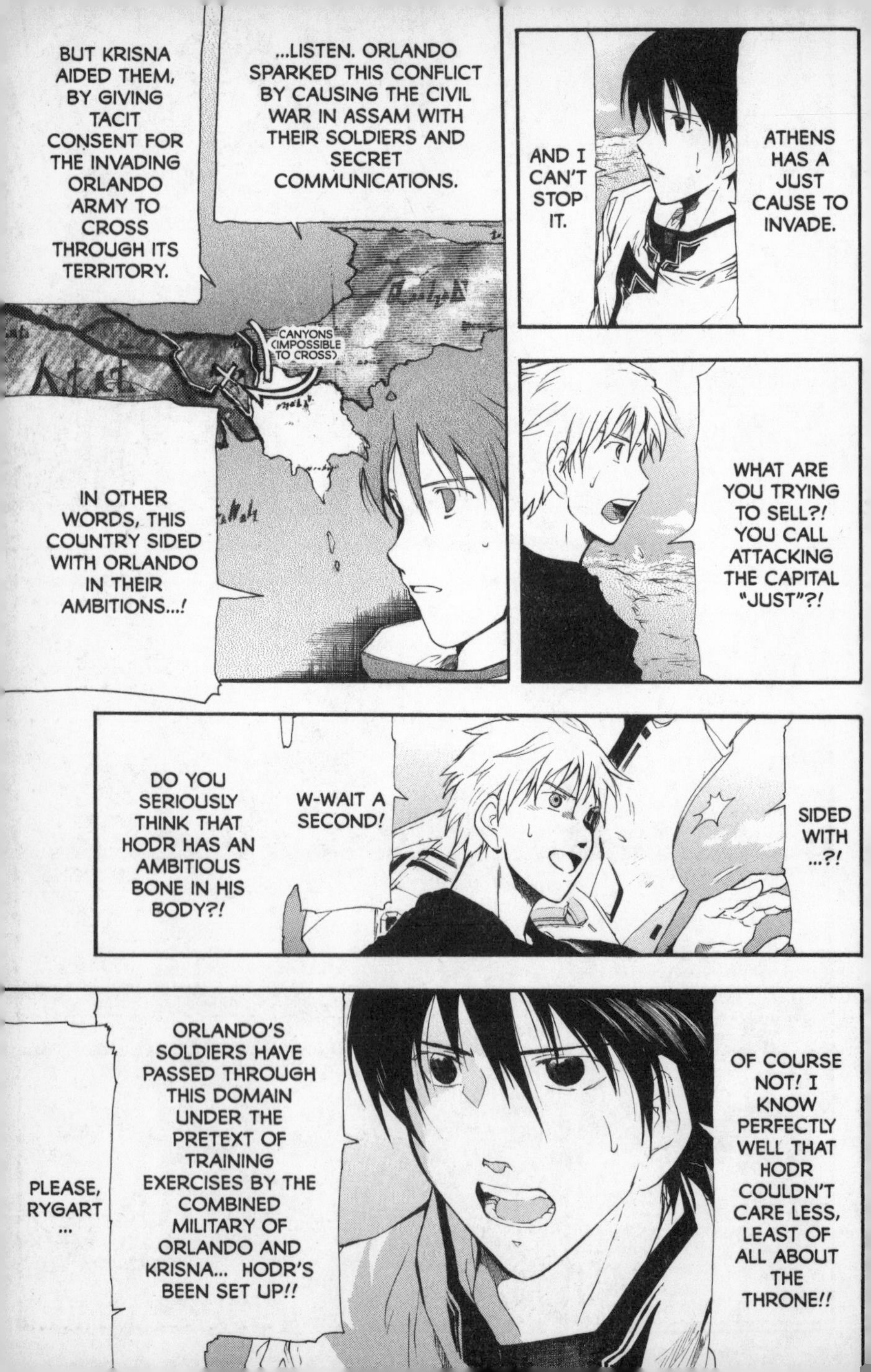

ATHENS HAS A JUST CAUSE TO INVADE.
AND I CAN'T STOP IT.
WHAT ARE YOU TRYING TO SELL?! YOU CALL ATTACKING THE CAPITAL "JUST"?!
...LISTEN. ORLANDO SPARKED THIS CONFLICT BY CAUSING THE CIVIL WAR IN ASSAM WITH THEIR SOLDIERS AND SECRET COMMUNICATIONS.
BUT KRISNA AIDED THEM, BY GIVING TACIT CONSENT FOR THE INVADING ORLANDO ARMY TO CROSS THROUGH ITS TERRITORY.
CANYONS (IMPOSSIBLE TO CROSS)
IN OTHER WORDS, THIS COUNTRY SIDED WITH ORLANDO IN THEIR AMBITIONS...!
SIDED WITH ...?!
W-WAIT A SECOND!
DO YOU SERIOUSLY THINK THAT HODR HAS AN AMBITIOUS BONE IN HIS BODY?!
OF COURSE NOT! I KNOW PERFECTLY WELL THAT HODR COULDN'T CARE LESS, LEAST OF ALL ABOUT THE THRONE!!
ORLANDO'S SOLDIERS HAVE PASSED THROUGH THIS DOMAIN UNDER THE PRETEXT OF TRAINING EXERCISES BY THE COMBINED MILITARY OF ORLANDO AND KRISNA... HODR'S BEEN SET UP!!
PLEASE, RYGART ...

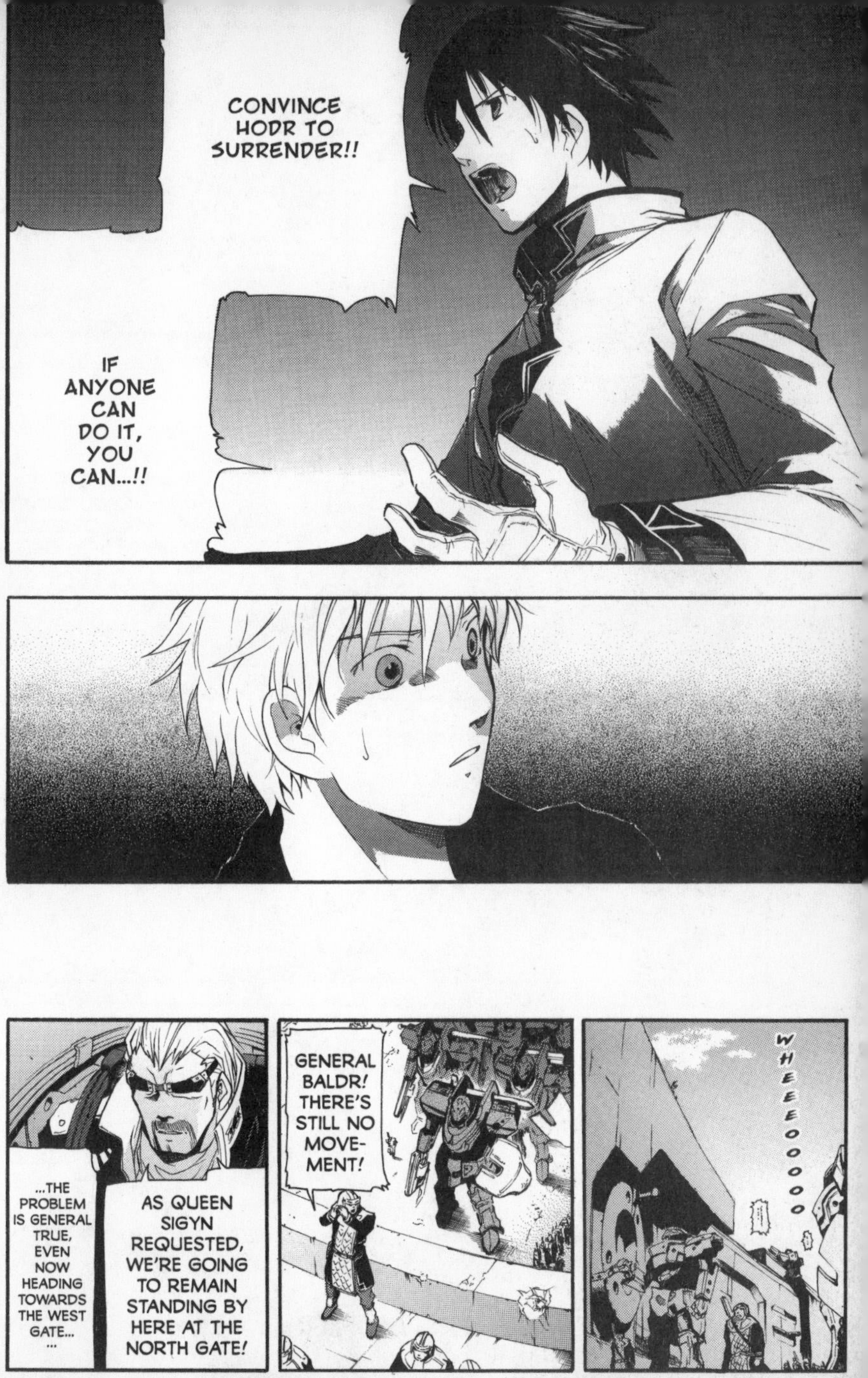
CONVINCE HODR TO SURRENDER!!
IF ANYONE CAN DO IT, YOU CAN...!!
WHEEEOOOOO
GENERAL BALDR! THERE'S STILL NO MOVEMENT!
AS QUEEN SIGYN REQUESTED, WE'RE GOING TO REMAIN STANDING BY HERE AT THE NORTH GATE!
...THE PROBLEM IS GENERAL TRUE, EVEN NOW HEADING TOWARDS THE WEST GATE... ...

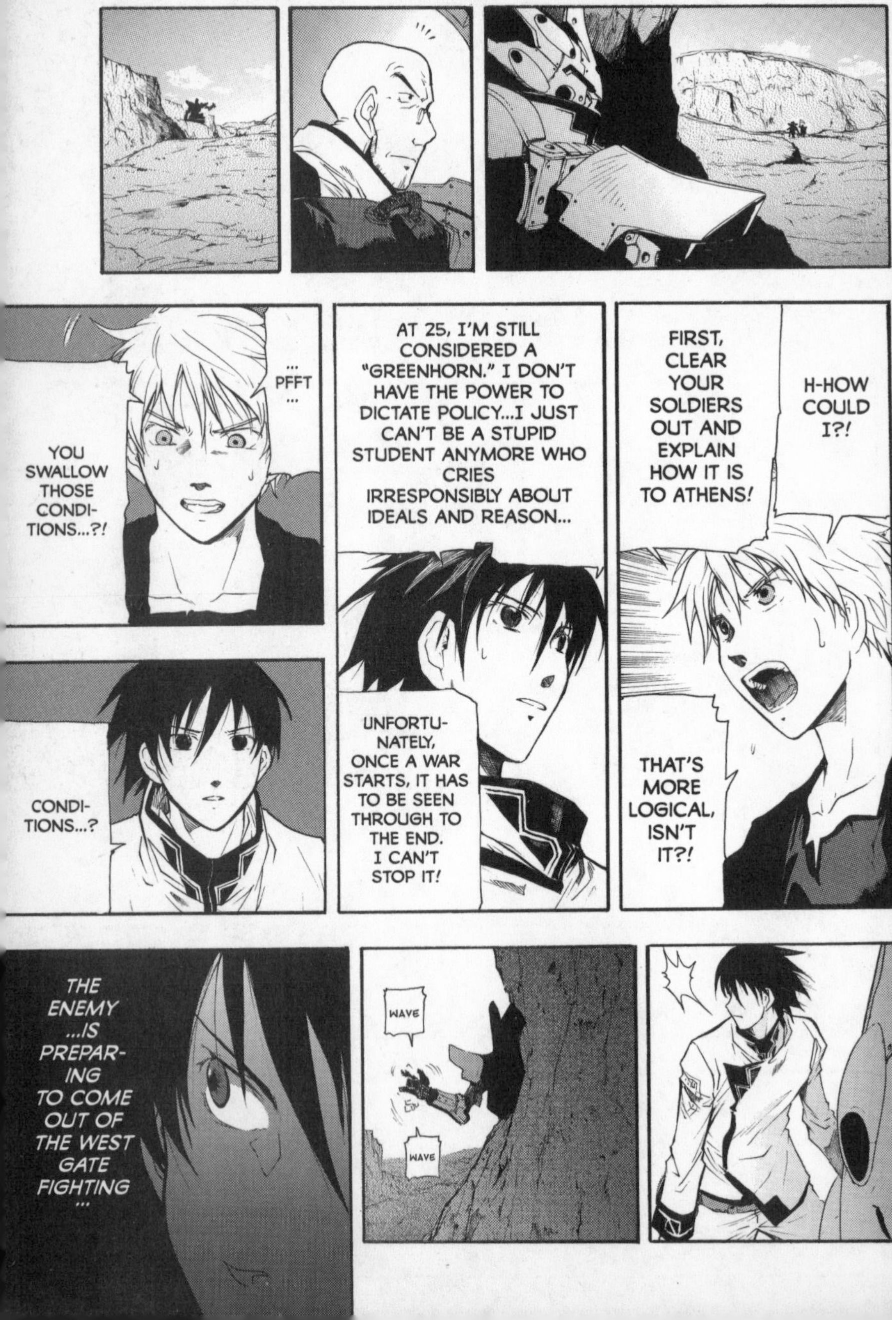
H-HOW COULD I?!
FIRST, CLEAR YOUR SOLDIERS OUT AND EXPLAIN HOW IT IS TO ATHENS!
THAT'S MORE LOGICAL, ISN'T IT?!
AT 25, I'M STILL CONSIDERED A "GREENHORN." I DON'T HAVE THE POWER TO DICTATE POLICY...I JUST CAN'T BE A STUPID STUDENT ANYMORE WHO CRIES IRRESPONSIBLY ABOUT IDEALS AND REASON...
UNFORTU-NATELY, ONCE A WAR STARTS, IT HAS TO BE SEEN THROUGH TO THE END. I CAN'T STOP IT!
... PFFT ...
YOU SWALLOW THOSE CONDI-TIONS...?!
CONDI-TIONS...?
WAVE
WAVE
THE ENEMY ...IS PREPAR-ING TO COME OUT OF THE WEST GATE FIGHTING ...

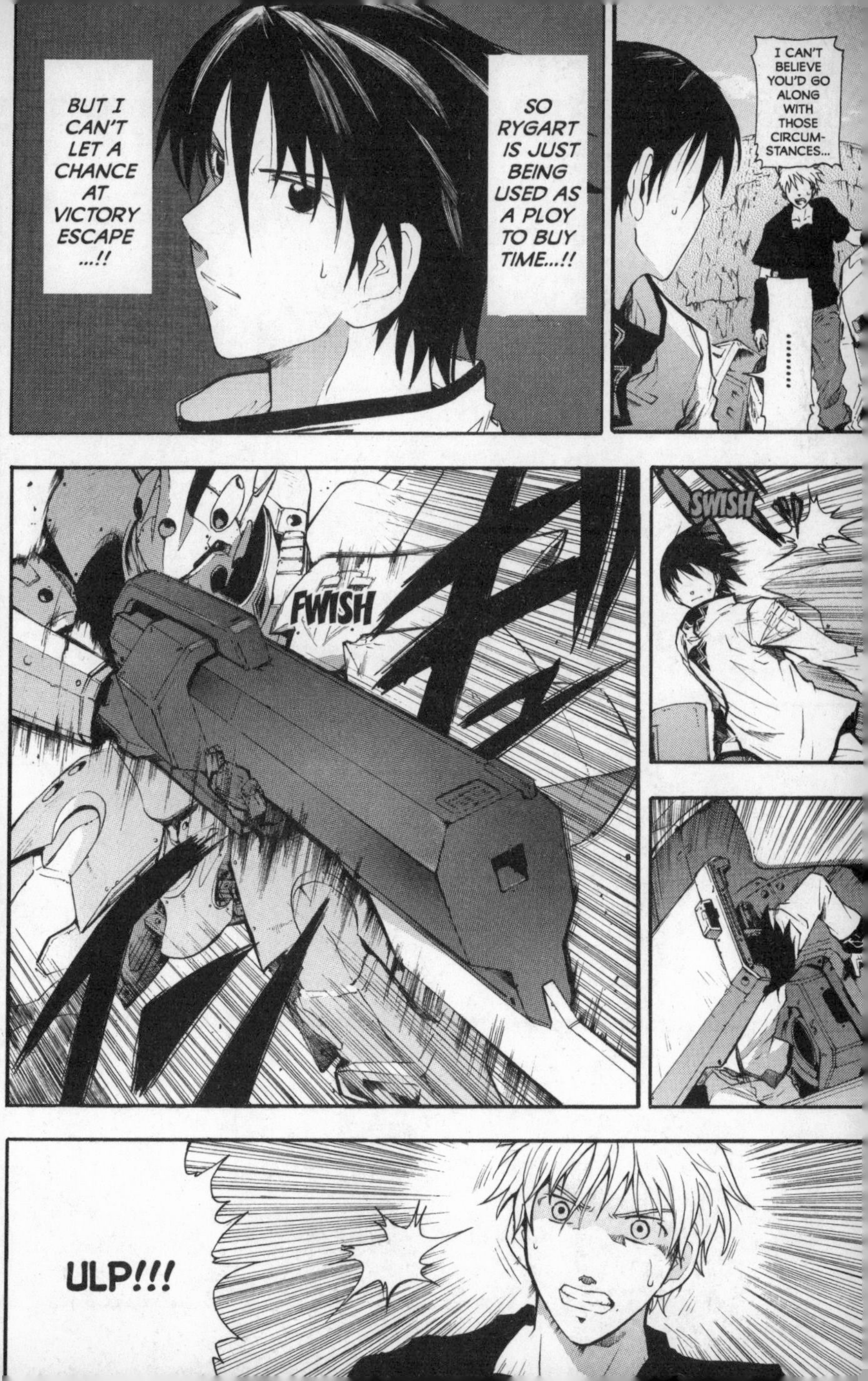
I CAN'T BELIEVE YOU'D GO ALONG WITH THOSE CIRCUM-STANCES...
......
SO RYGART IS JUST BEING USED AS A PLOY TO BUY TIME...!!
BUT I CAN'T LET A CHANCE AT VICTORY ESCAPE ...!!
SWISH
FWISH
ULP!!!

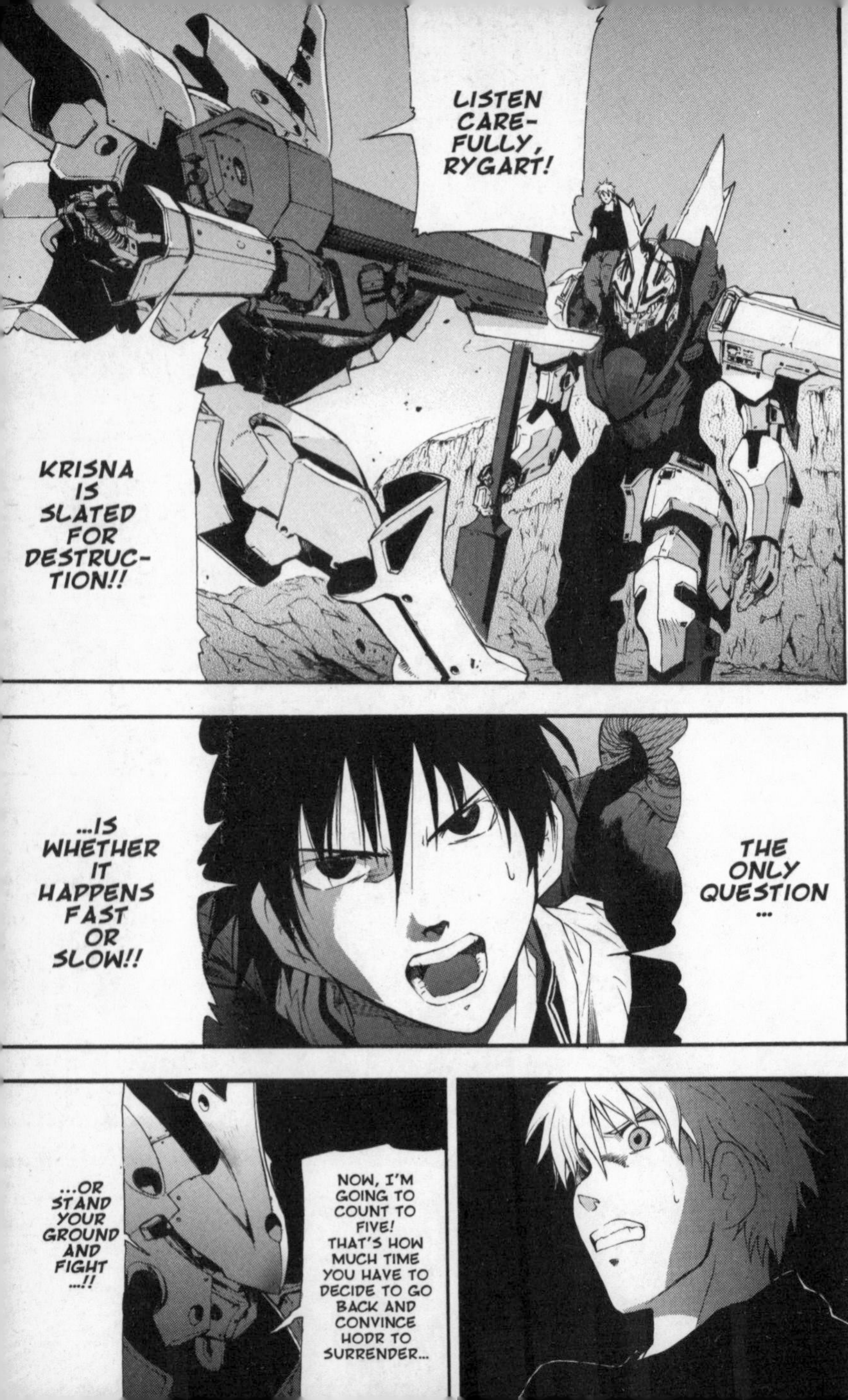
LISTEN CARE-FULLY, RYGART!
KRISNA IS SLATED FOR DESTRUC-TION!!
THE ONLY QUESTION ...
...IS WHETHER IT HAPPENS FAST OR SLOW!!
NOW, I'M GOING TO COUNT TO FIVE! THAT'S HOW MUCH TIME YOU HAVE TO DECIDE TO GO BACK AND CONVINCE HODR TO SURRENDER...
...OR STAND YOUR GROUND AND FIGHT ...!!

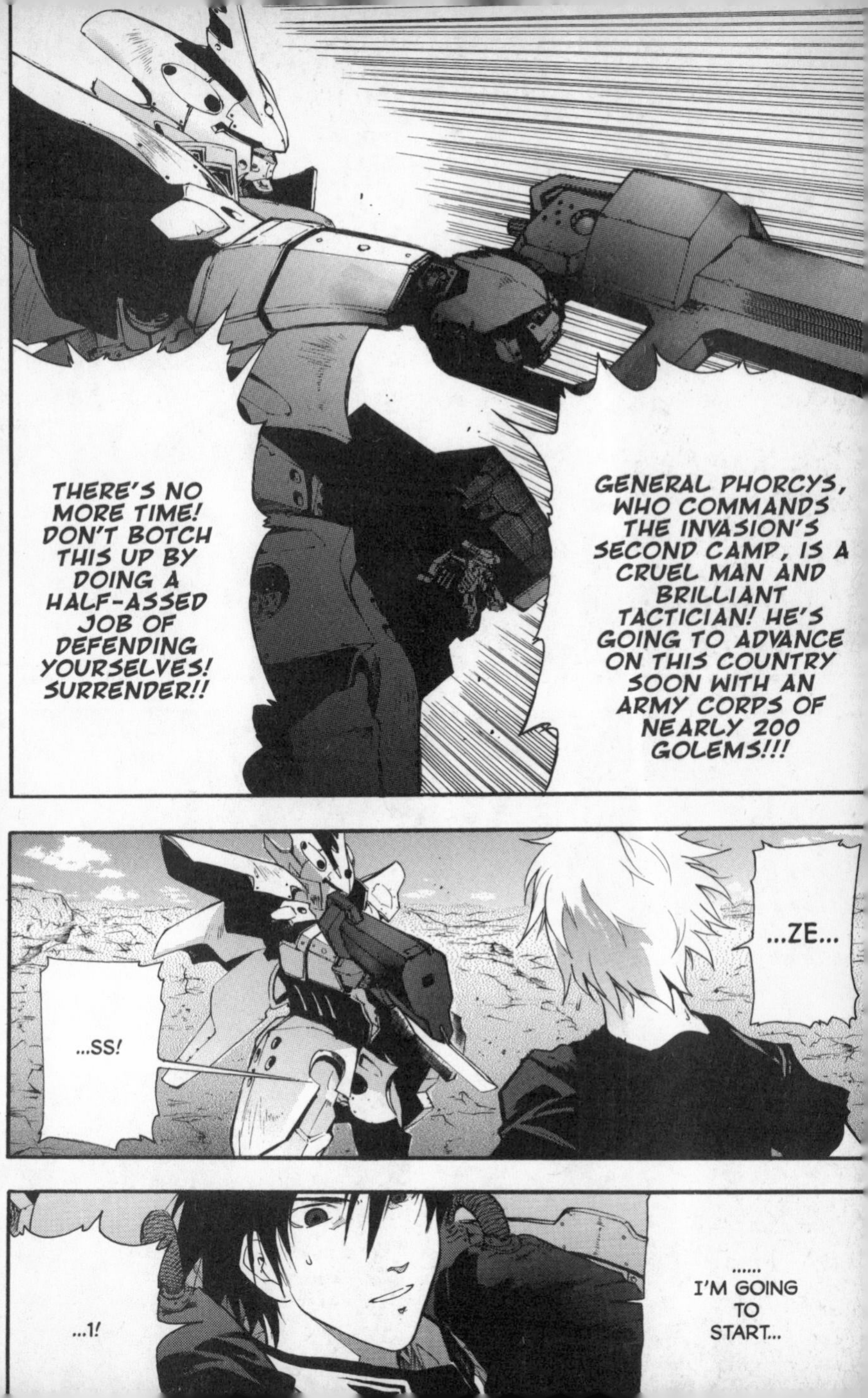
GENERAL PHORCYS, WHO COMMANDS THE INVASION'S SECOND CAMP, IS A CRUEL MAN AND BRILLIANT TACTICIAN! HE'S GOING TO ADVANCE ON THIS COUNTRY SOON WITH AN ARMY CORPS OF NEARLY 200 GOLEMS!!!
THERE'S NO MORE TIME! DON'T BOTCH THIS UP BY DOING A HALF-ASSED JOB OF DEFENDING YOURSELVES! SURRENDER!!
...ZE...
...SS!
...... I'M GOING TO START...
...1!

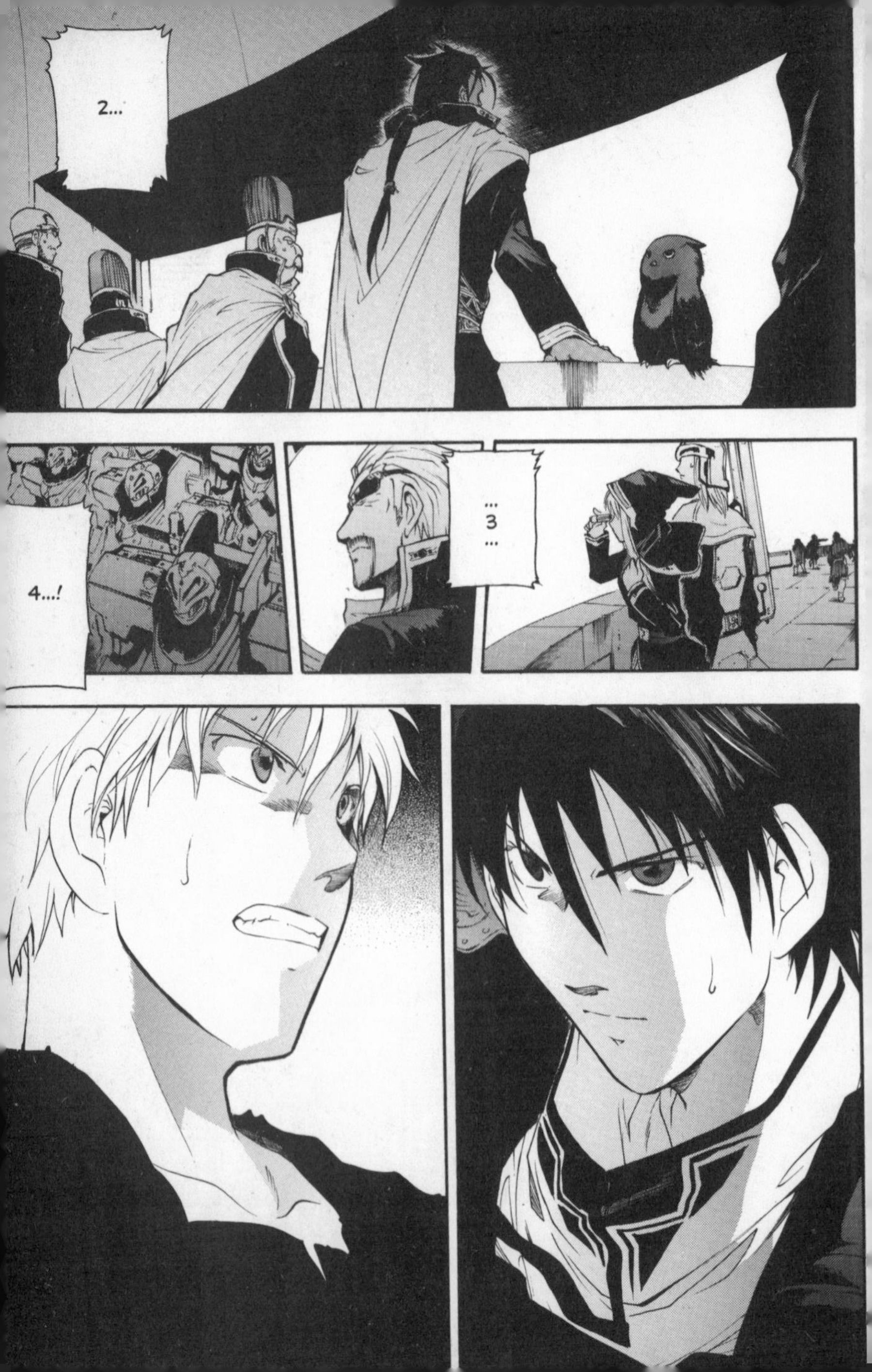
2...
...3...
4...!

BROKEN BLADE

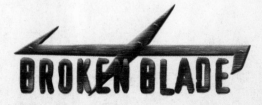

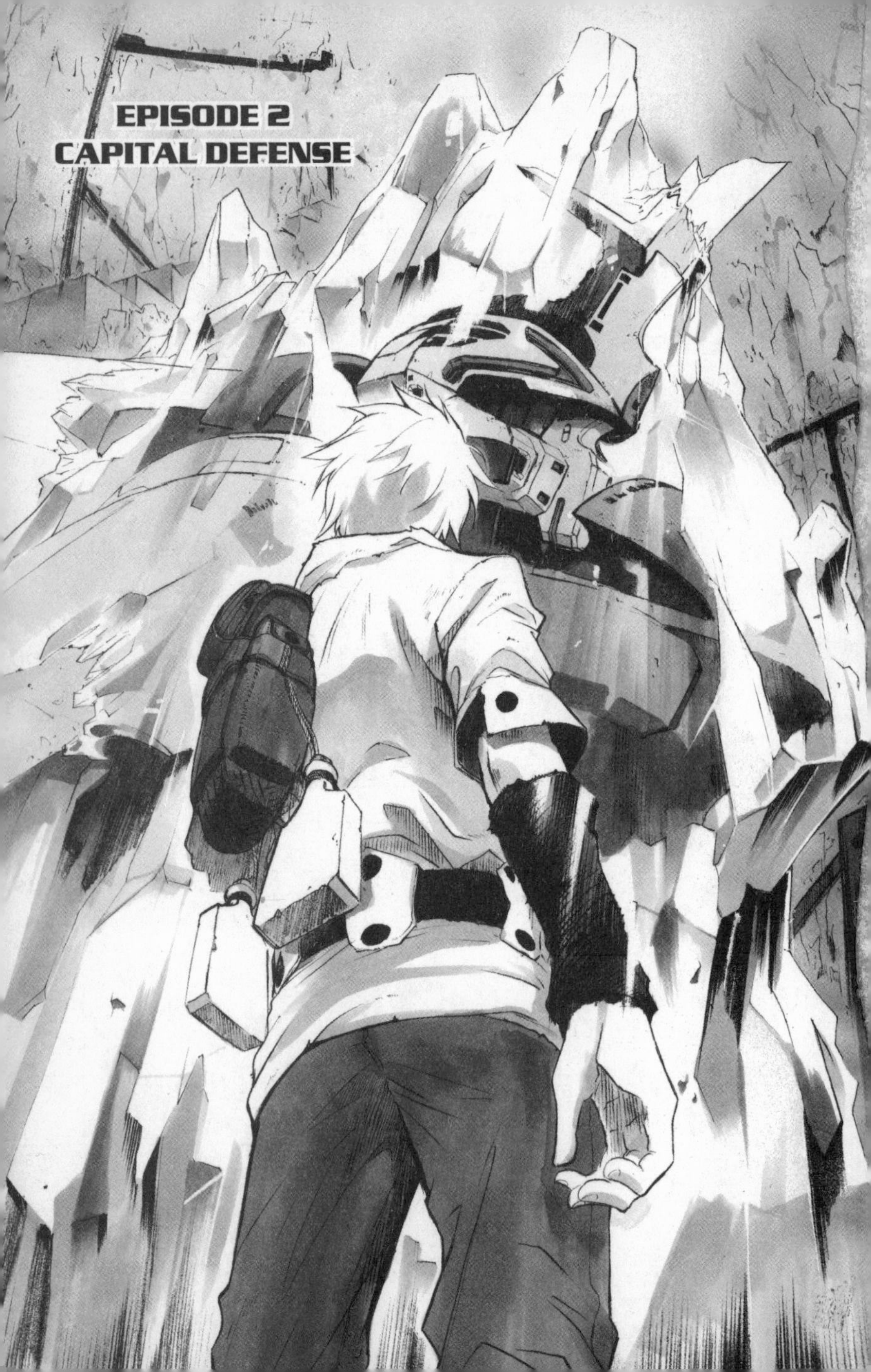
EPISODE 2
CAPITAL DEFENSE

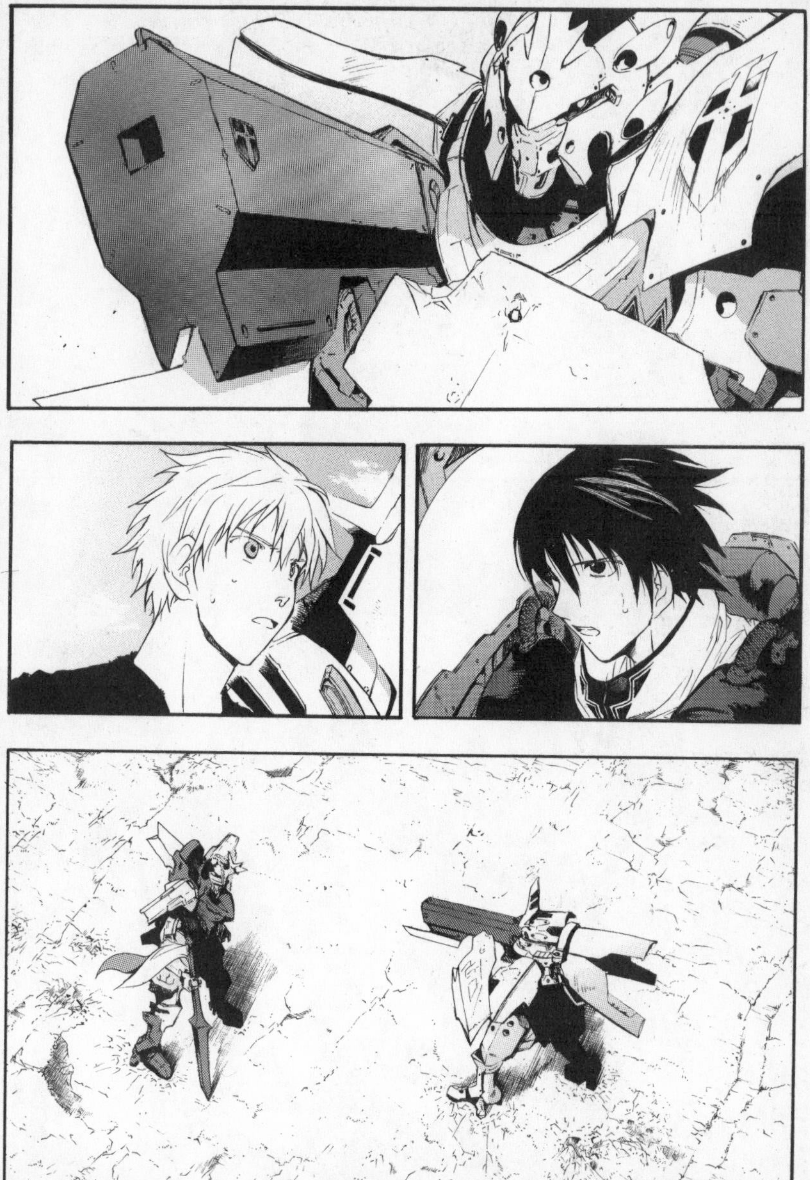

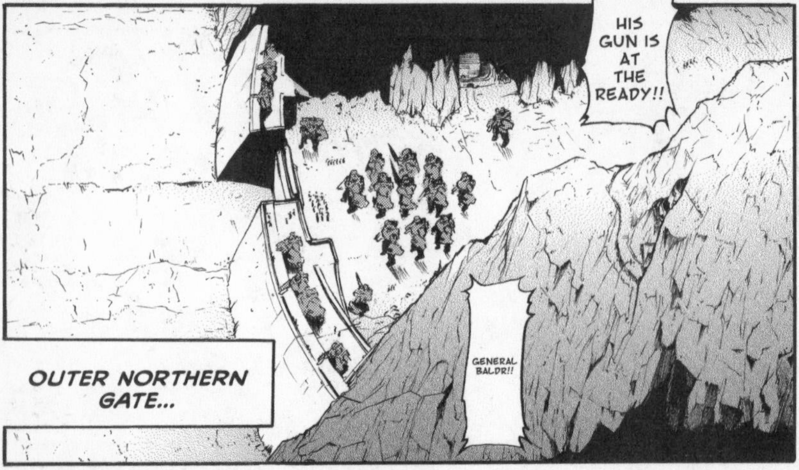
HIS GUN IS AT THE READY!!
GENERAL BALDR!!
OUTER NORTHERN GATE...

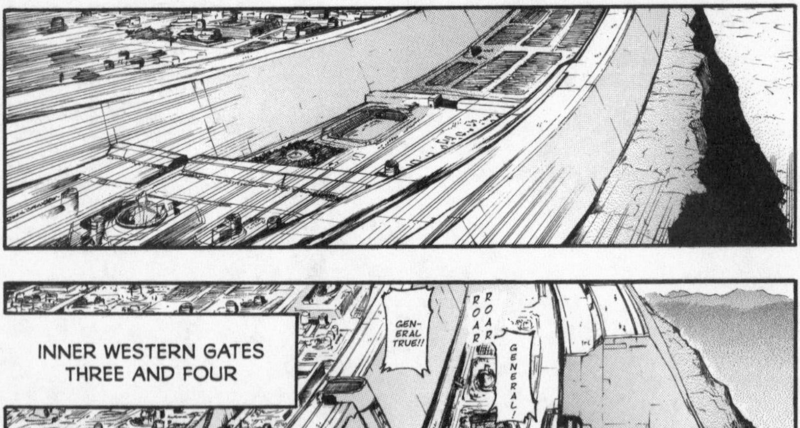

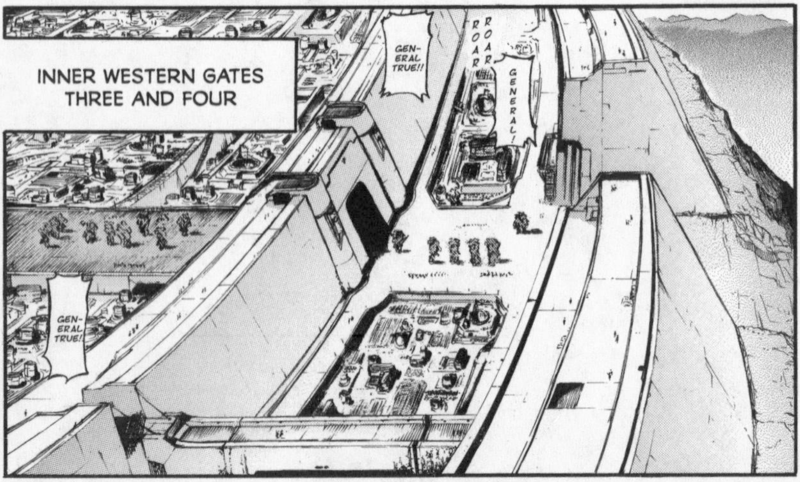
ROAR ROAR
GENERAL!
GEN-ERAL TRUE!!
INNER WESTERN GATES THREE AND FOUR
GEN-ERAL TRUE!!

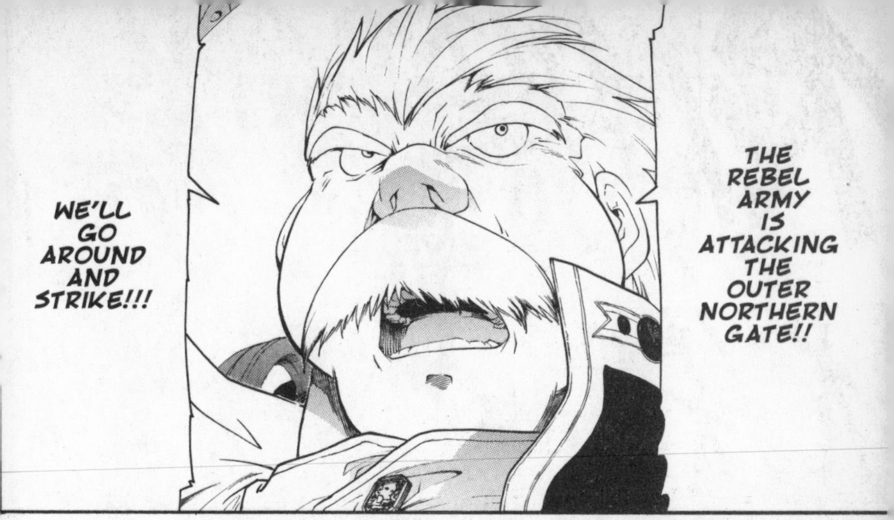
THE REBEL ARMY IS ATTACKING THE OUTER NORTHERN GATE!!
WE'LL GO AROUND AND STRIKE!!!
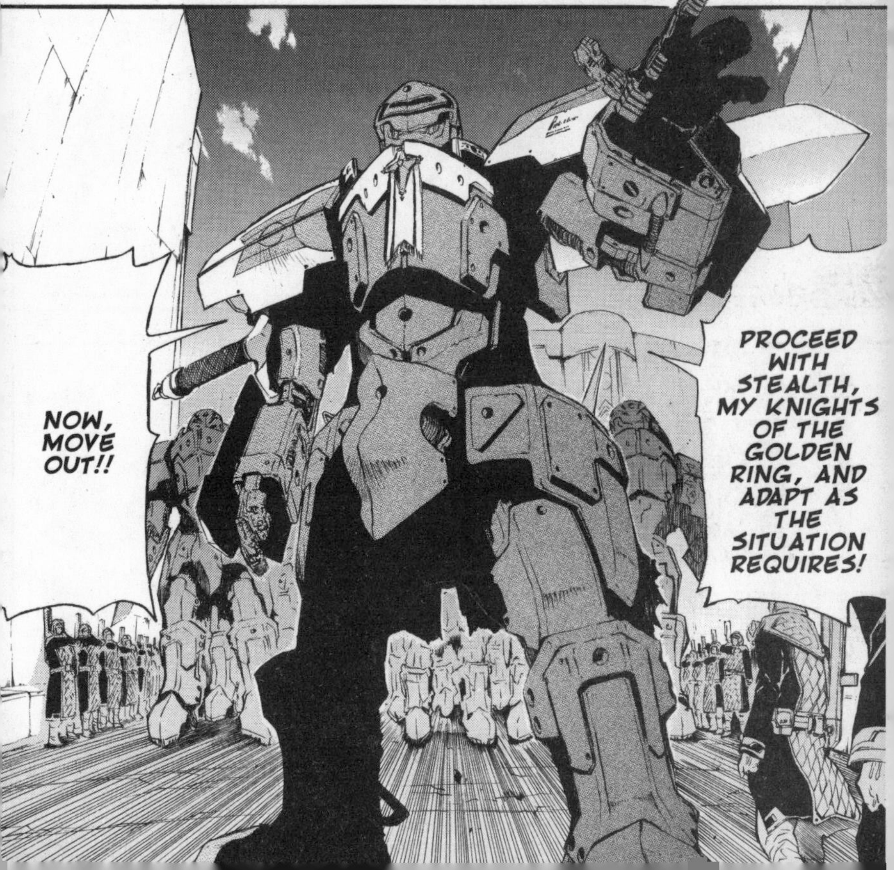
PROCEED WITH STEALTH, MY KNIGHTS OF THE GOLDEN RING, AND ADAPT AS THE SITUATION REQUIRES!
NOW, MOVE OUT!!

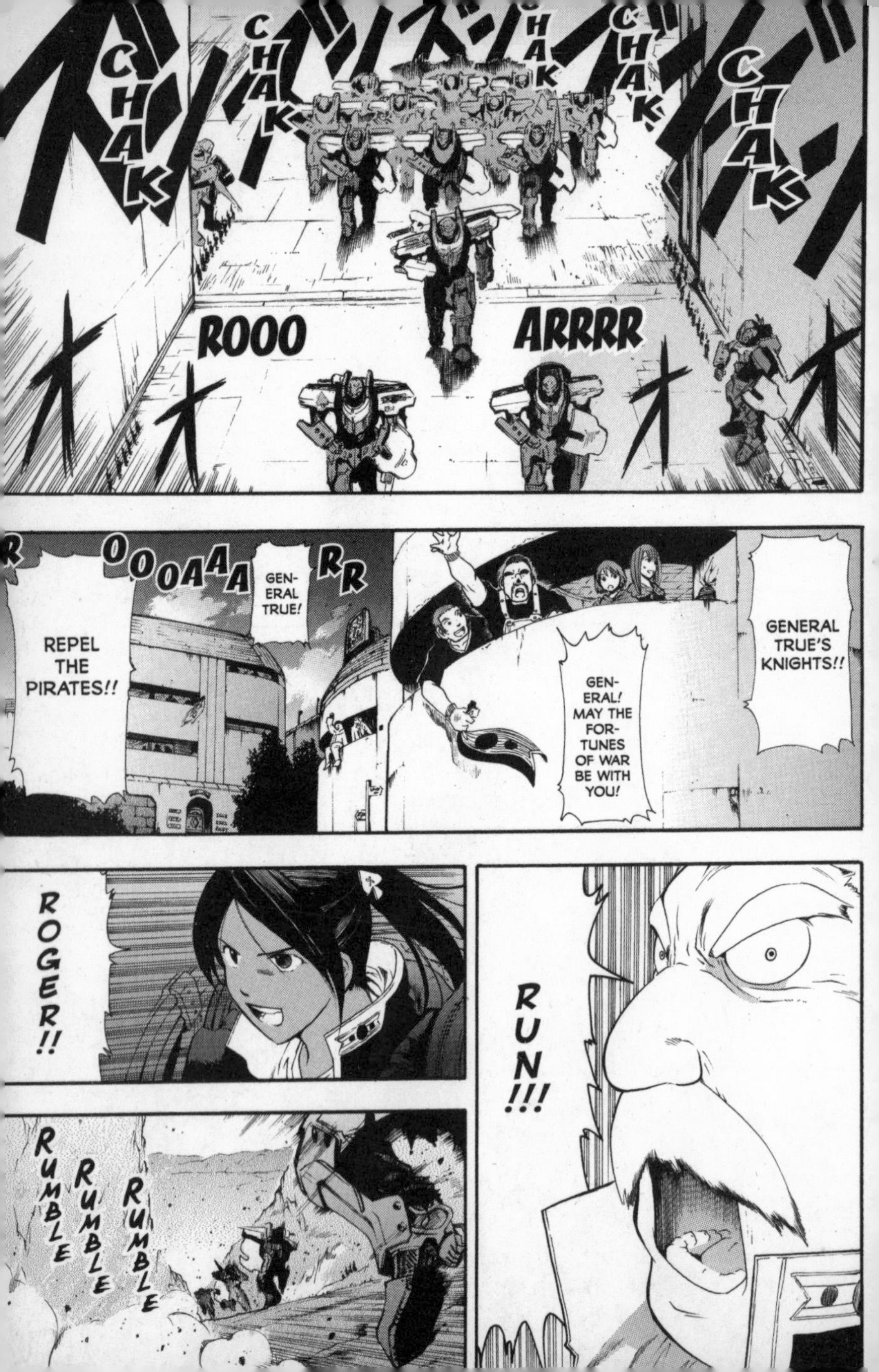
CHAK
CHAK
CHAK
CHAK
CHAK
CHAK
ROOO
ARRRR
GENERAL TRUE'S KNIGHTS!!
GEN-ERAL! MAY THE FOR-TUNES OF WAR BE WITH YOU!
ROOOAAARR
GEN-ERAL TRUE!
REPEL THE PIRATES!!
RUN!!!
ROGER!!
RUMBLE
RUMBLE
RUMBLE

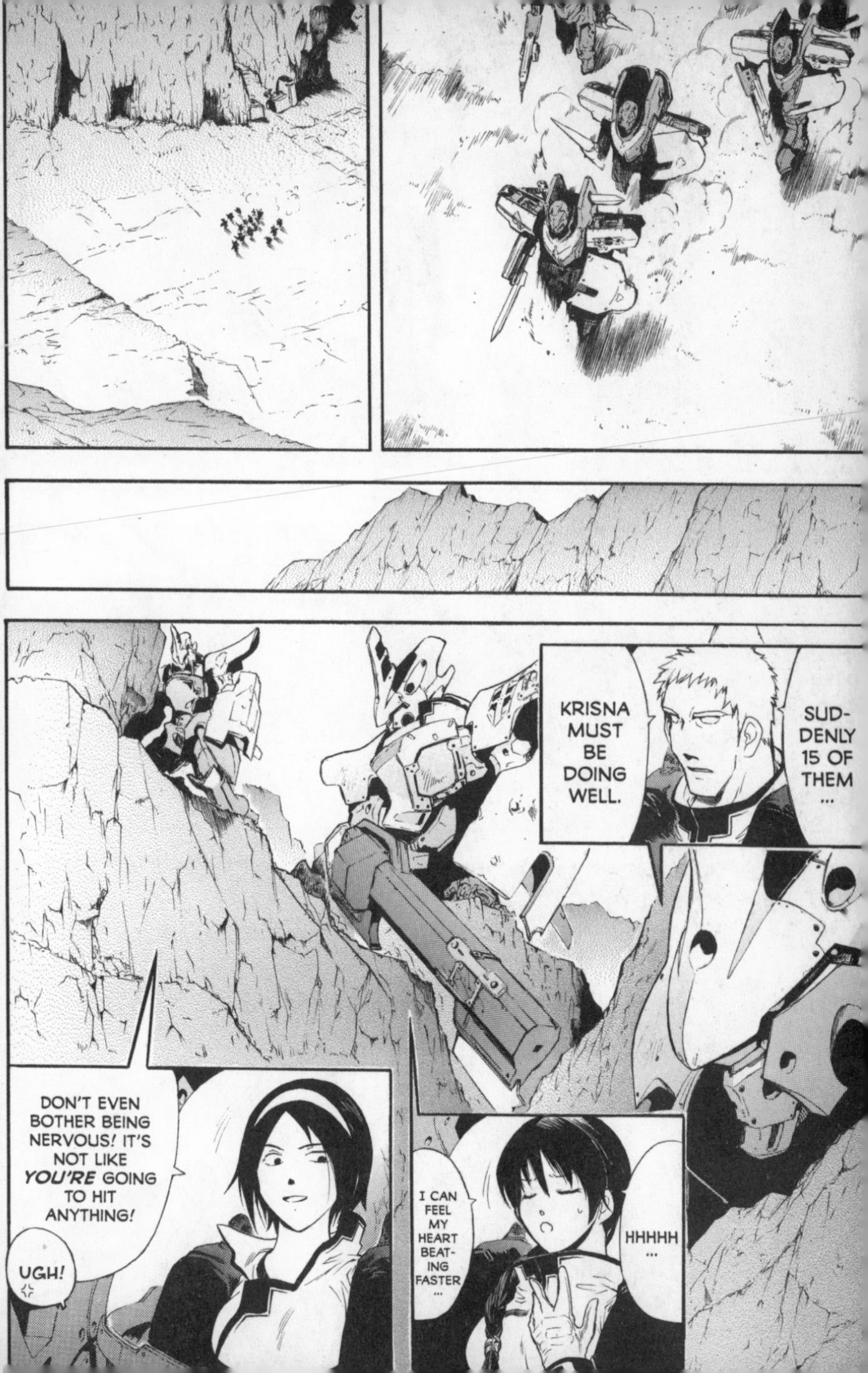
SUD-DENLY 15 OF THEM ...
KRISNA MUST BE DOING WELL.
HHHHH ...
I CAN FEEL MY HEART BEAT-ING FASTER ...
DON'T EVEN BOTHER BEING NERVOUS! IT'S NOT LIKE *YOU'RE* GOING TO HIT ANYTHING!
UGH!

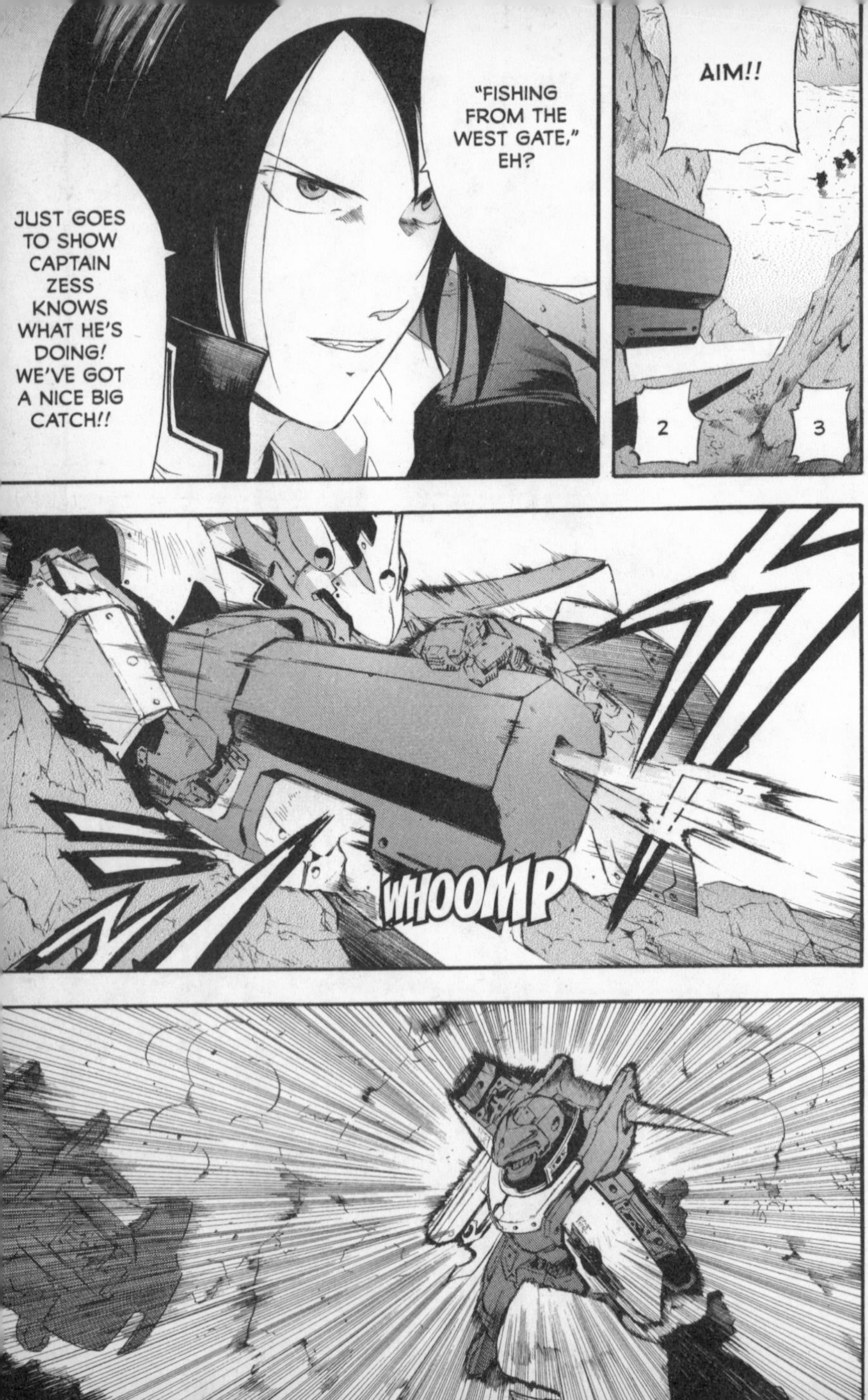
AIM!!
2
3
"FISHING FROM THE WEST GATE," EH?
JUST GOES TO SHOW CAPTAIN ZESS KNOWS WHAT HE'S DOING! WE'VE GOT A NICE BIG CATCH!!
WHOOMP

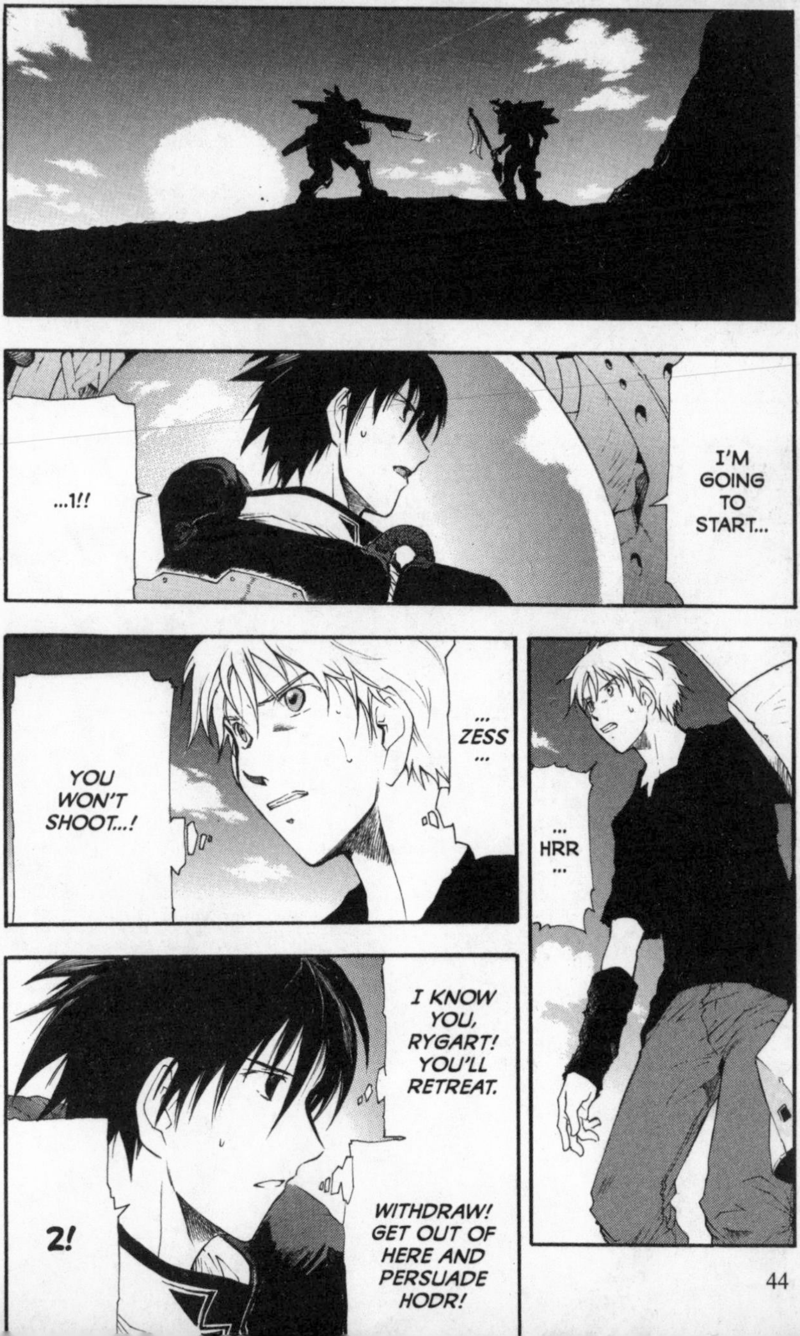
I'M GOING TO START...
...1!!
...
HRR
...
...
ZESS
...
YOU WON'T SHOOT...!
I KNOW YOU, RYGART! YOU'LL RETREAT.
WITHDRAW! GET OUT OF HERE AND PERSUADE HODR!
2!

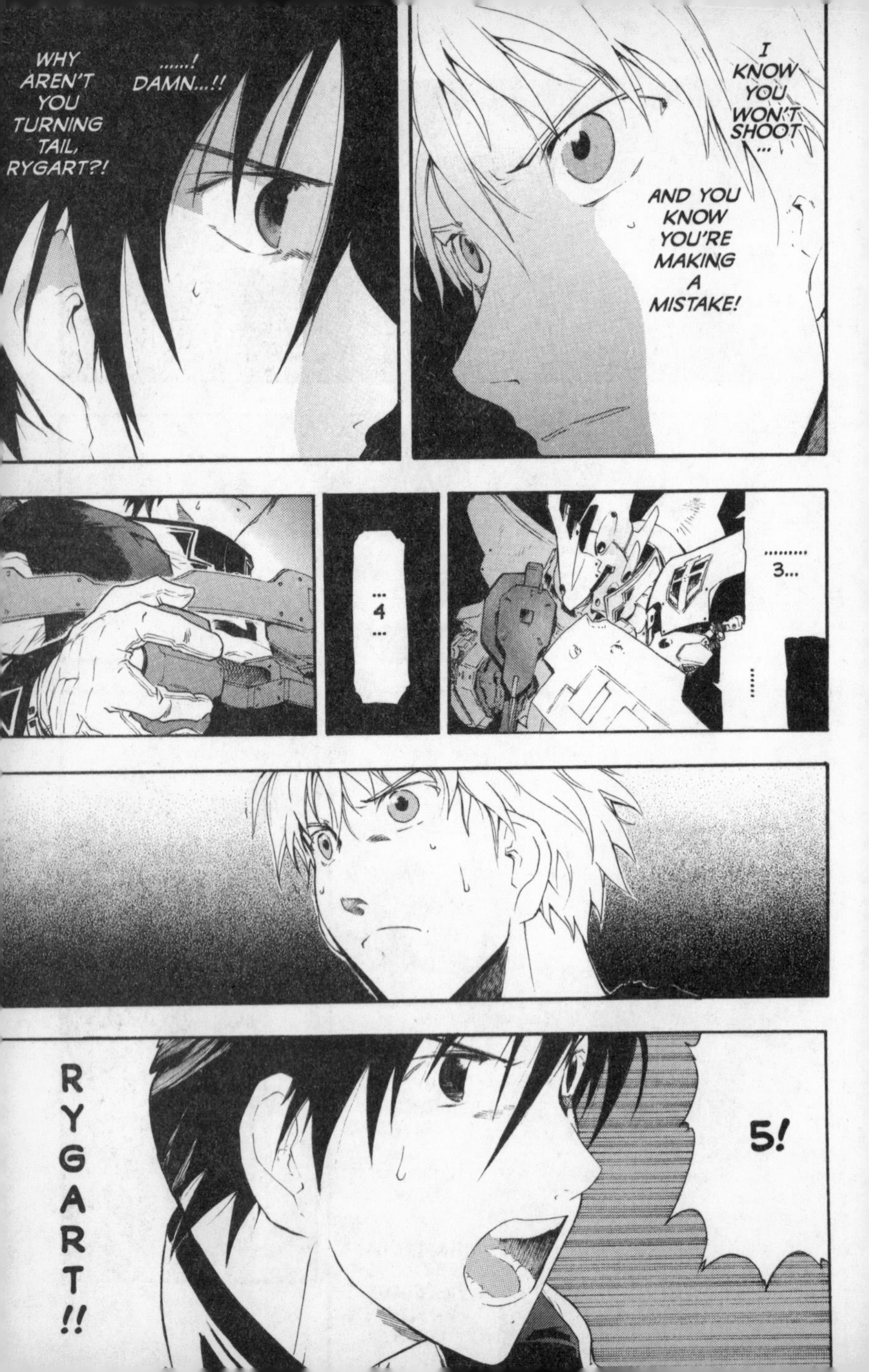
I KNOW YOU WON'T SHOOT...
AND YOU KNOW YOU'RE MAKING A MISTAKE!
......! DAMN...!!
WHY AREN'T YOU TURNING TAIL, RYGART?!
.... 3...
......
...4...
5!
RYGART!!

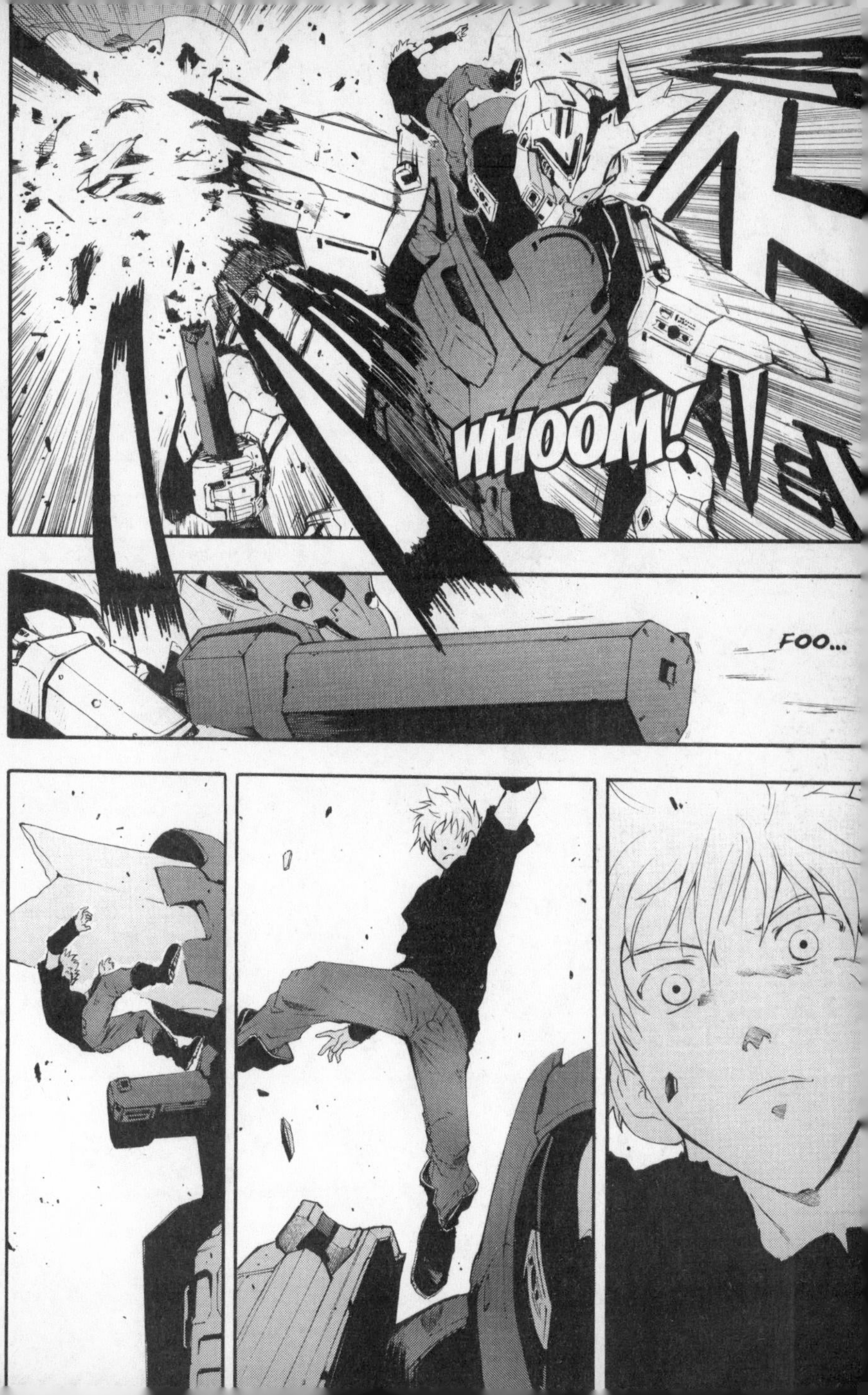
WHOOM!
FOO...

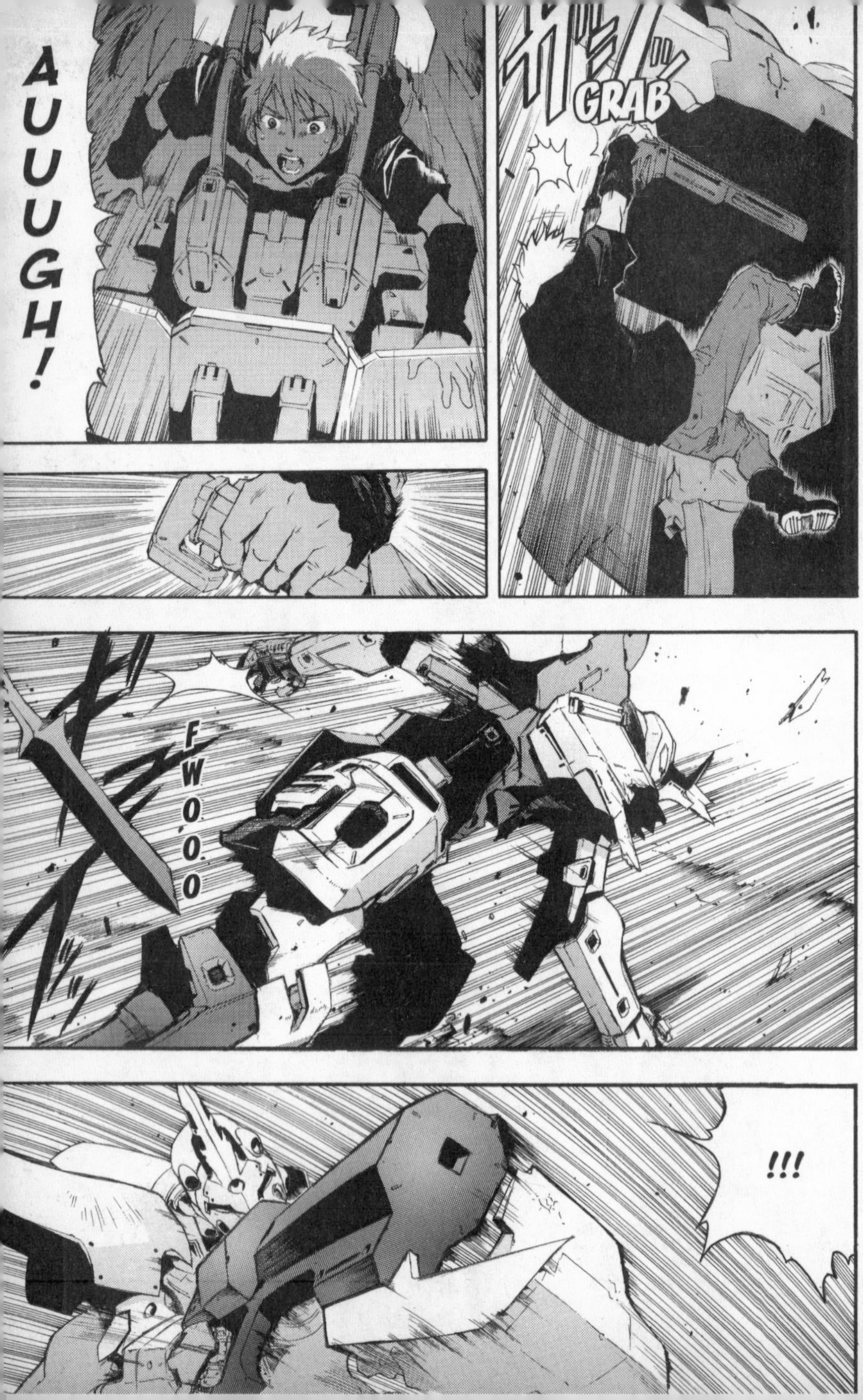

GRAB
AUUUGH!
FWOOO
!!!

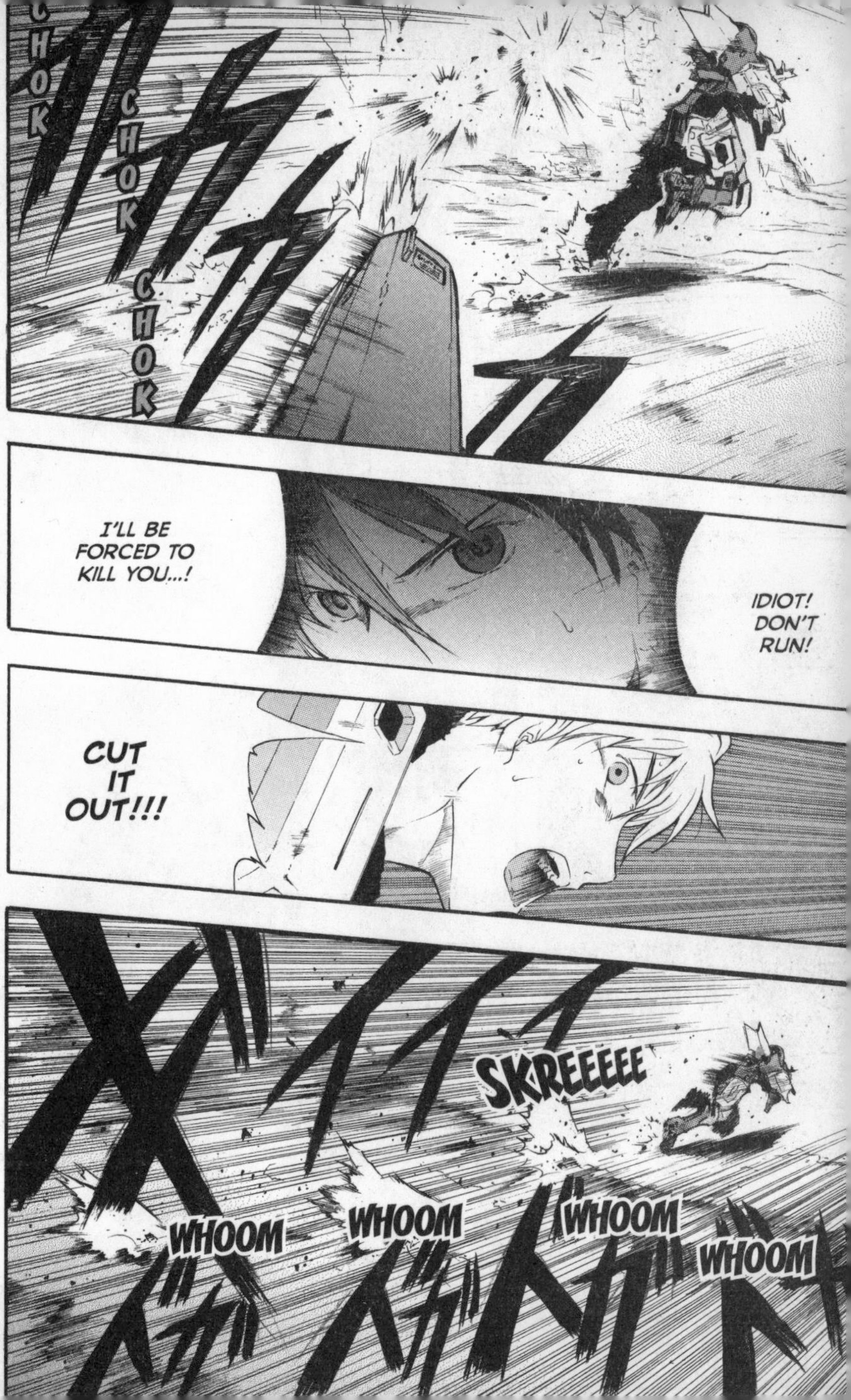
CHOK
CHOK
CHOK
IDIOT! DON'T RUN!
I'LL BE FORCED TO KILL YOU...!
CUT IT OUT!!!
SKREEEEE
WHOOM
WHOOM
WHOOM
WHOOM

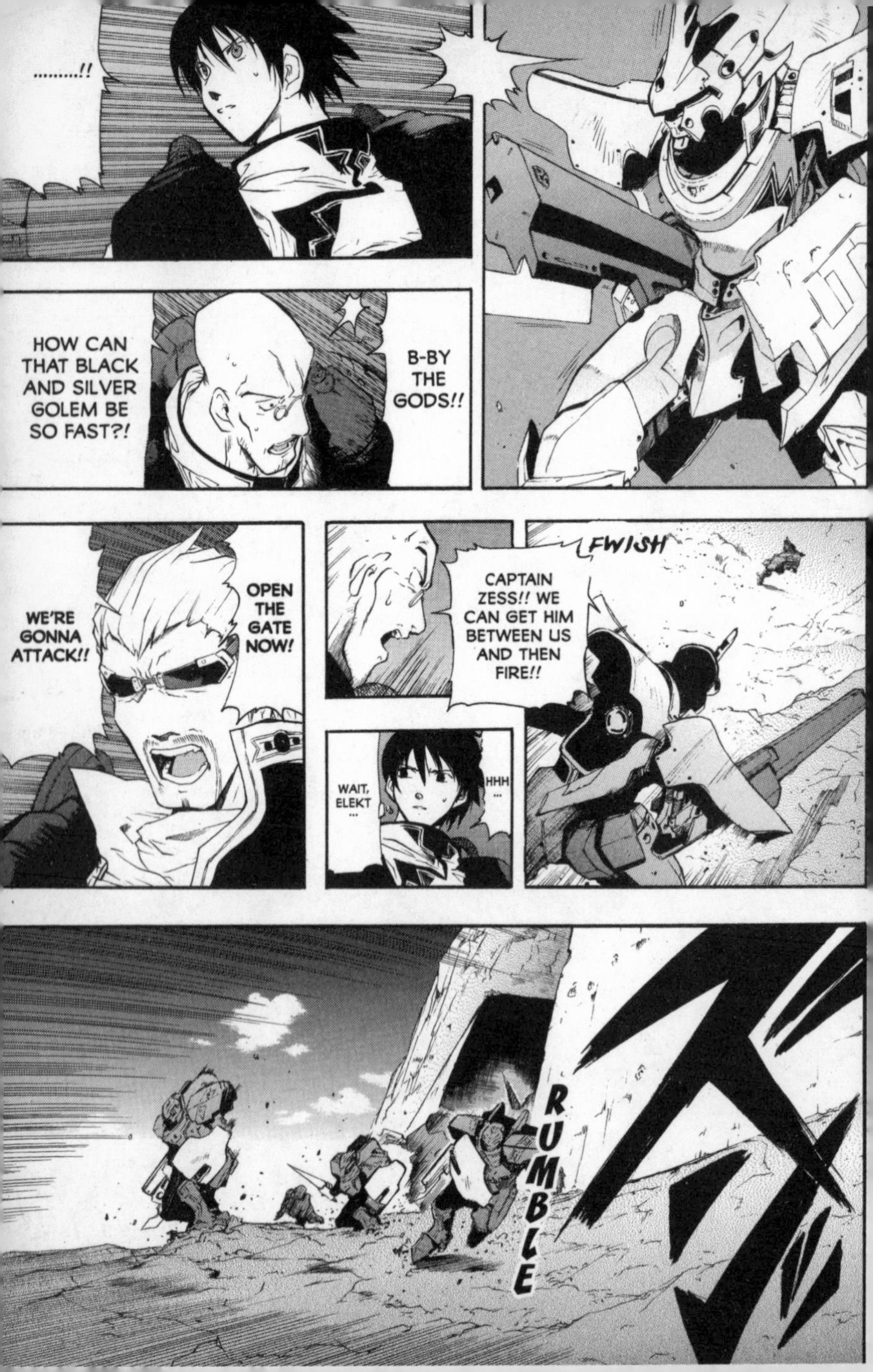

........!!
B-BY THE GODS!!
HOW CAN THAT BLACK AND SILVER GOLEM BE SO FAST?!
FWISH
CAPTAIN ZESS!! WE CAN GET HIM BETWEEN US AND THEN FIRE!!
HHH ...
WAIT, ELEKT ...
OPEN THE GATE NOW!
WE'RE GONNA ATTACK!!
RUMBLE

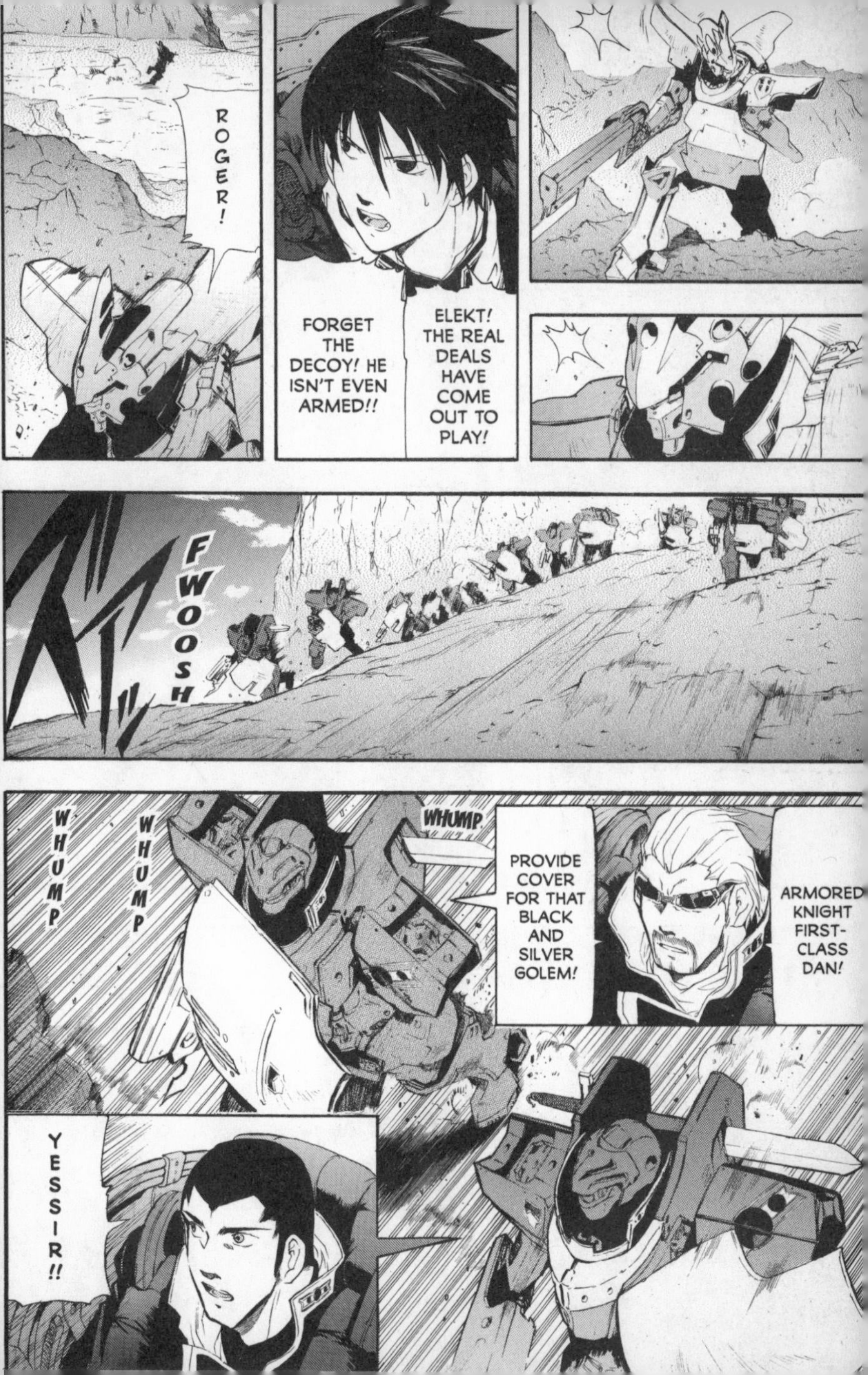
ELEKT! THE REAL DEALS HAVE COME OUT TO PLAY!
FORGET THE DECOY! HE ISN'T EVEN ARMED!!
ROGER!
FWOOSH
ARMORED KNIGHT FIRST-CLASS DAN!
PROVIDE COVER FOR THAT BLACK AND SILVER GOLEM!
WHUMP
WHUMP
WHUMP
YESSIR!!

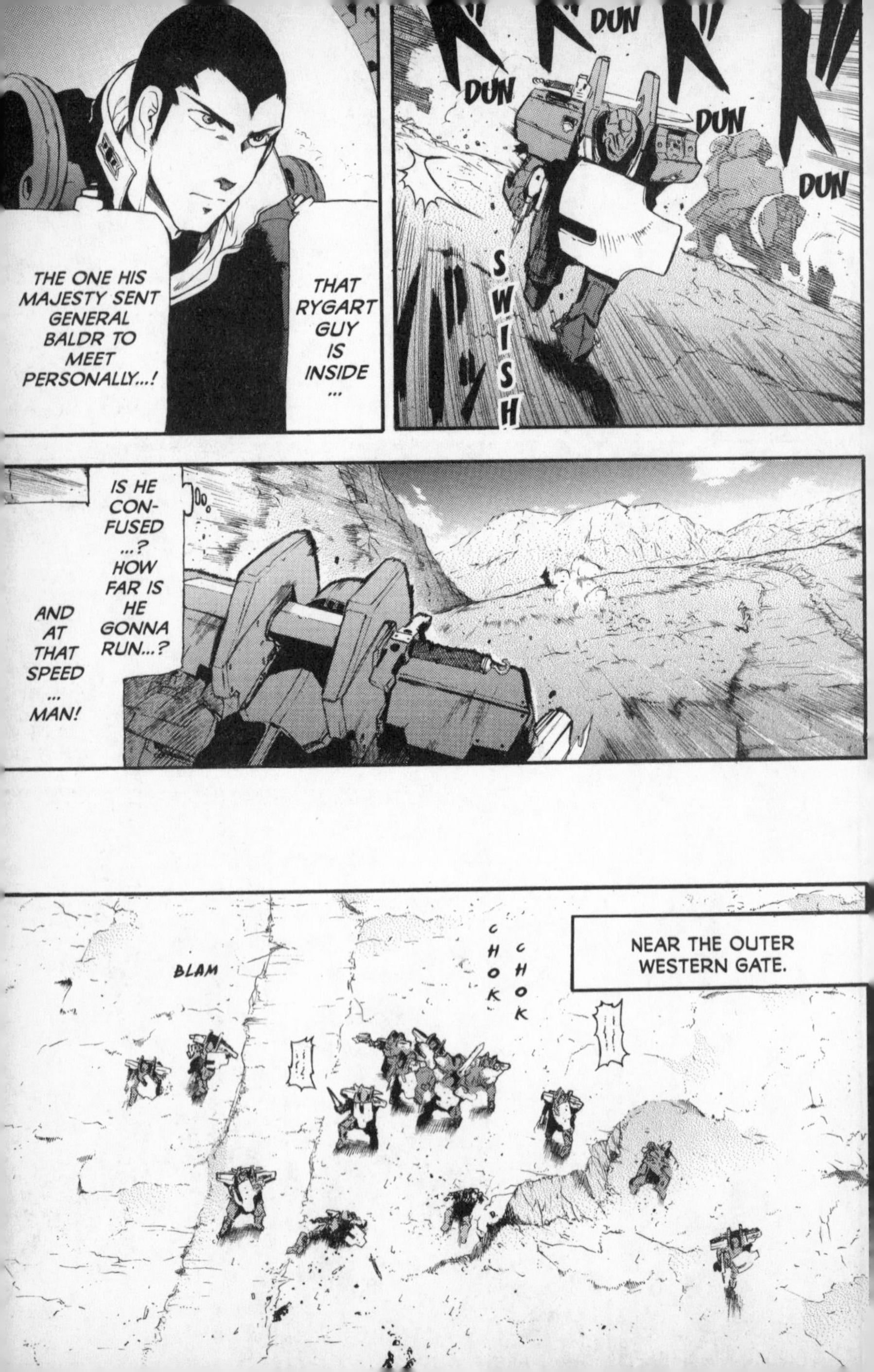
DUN
DUN
DUN
DUN
SWISH
THAT RYGART GUY IS INSIDE...
THE ONE HIS MAJESTY SENT GENERAL BALDR TO MEET PERSONALLY...!
IS HE CONFUSED...? HOW FAR IS HE GONNA RUN...?
AND AT THAT SPEED... MAN!
NEAR THE OUTER WESTERN GATE.
CHOK CHOK
BLAM

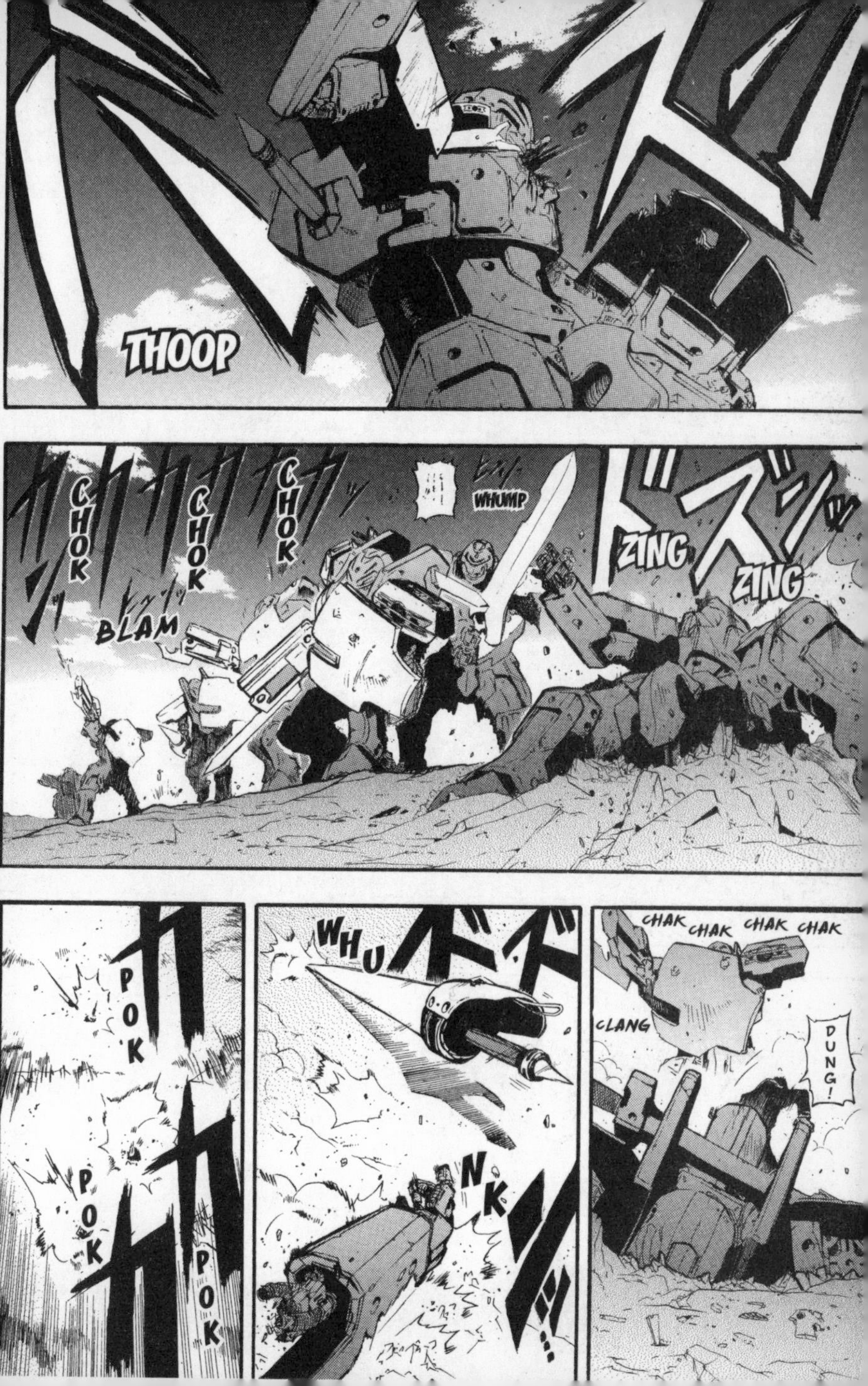
THOOP
ZING
ZING
WHUMP
CHOK
CHOK
CHOK
BLAM
CHAK CHAK CHAK CHAK
DUNG!
CLANG
WHU
NK
POK
POK
POK
POK

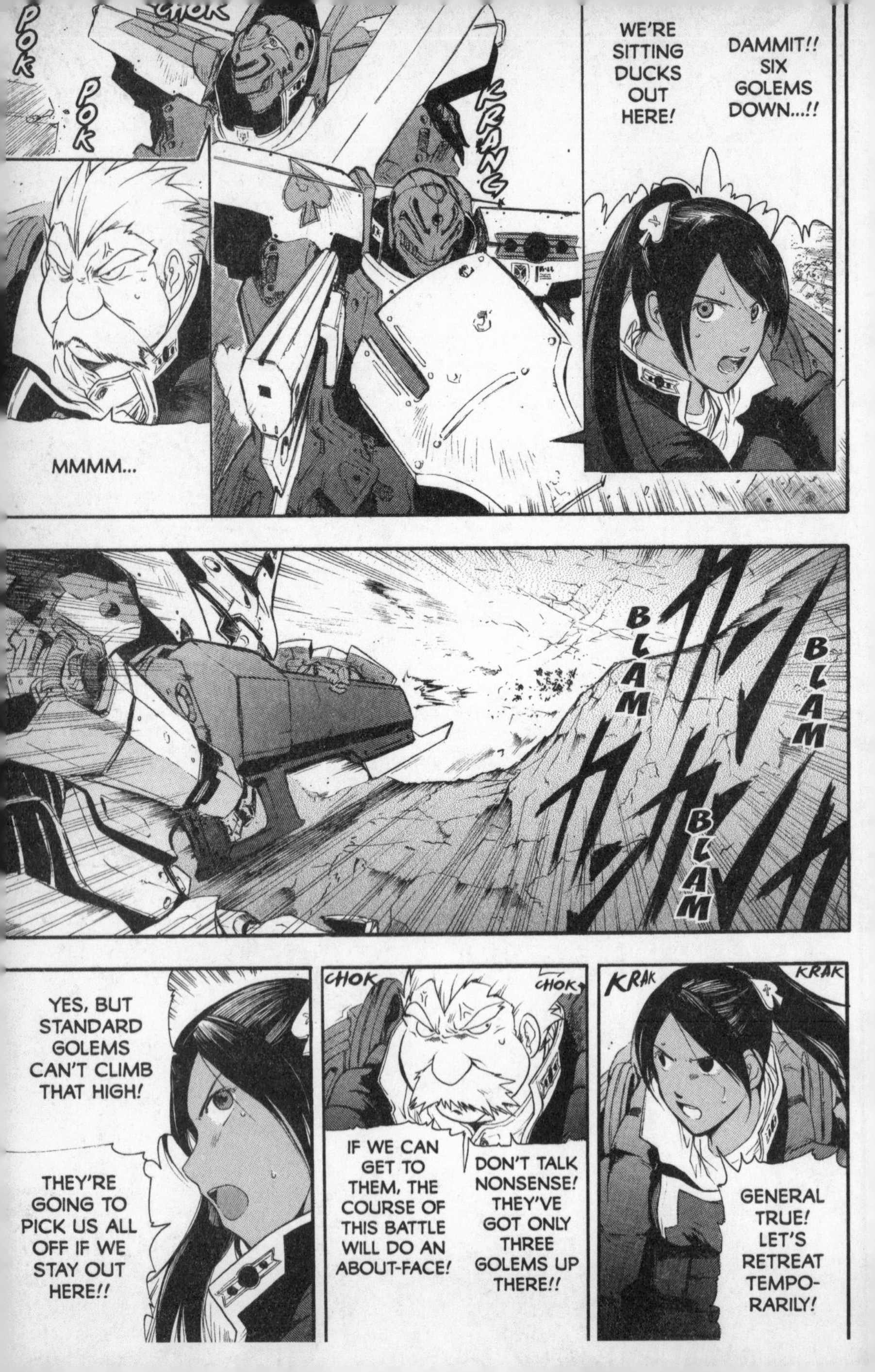
DAMMIT!! SIX GOLEMS DOWN...!!
WE'RE SITTING DUCKS OUT HERE!
KRANG
CHOK
POK
POK
POK
MMMM...
BLAM
BLAM
BLAM
BLAM
KRAK
KRAK
GENERAL TRUE! LET'S RETREAT TEMPO-RARILY!
CHOK
CHOK
DON'T TALK NONSENSE! THEY'VE GOT ONLY THREE GOLEMS UP THERE!!
IF WE CAN GET TO THEM, THE COURSE OF THIS BATTLE WILL DO AN ABOUT-FACE!
YES, BUT STANDARD GOLEMS CAN'T CLIMB THAT HIGH!
THEY'RE GOING TO PICK US ALL OFF IF WE STAY OUT HERE!!

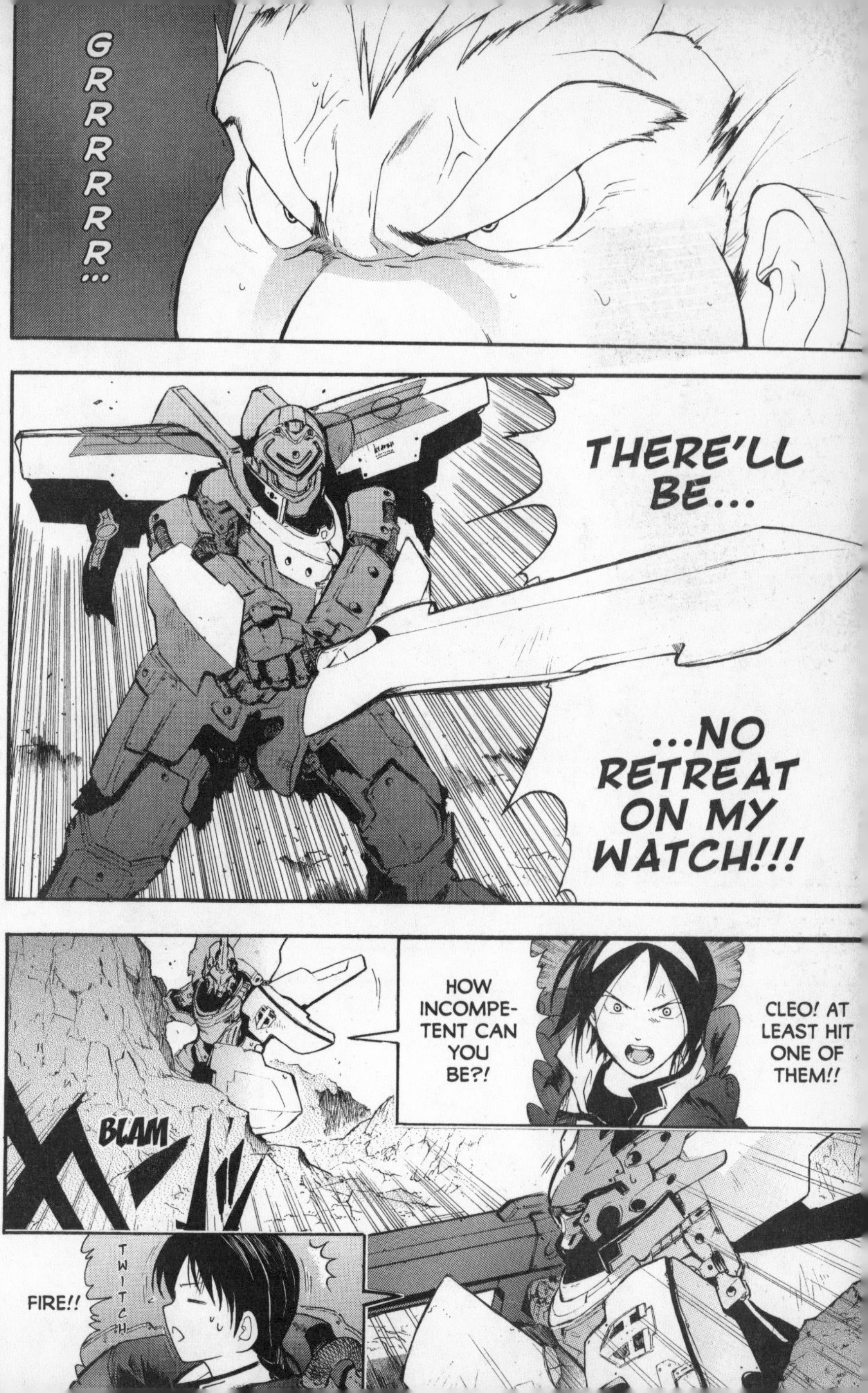
GRRRRRRR...
THERE'LL BE...
...NO RETREAT ON MY WATCH!!!
CLEO! AT LEAST HIT ONE OF THEM!!
HOW INCOMPE-TENT CAN YOU BE?!
BLAM
TWITCH
FIRE!!

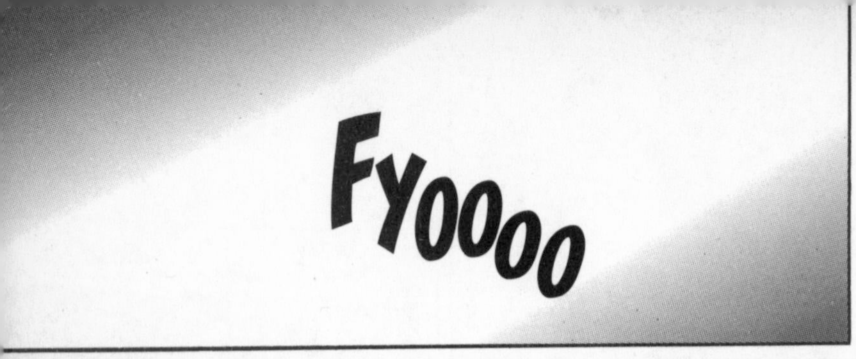
FYOOOO

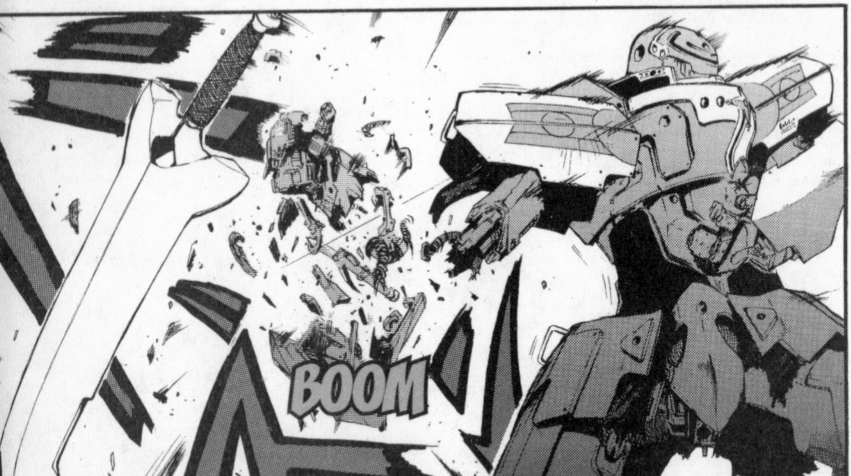
BOOM

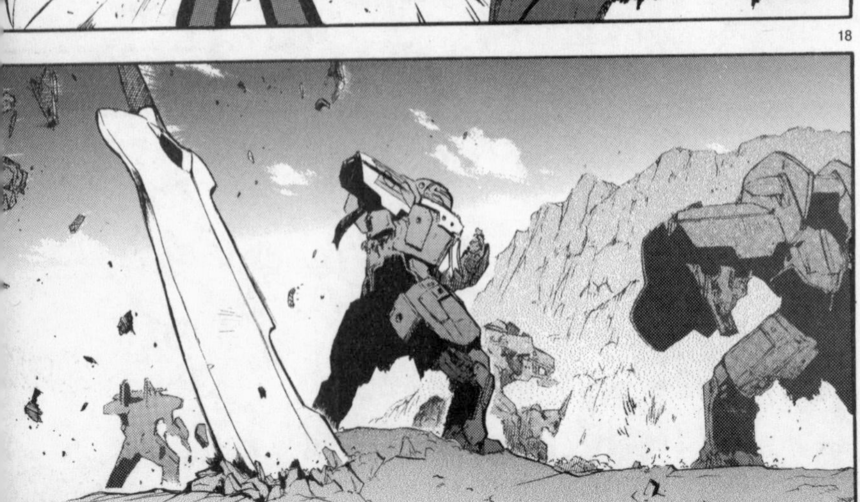

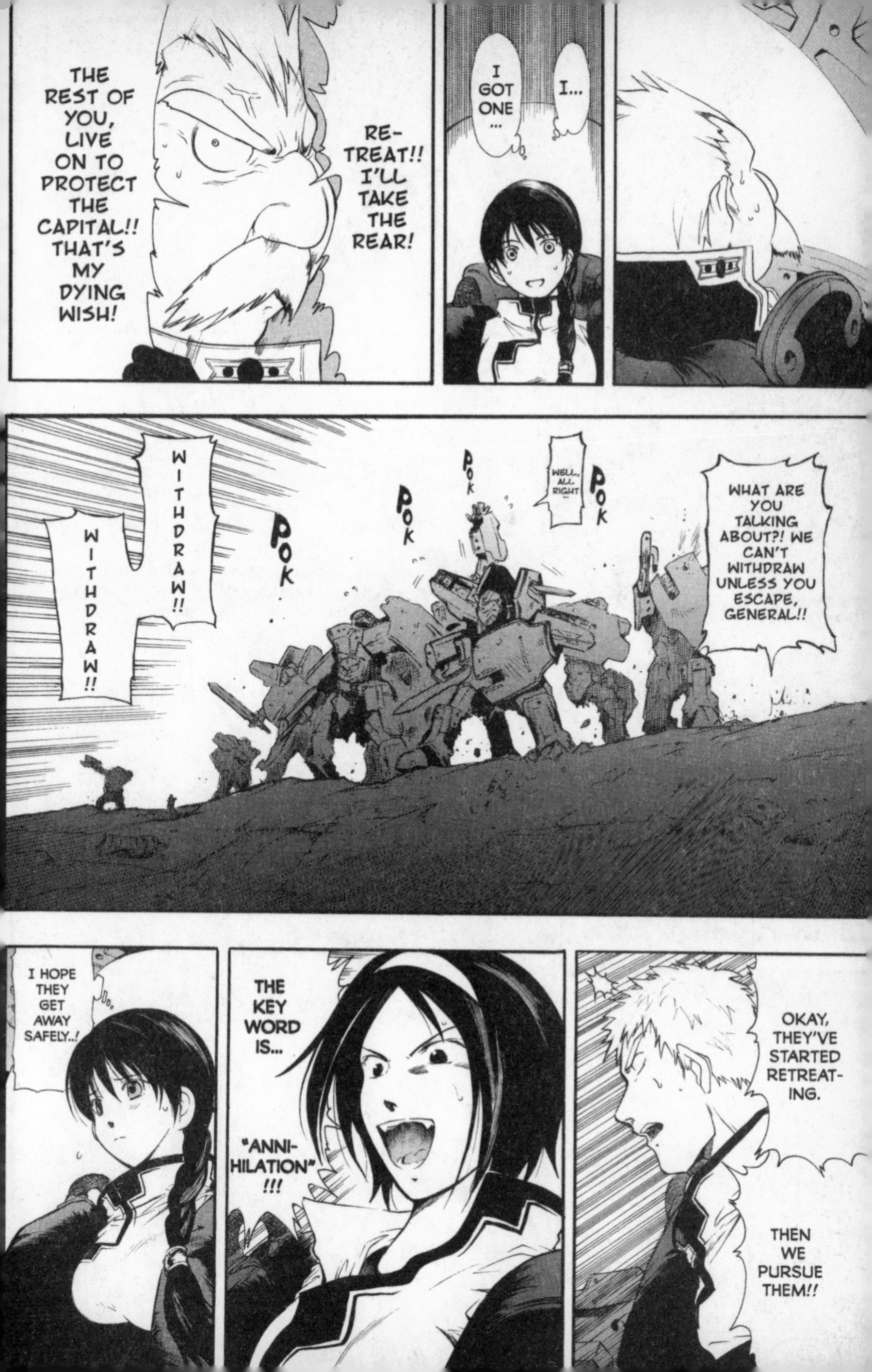

I...
I GOT ONE ...
RE-TREAT!! I'LL TAKE THE REAR!
THE REST OF YOU, LIVE ON TO PROTECT THE CAPITAL!! THAT'S MY DYING WISH!
WHAT ARE YOU TALKING ABOUT?! WE CAN'T WITHDRAW UNLESS YOU ESCAPE, GENERAL!!
POK
WELL, ALL RIGHT...
POK
POK
POK
WITHDRAW!!
WITHDRAW!!
OKAY, THEY'VE STARTED RETREAT-ING.
THEN WE PURSUE THEM!!
THE KEY WORD IS...
"ANNI-HILATION" !!!
I HOPE THEY GET AWAY SAFELY..!

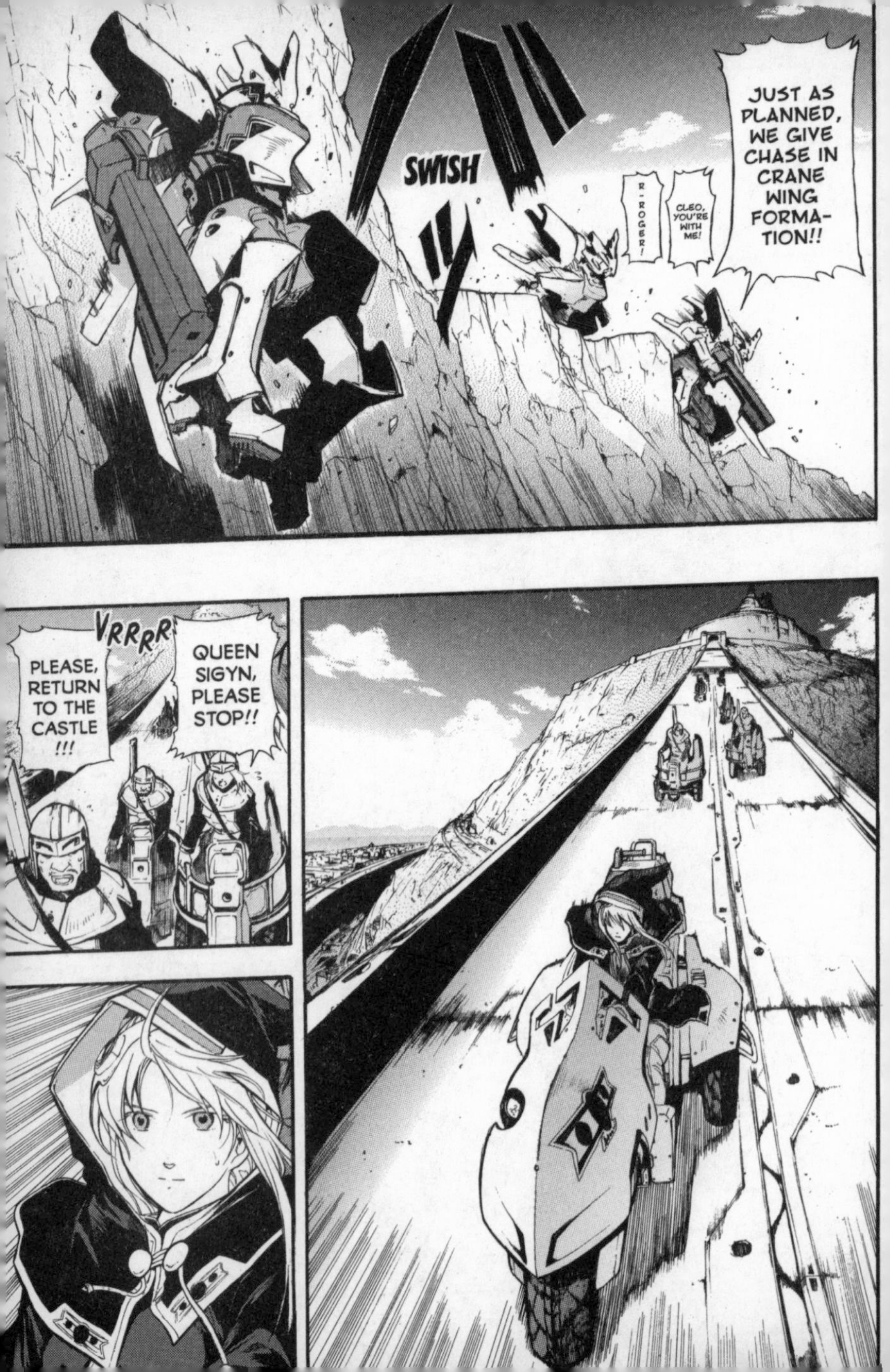
JUST AS PLANNED, WE GIVE CHASE IN CRANE WING FORMATION!!
CLEO, YOU'RE WITH ME!
R-ROGER!
SWISH
VRRRR
QUEEN SIGYN, PLEASE STOP!!
PLEASE, RETURN TO THE CASTLE!!!

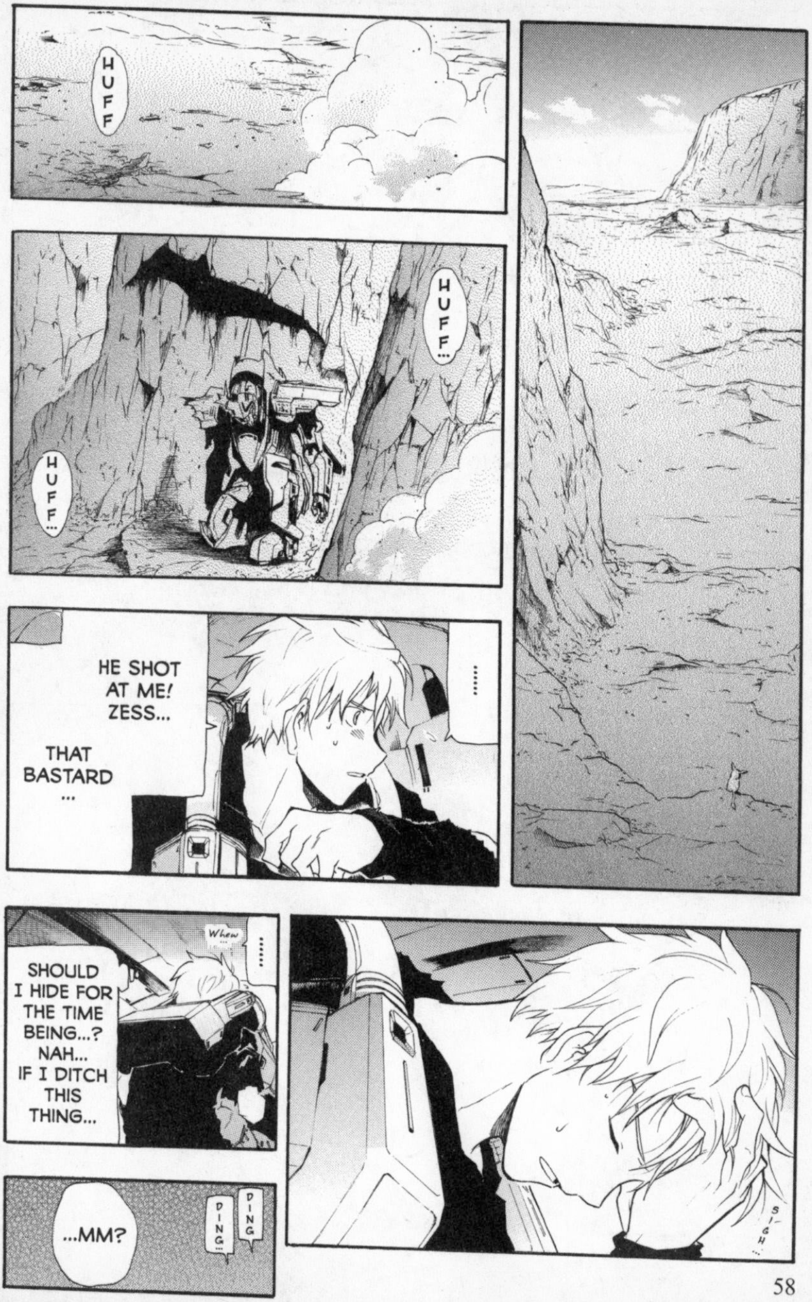
HUFF
HUFF...
HUFF...
......
HE SHOT AT ME! ZESS...
THAT BASTARD...
SIGH...
......
Whew...
SHOULD I HIDE FOR THE TIME BEING...? NAH... IF I DITCH THIS THING...
DING
DING...
...MM?

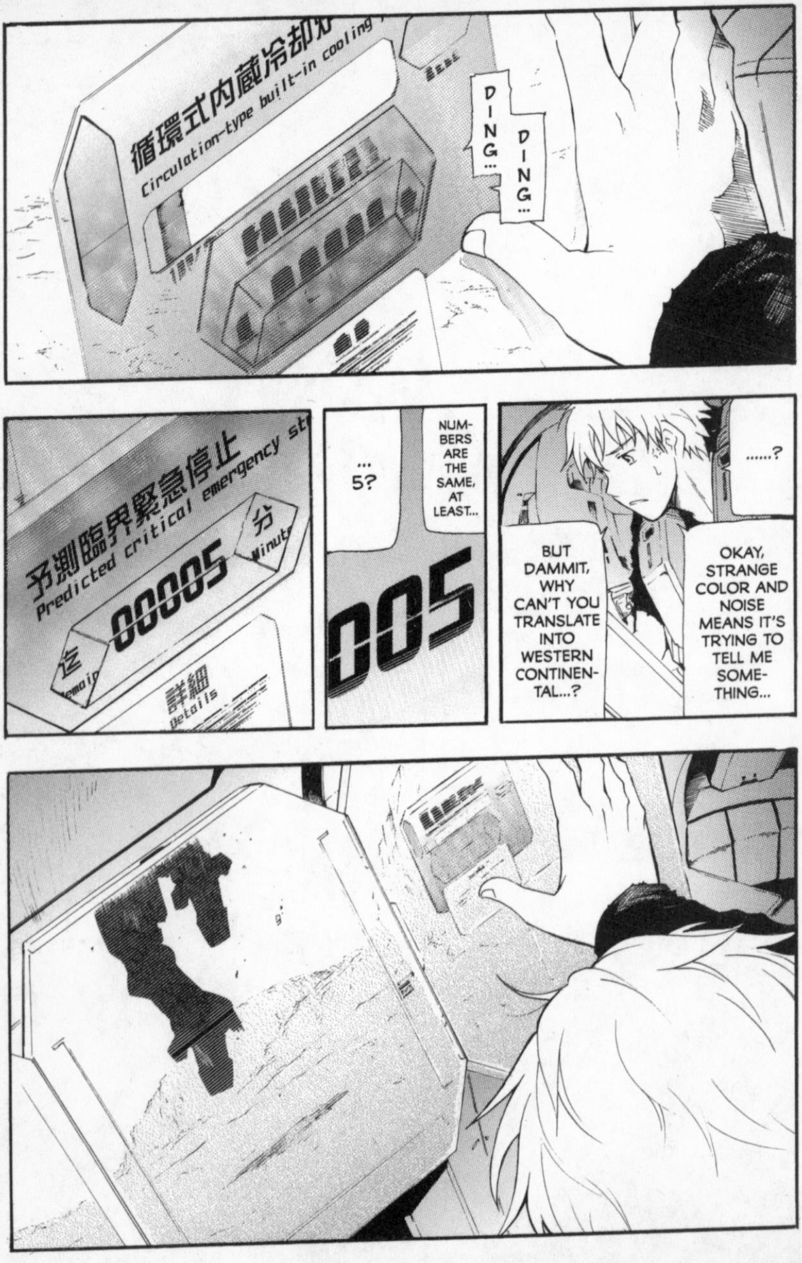
循環式内蔵冷却
Circulation-type built-in cooling
DING...
DING...
......?
OKAY, STRANGE COLOR AND NOISE MEANS IT'S TRYING TO TELL ME SOME-THING...
BUT DAMMIT, WHY CAN'T YOU TRANSLATE INTO WESTERN CONTINEN-TAL...?
NUM-BERS ARE THE SAME, AT LEAST...
... 5?
005
予測臨界緊急停止
Predicted critical emergency
分
00005
詳細
Details

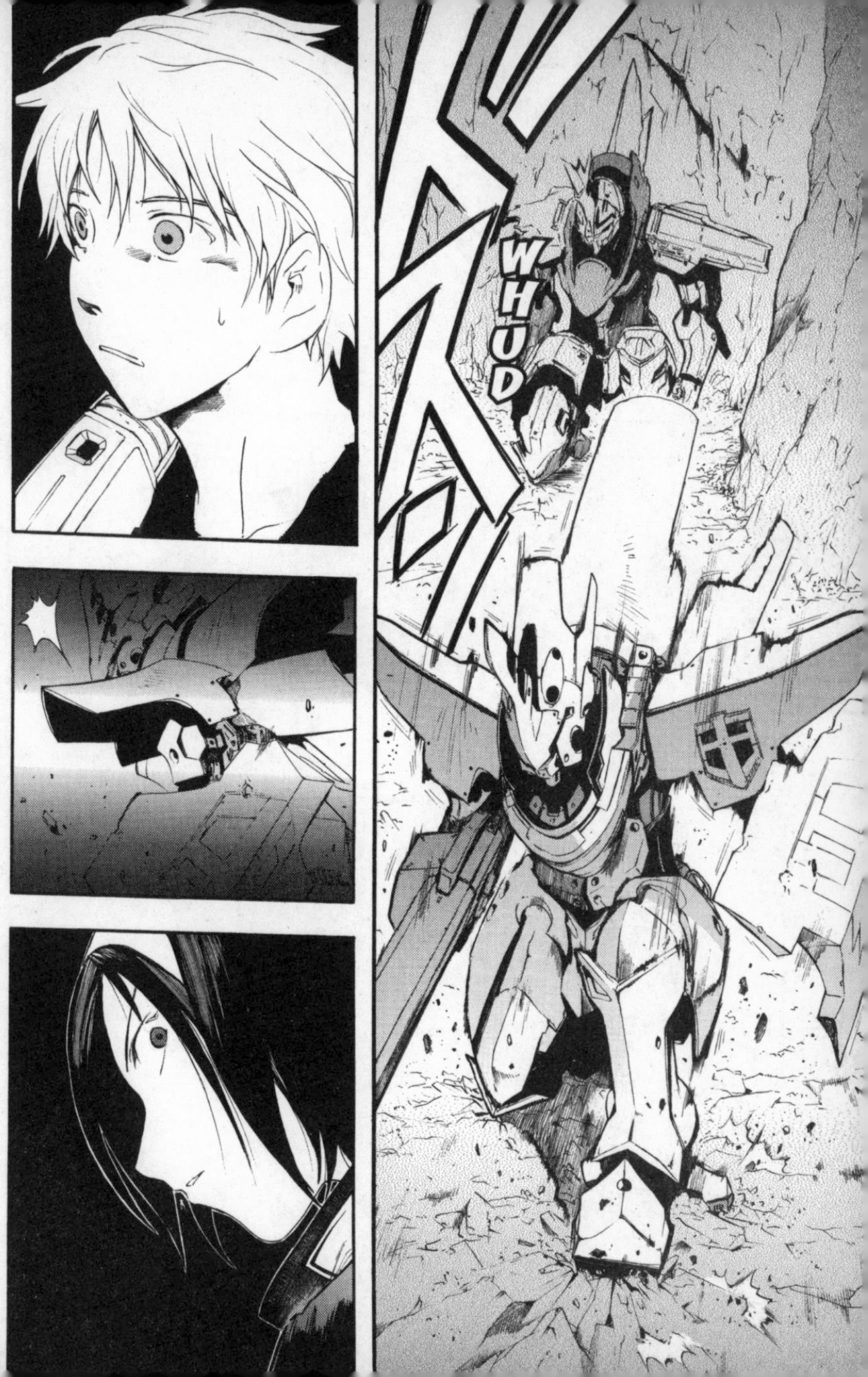
WHUD

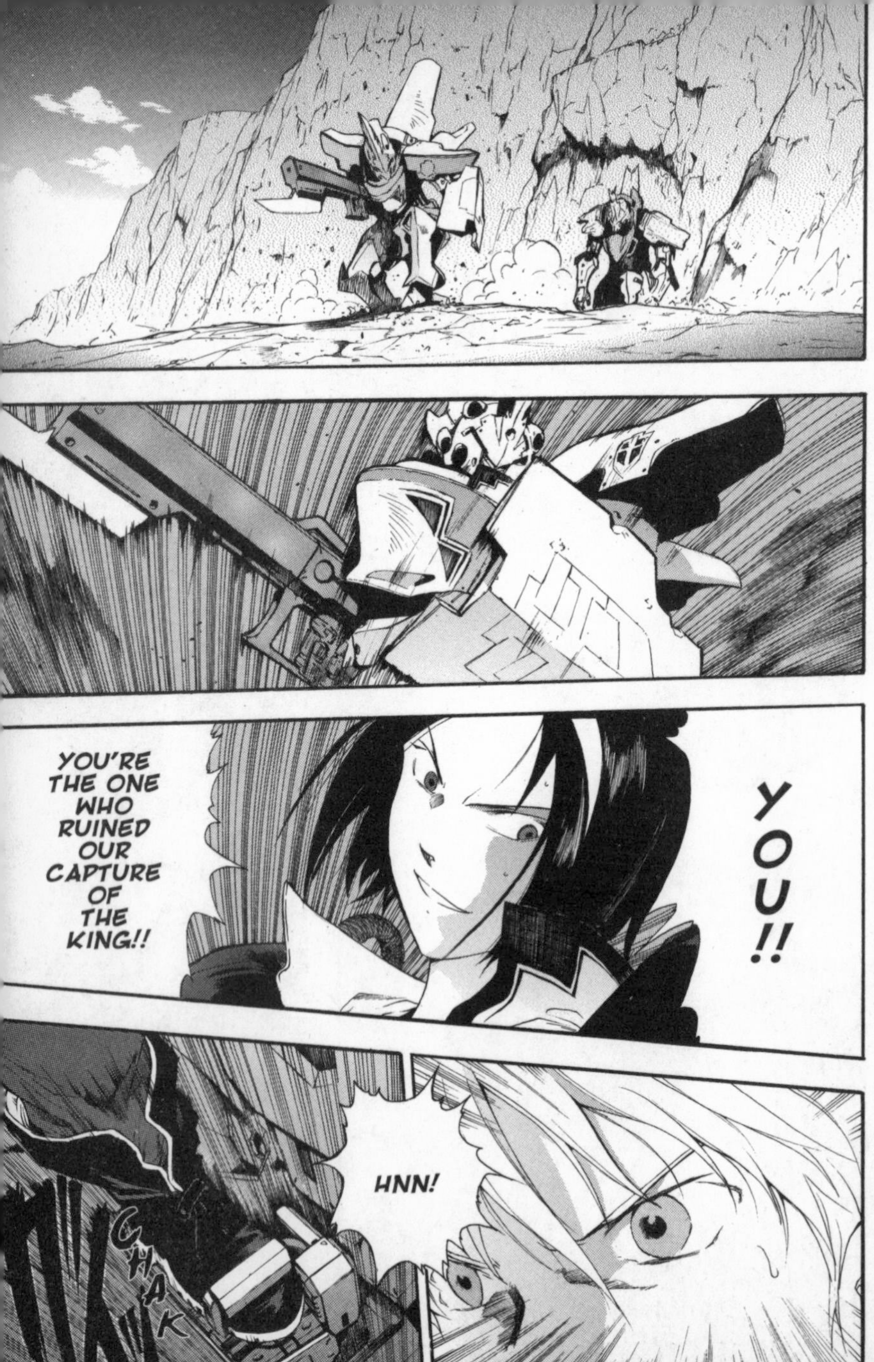
YOU!!
YOU'RE THE ONE WHO RUINED OUR CAPTURE OF THE KING!!
HNN!
CHAK

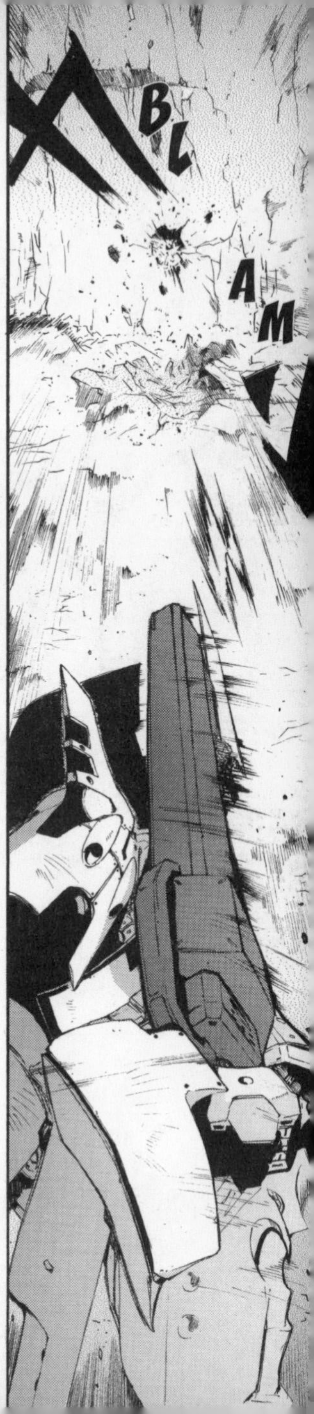
BLAM
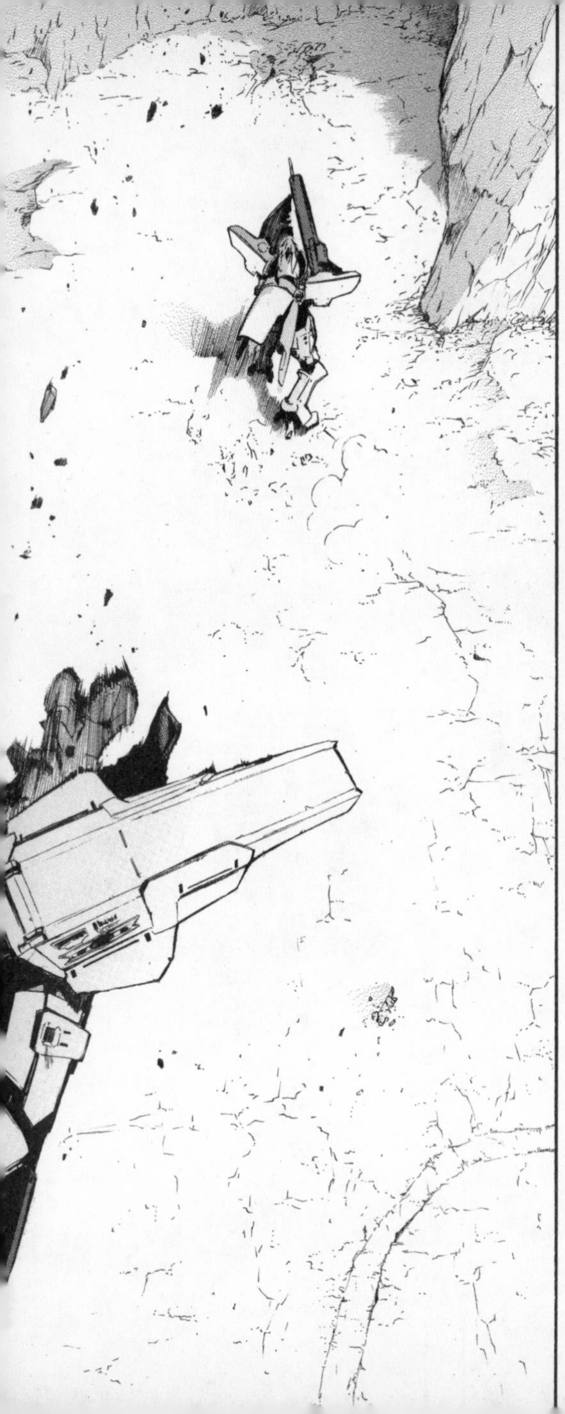

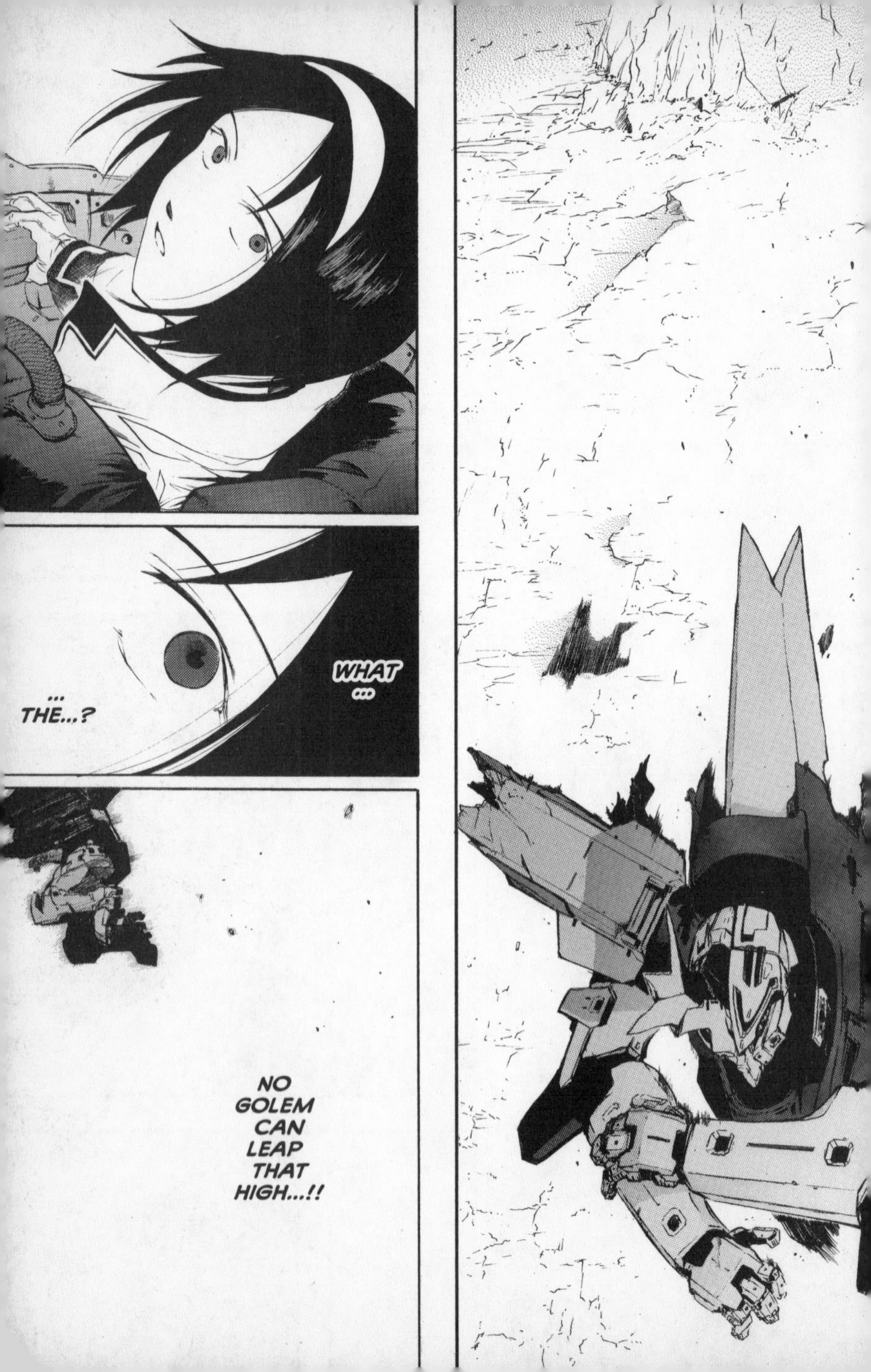
WHAT ...
... THE...?
NO GOLEM CAN LEAP THAT HIGH...!!

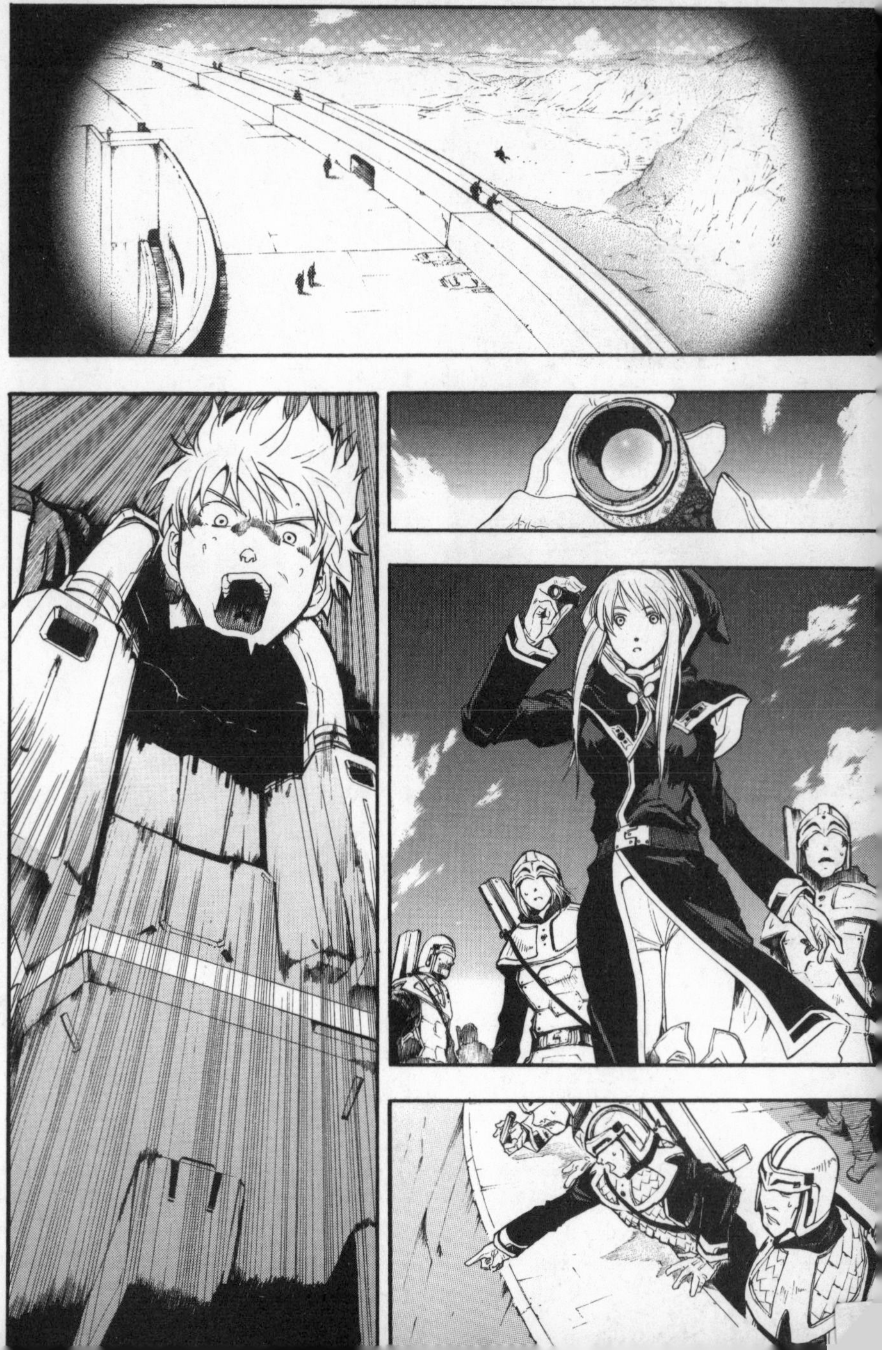

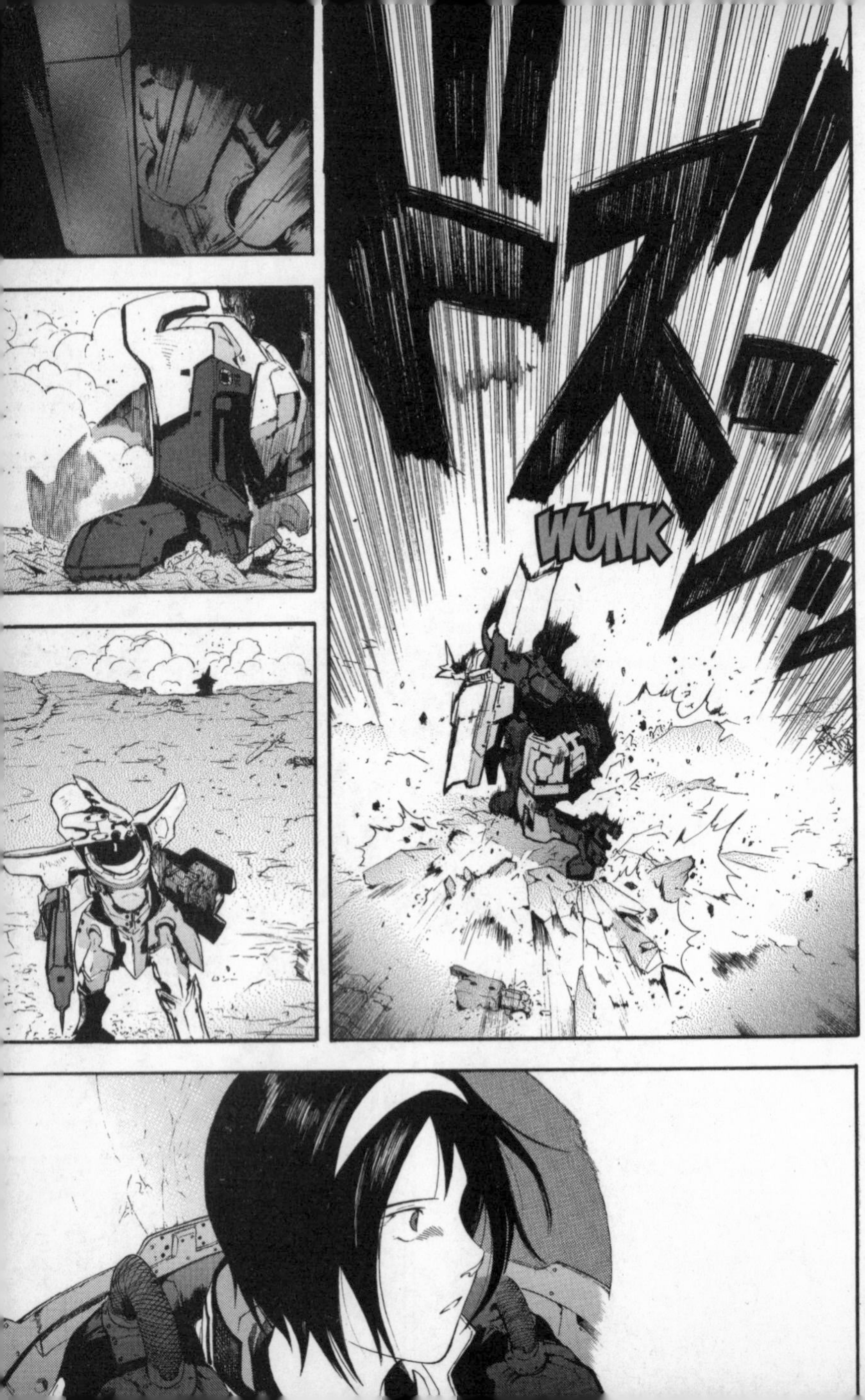
WUNK

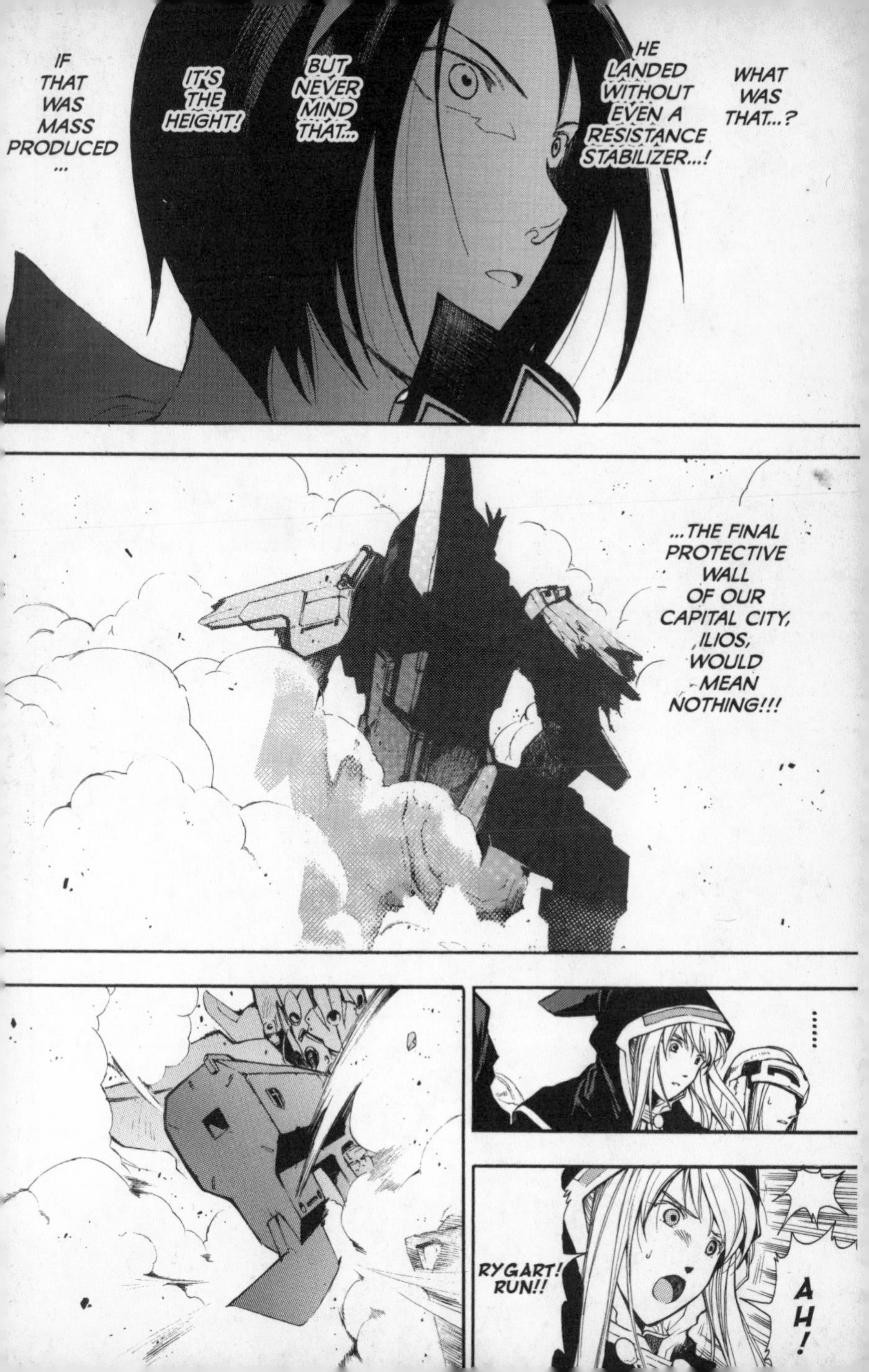
WHAT WAS THAT...?
HE LANDED WITHOUT EVEN A RESISTANCE STABILIZER...!
BUT NEVER MIND THAT...
IT'S THE HEIGHT!
IF THAT WAS MASS PRODUCED ...
...THE FINAL PROTECTIVE WALL OF OUR CAPITAL CITY, ILIOS, WOULD MEAN NOTHING!!!
......
AH!
RYGART! RUN!!

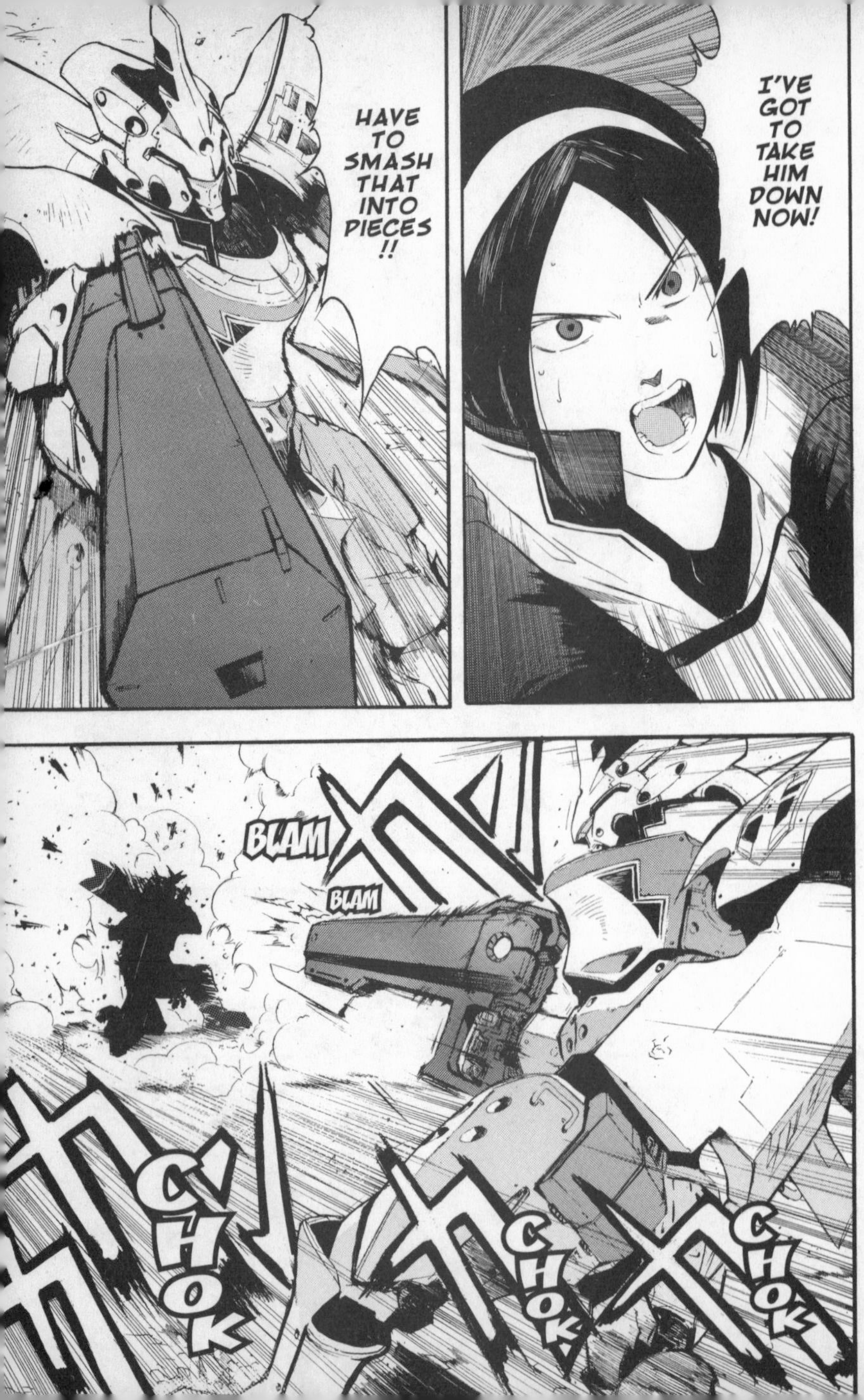
I'VE GOT TO TAKE HIM DOWN NOW!
HAVE TO SMASH THAT INTO PIECES!!
BLAM
BLAM
CHOK
CHOK
CHOK

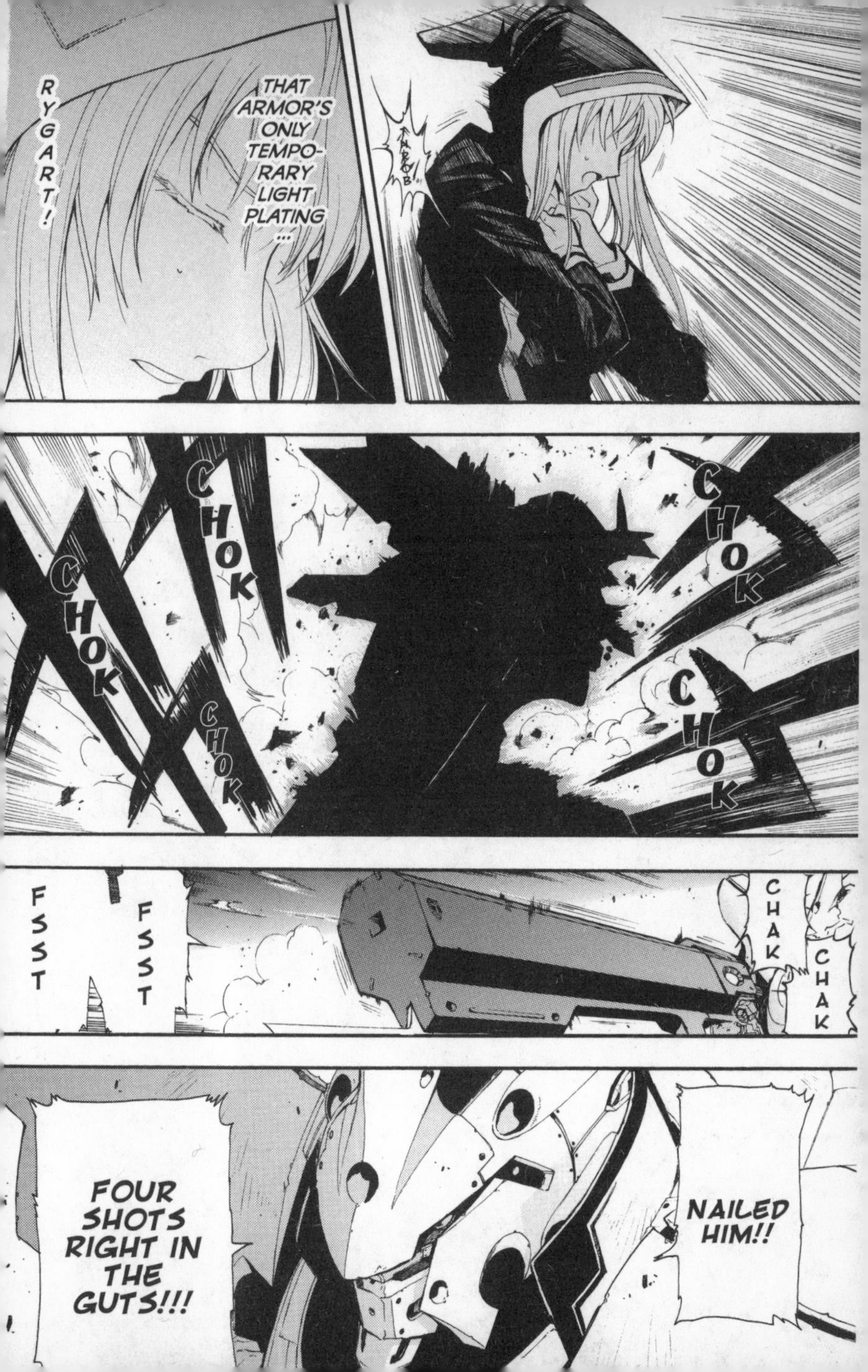
THROB
THAT ARMOR'S ONLY TEMPORARY LIGHT PLATING ...
RYGART!
CHOK
CHOK
CHOK
CHOK
CHOK
CHOK
CHAK
CHAK
FSST
FSST
NAILED HIM!!
FOUR SHOTS RIGHT IN THE GUTS!!!

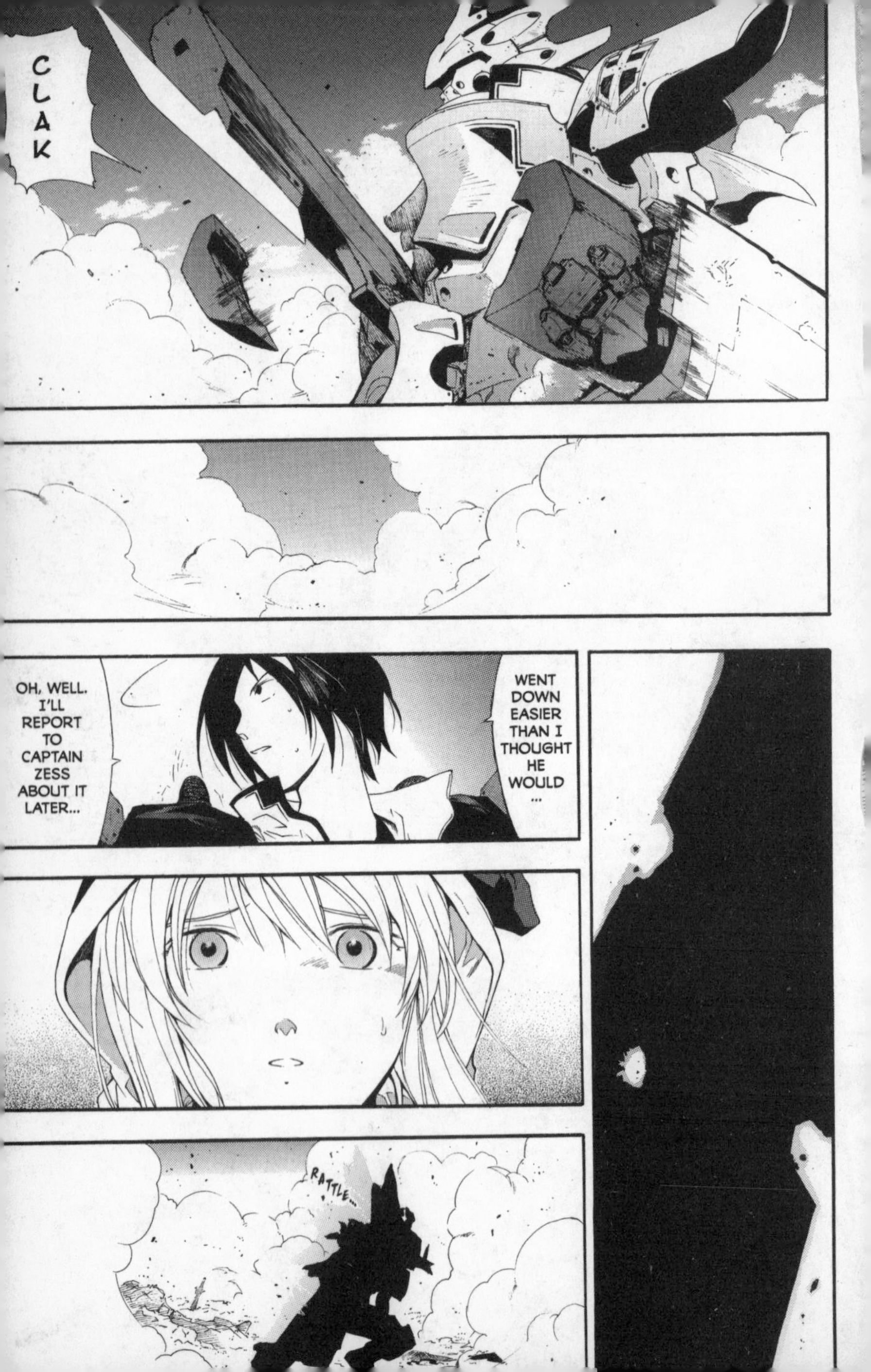
CLAK
WENT DOWN EASIER THAN I THOUGHT HE WOULD ...
OH, WELL. I'LL REPORT TO CAPTAIN ZESS ABOUT IT LATER...
RATTLE...

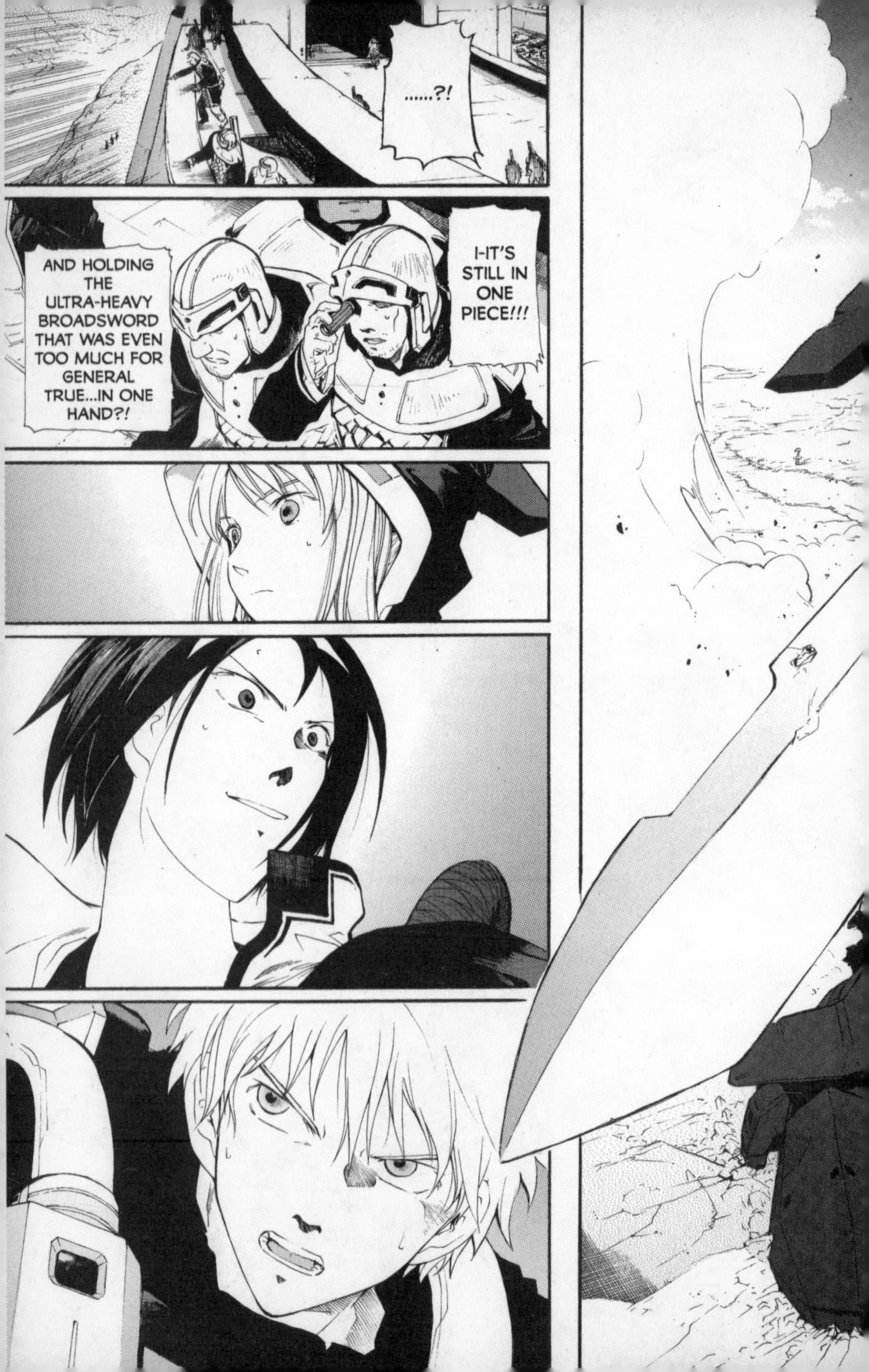

......?!
I-IT'S STILL IN ONE PIECE!!!
AND HOLDING THE ULTRA-HEAVY BROADSWORD THAT WAS EVEN TOO MUCH FOR GENERAL TRUE...IN ONE HAND?!

BROKEN BLADE

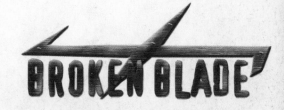

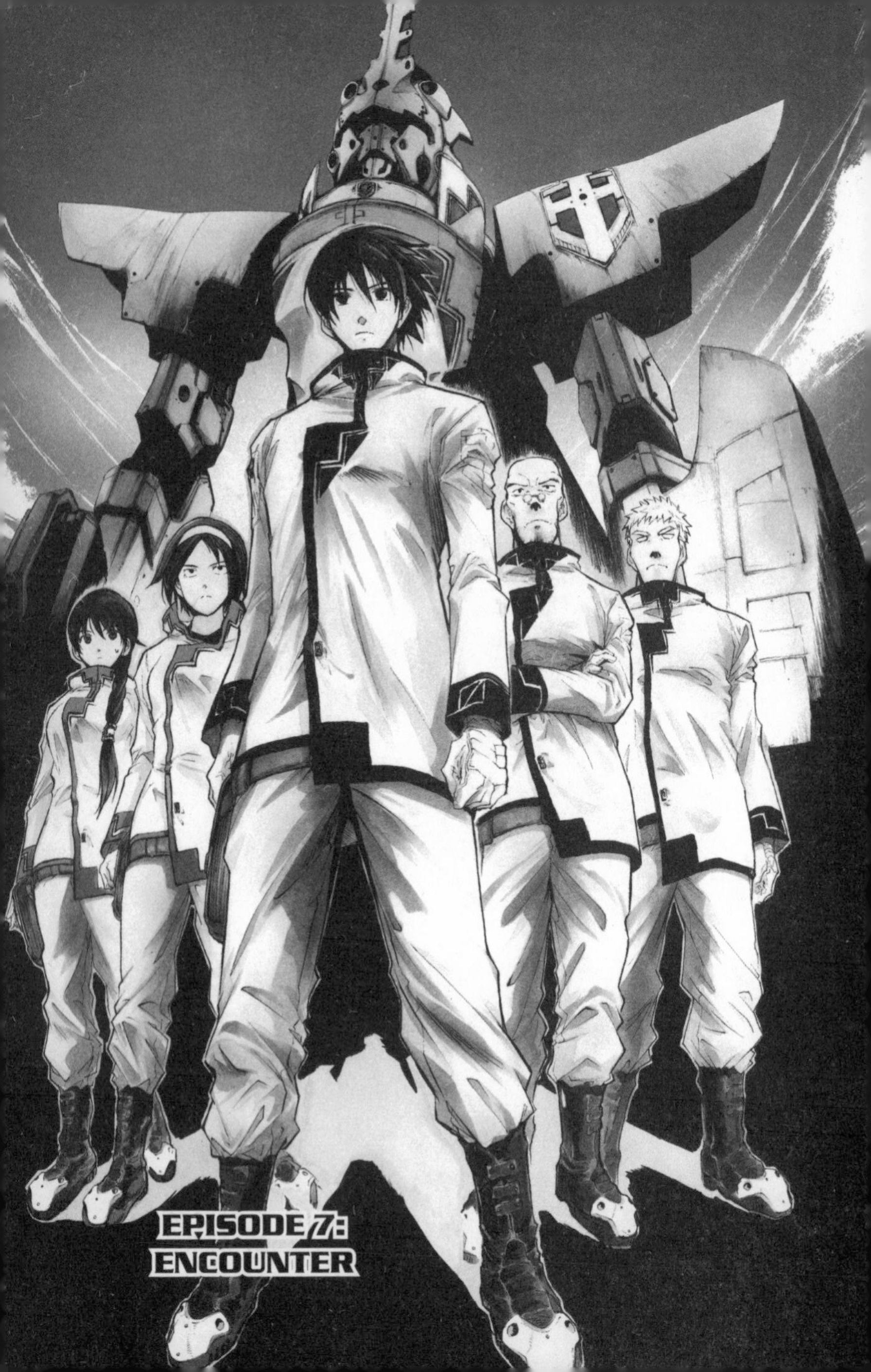
EPISODE 7:
ENCOUNTER

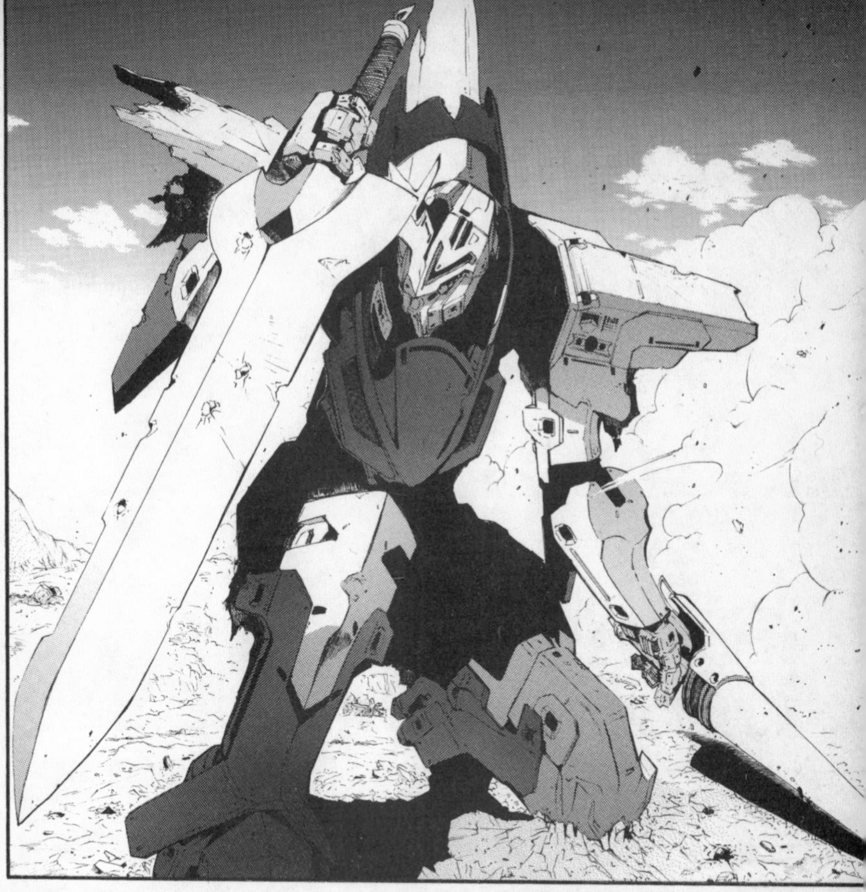
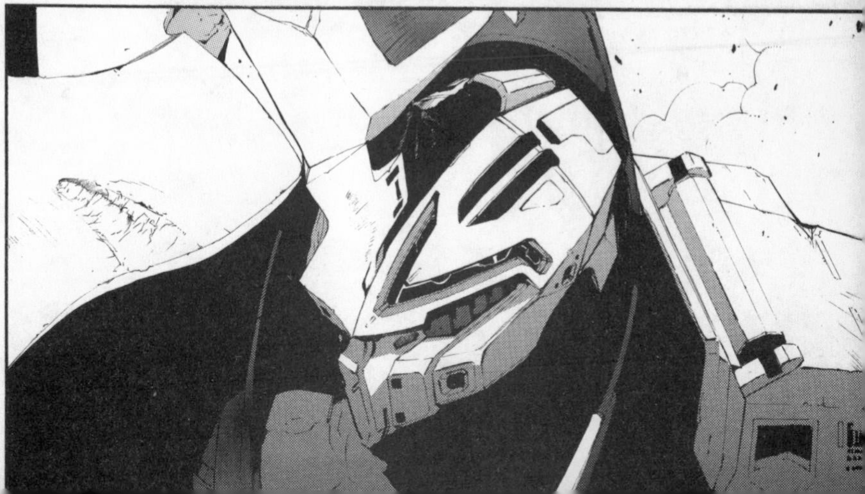

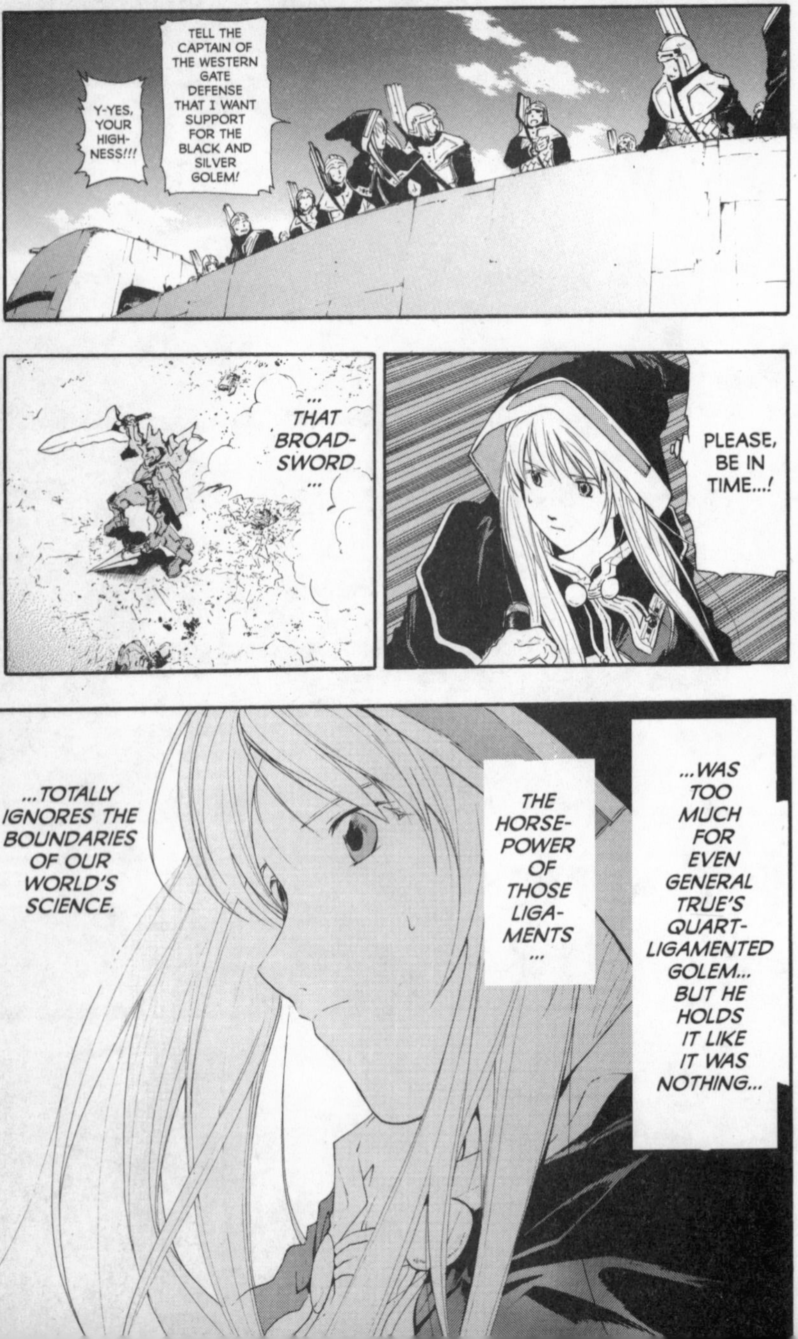
TELL THE CAPTAIN OF THE WESTERN GATE DEFENSE THAT I WANT SUPPORT FOR THE BLACK AND SILVER GOLEM!
Y-YES, YOUR HIGH-NESS!!!
PLEASE, BE IN TIME...!
...THAT BROAD-SWORD...
...WAS TOO MUCH FOR EVEN GENERAL TRUE'S QUART-LIGAMENTED GOLEM... BUT HE HOLDS IT LIKE IT WAS NOTHING...
THE HORSE-POWER OF THOSE LIGA-MENTS...
...TOTALLY IGNORES THE BOUNDARIES OF OUR WORLD'S SCIENCE.

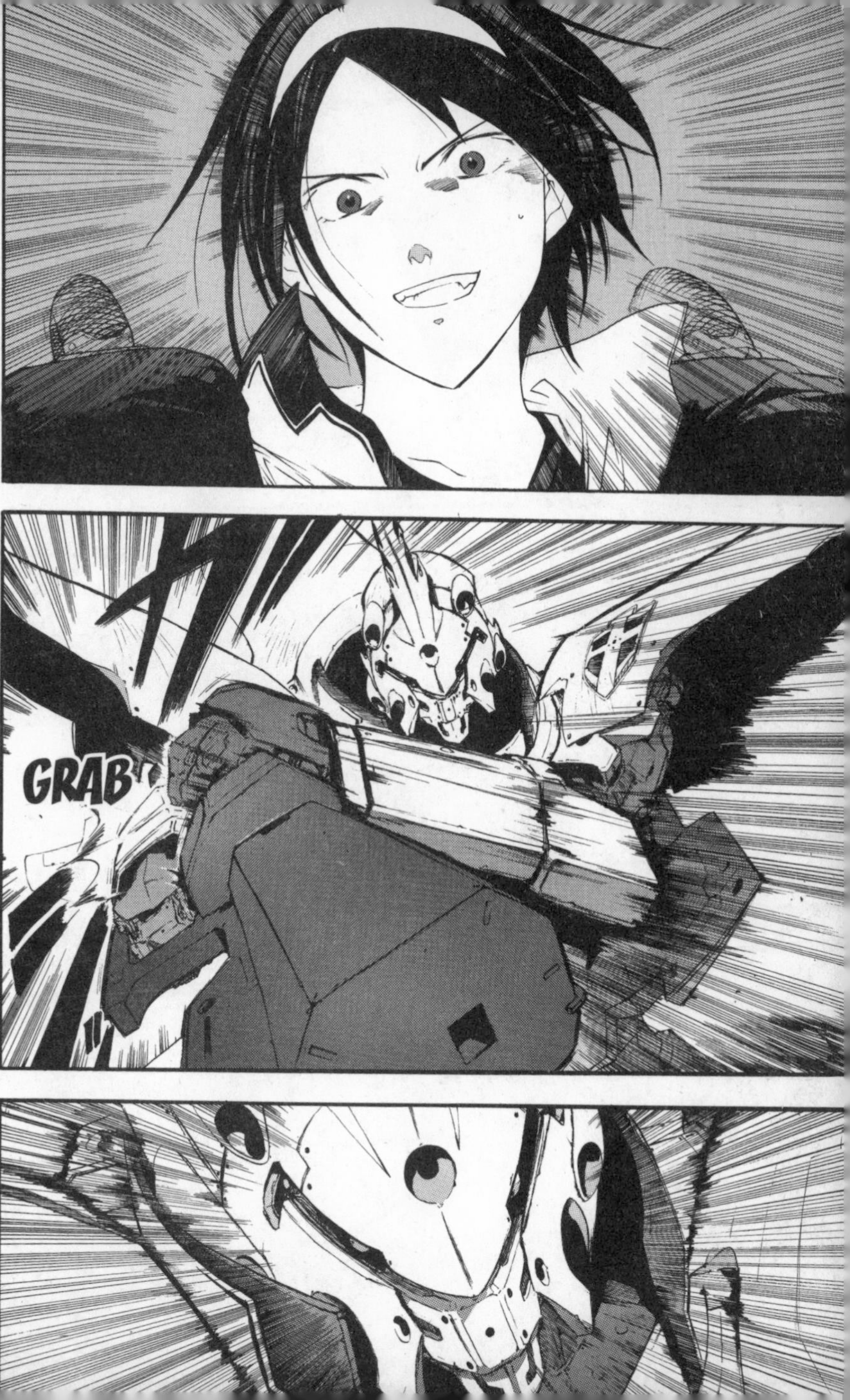
GRAB

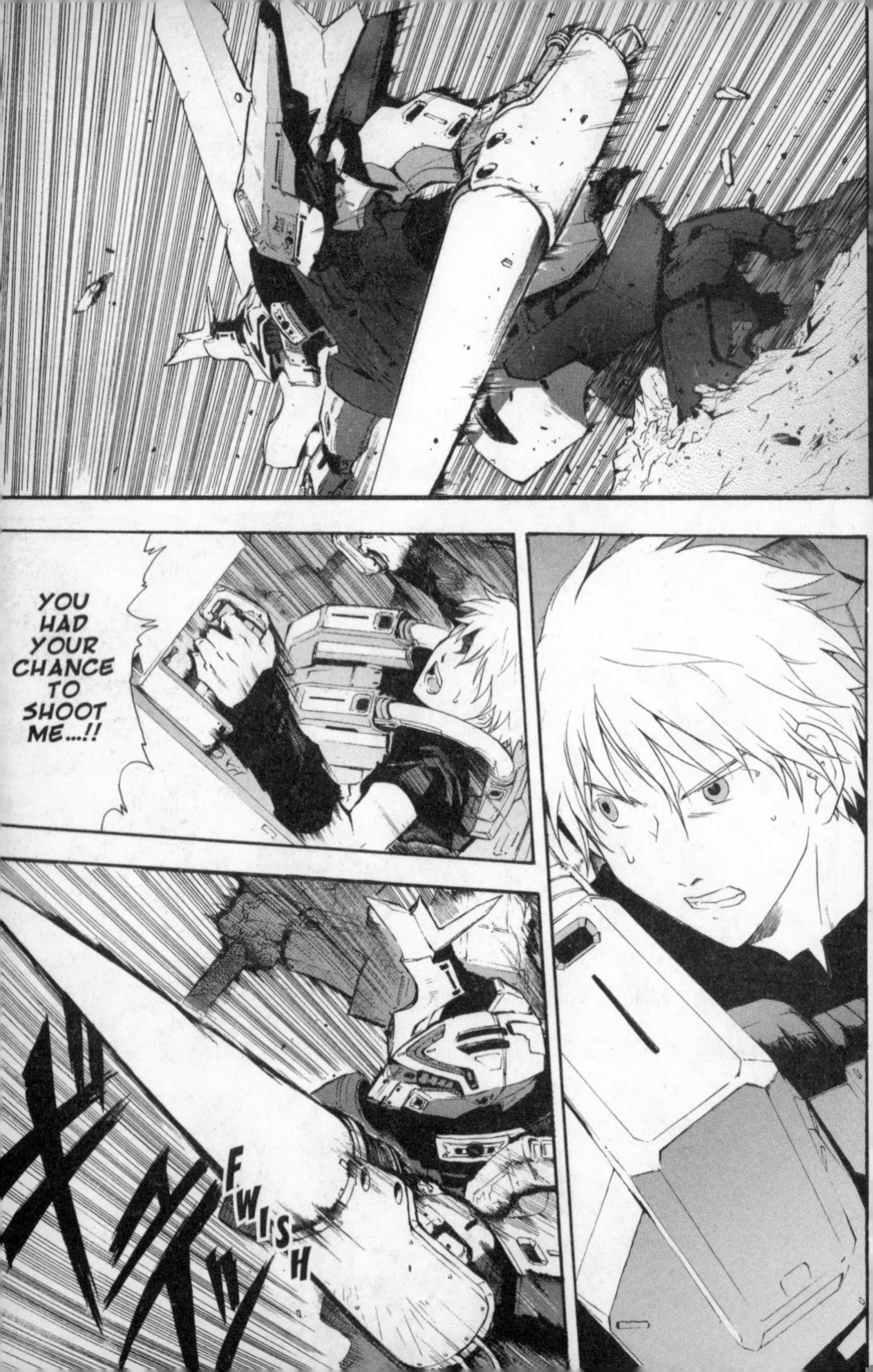
YOU HAD YOUR CHANCE TO SHOOT ME...!!
FWISH

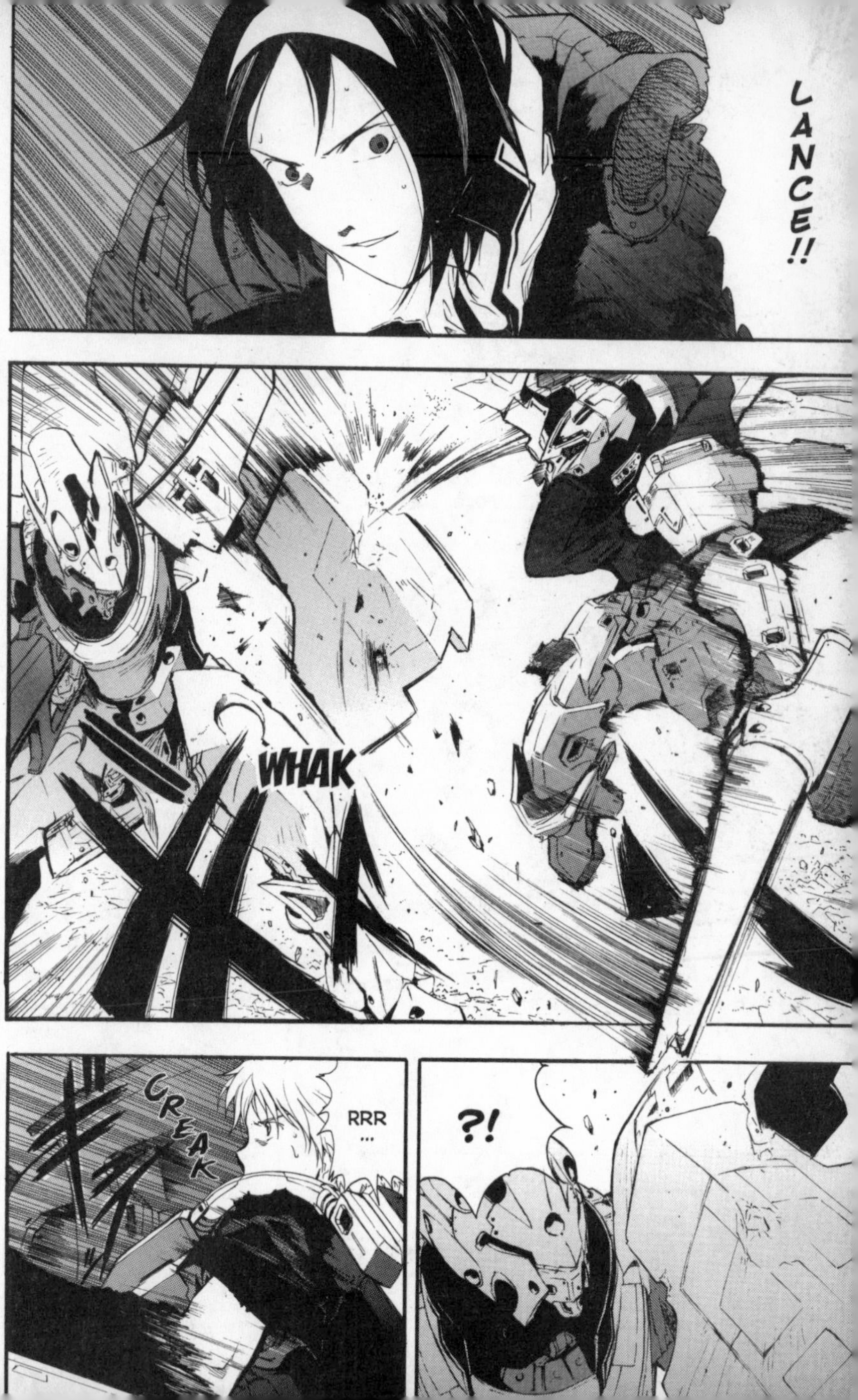
LANCE!!
WHAK
?!
RRR ...
CREAK

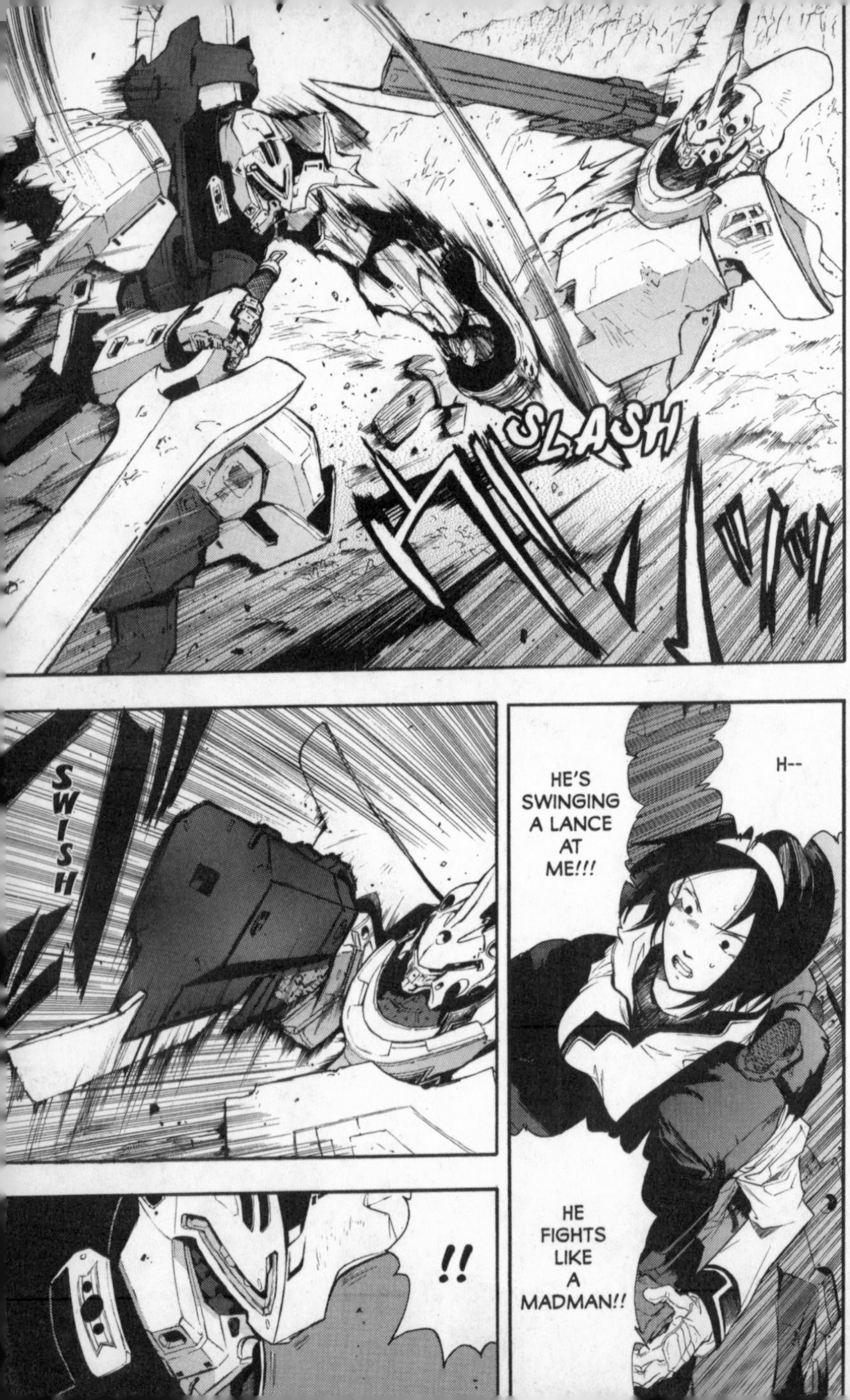
SLASH
H--
HE'S SWINGING A LANCE AT ME!!!
HE FIGHTS LIKE A MADMAN!!
SWISH
!!

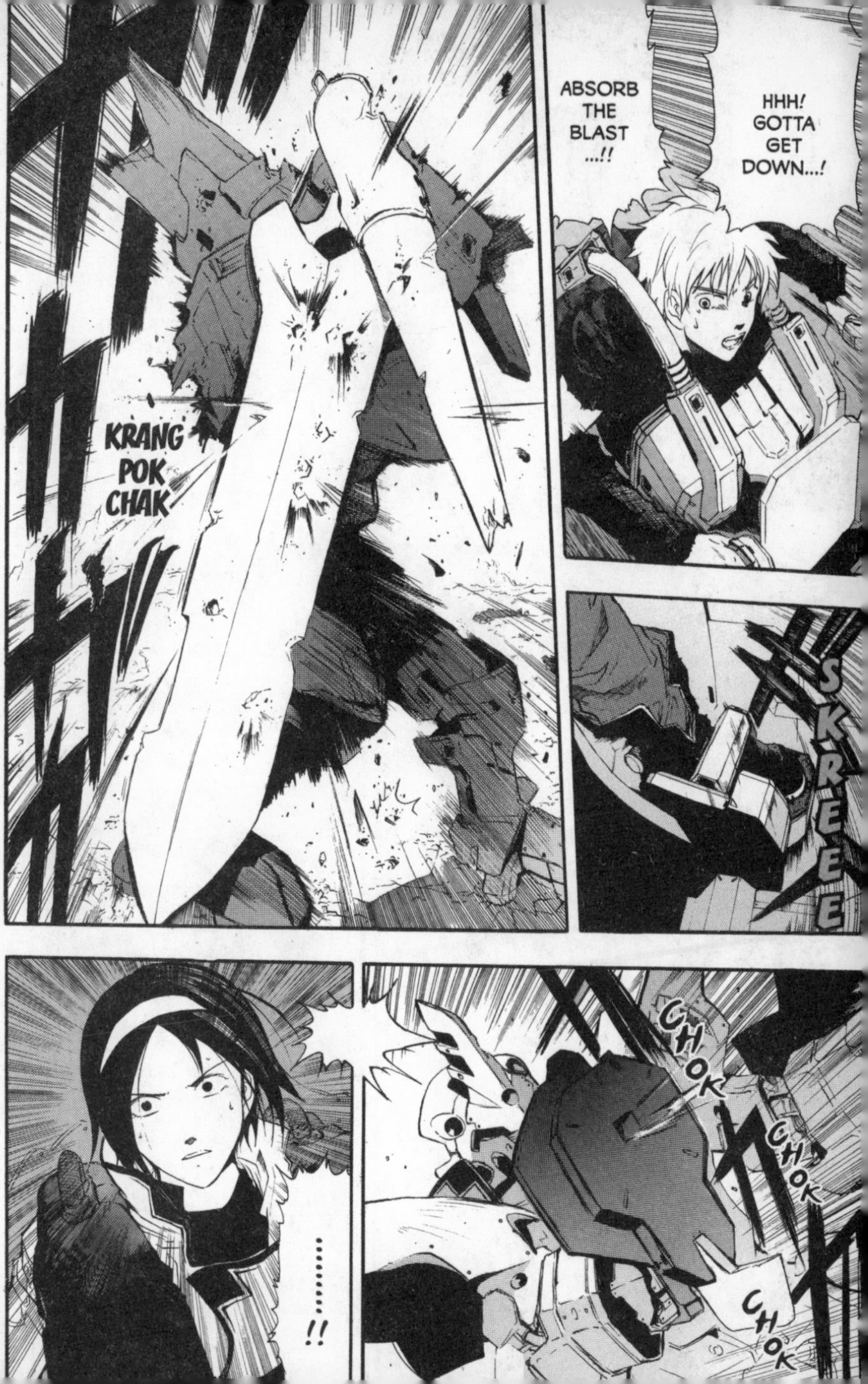
HHH! GOTTA GET DOWN...!
ABSORB THE BLAST ...!!
SKREEE
KRANG POK CHAK
CHOK CHOK CHOK CHOK
......!!

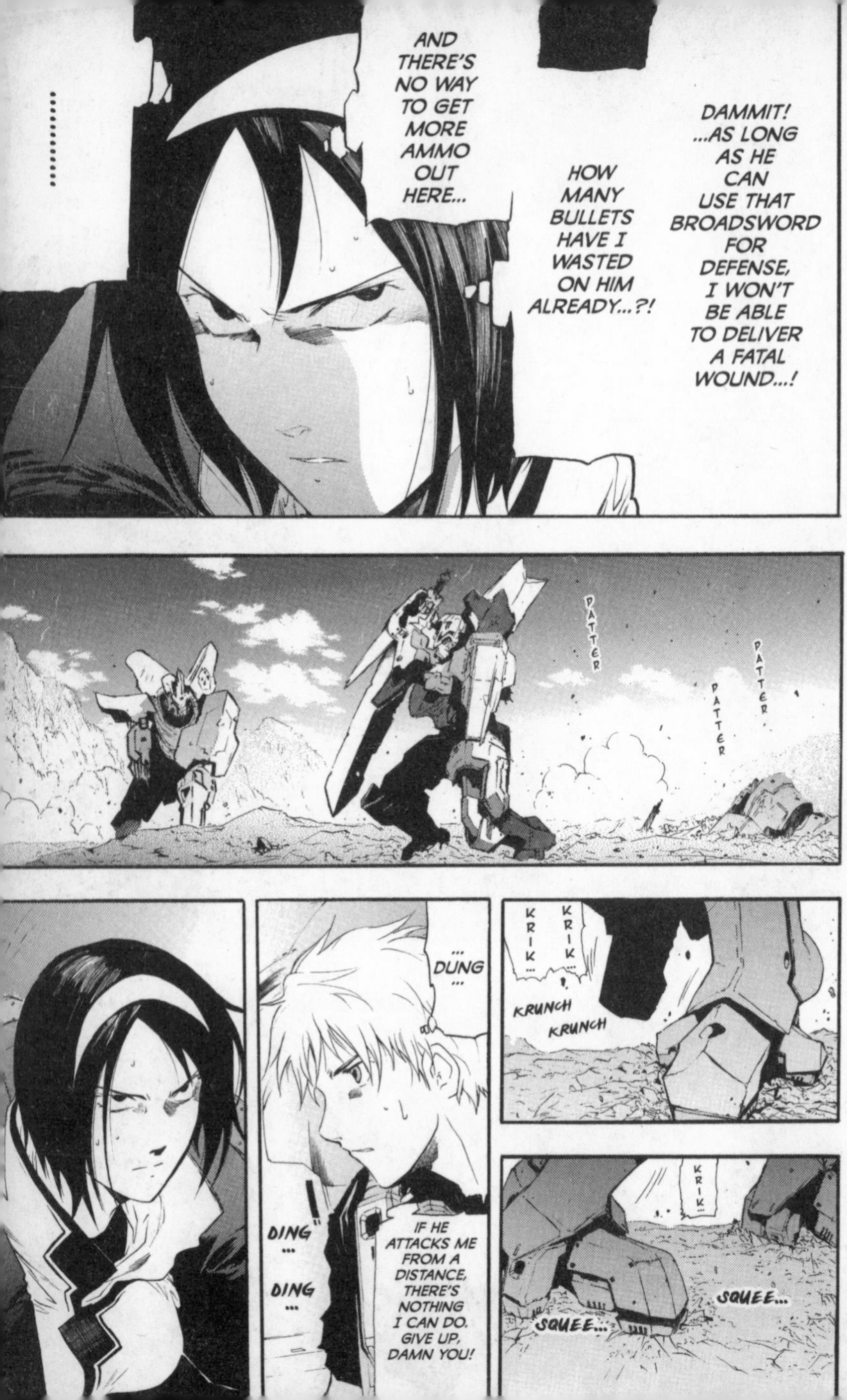
DAMMIT! ...AS LONG AS HE CAN USE THAT BROADSWORD FOR DEFENSE, I WON'T BE ABLE TO DELIVER A FATAL WOUND...!
HOW MANY BULLETS HAVE I WASTED ON HIM ALREADY...?!
AND THERE'S NO WAY TO GET MORE AMMO OUT HERE...
....
PATTER
PATTER
PATTER
KRIK...
KRIK...
KRUNCH
KRUNCH
KRIK...
SQUEE...
SQUEE...
...DUNG...
DING...
DING...
IF HE ATTACKS ME FROM A DISTANCE, THERE'S NOTHING I CAN DO. GIVE UP, DAMN YOU!

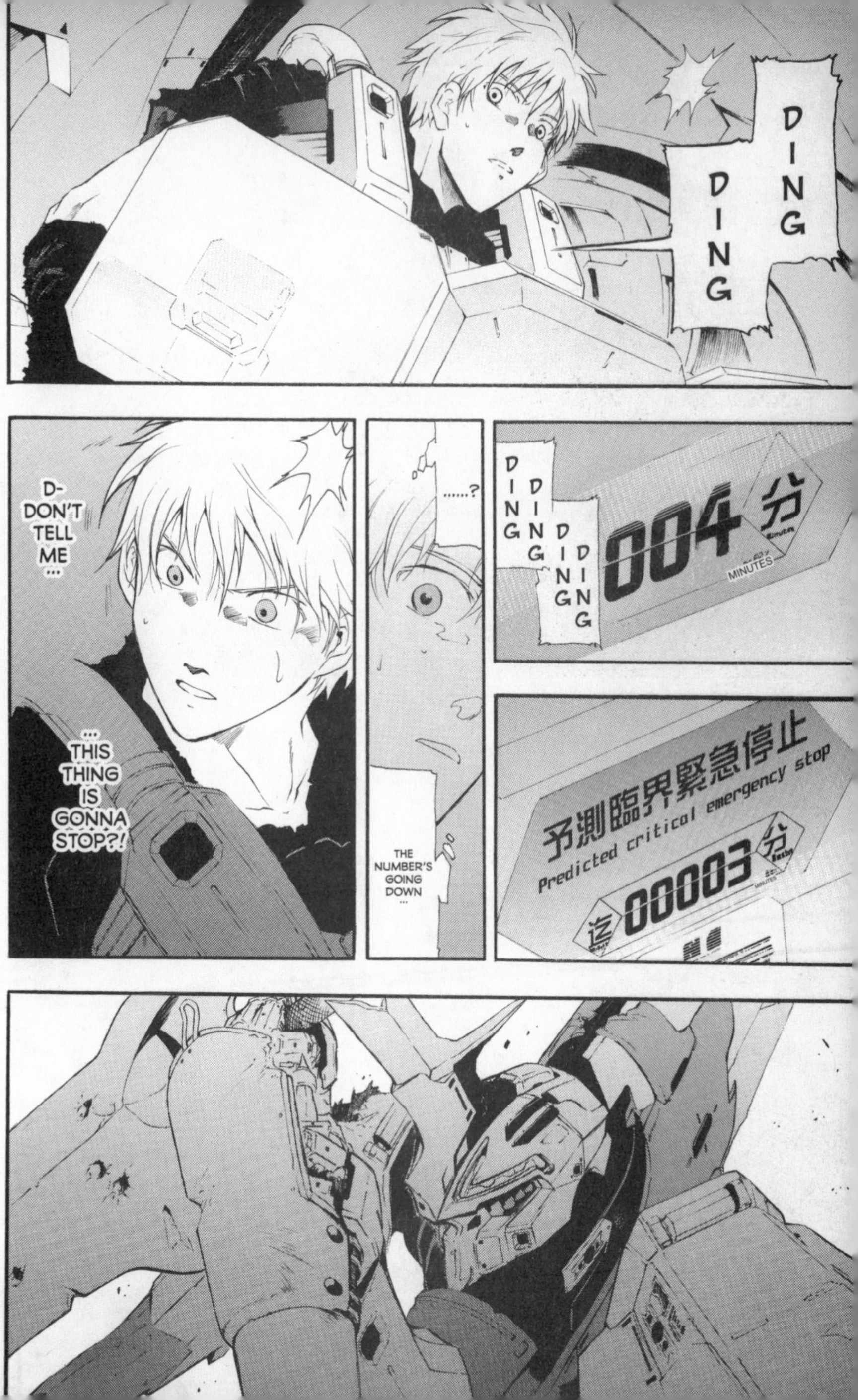
DING
DING
DING
DING
DING
DING
004 分
MINUTES
予測臨界緊急停止
Predicted critical emergency stop
迄 00003 分
MINUTES
......?
THE NUMBER'S GOING DOWN ...
D- DON'T TELL ME ...
... THIS THING IS GONNA STOP?!

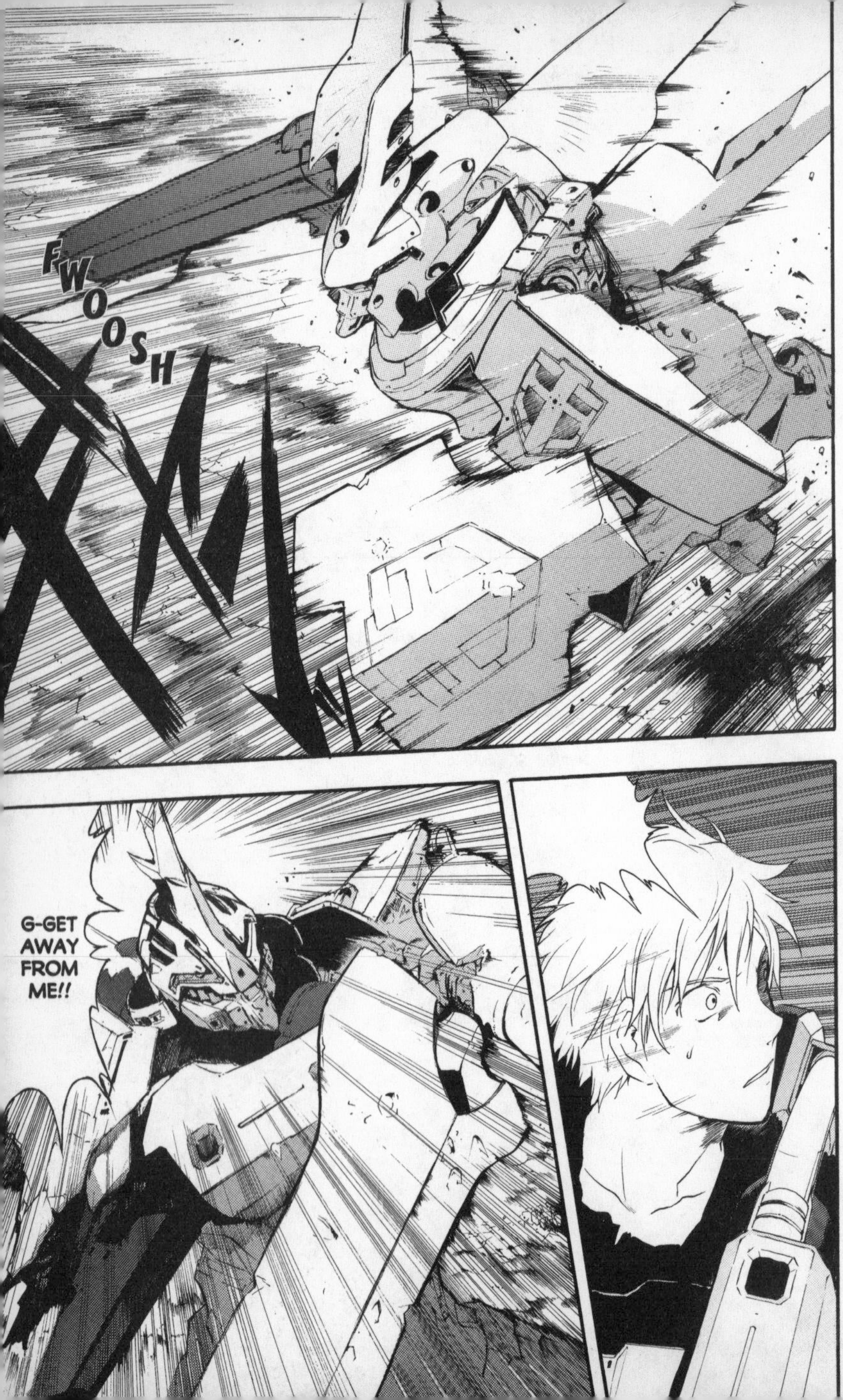
FWOOSH
G-GET AWAY FROM ME!!

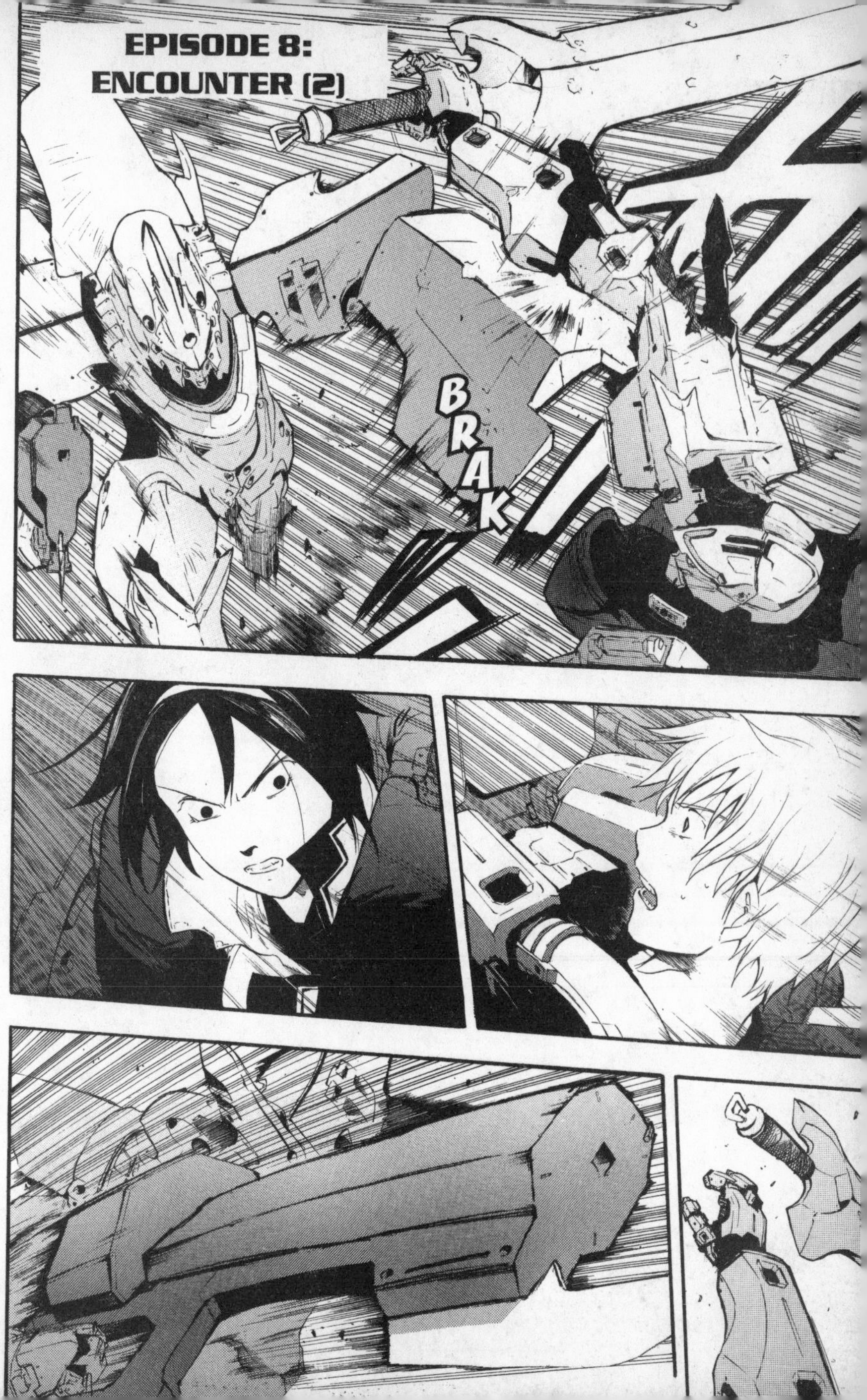
EPISODE 8:
ENCOUNTER (2)
BRAK

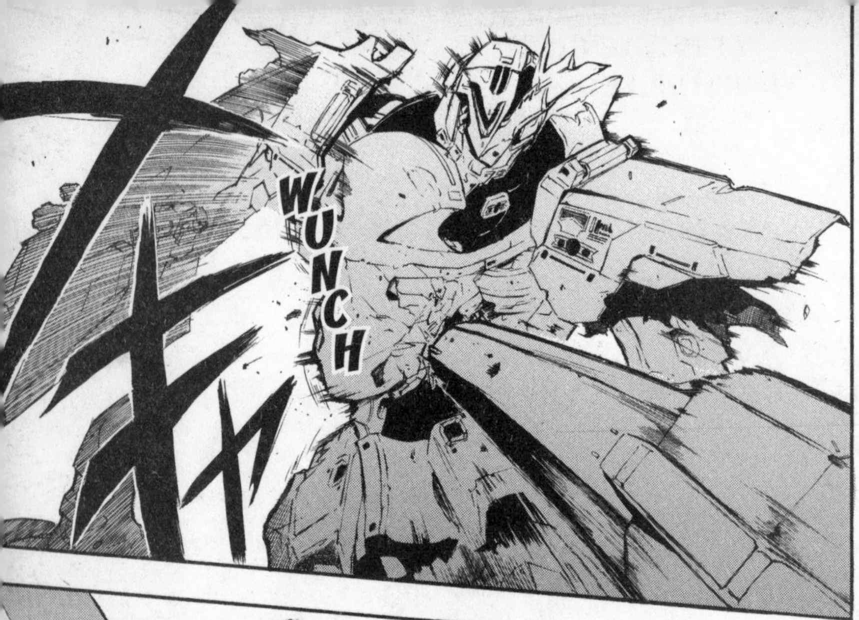
WUNCH
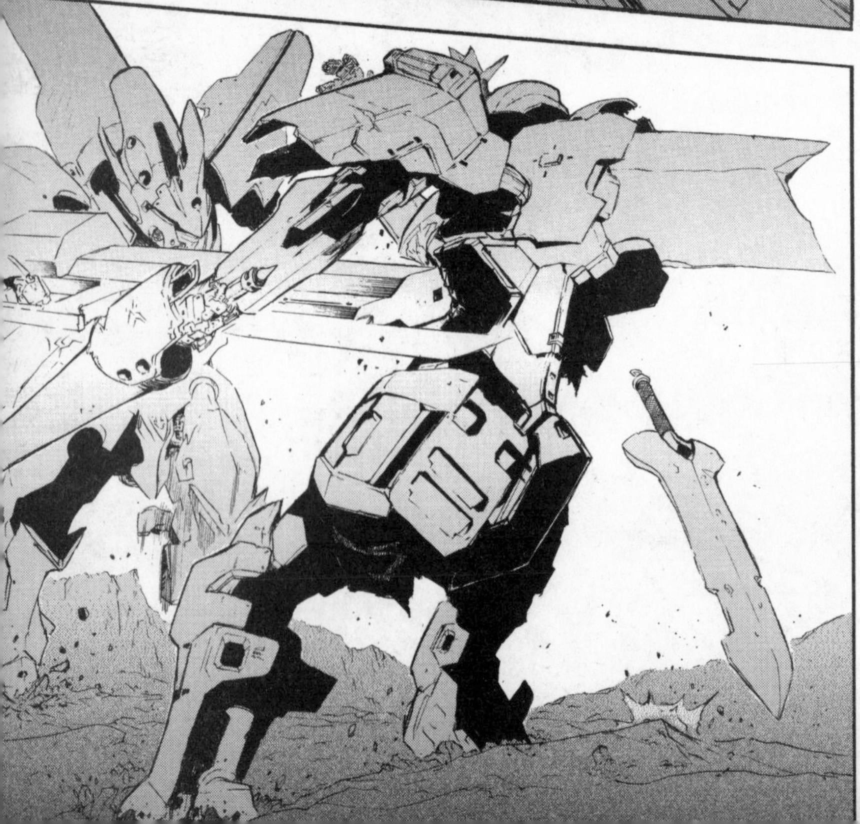

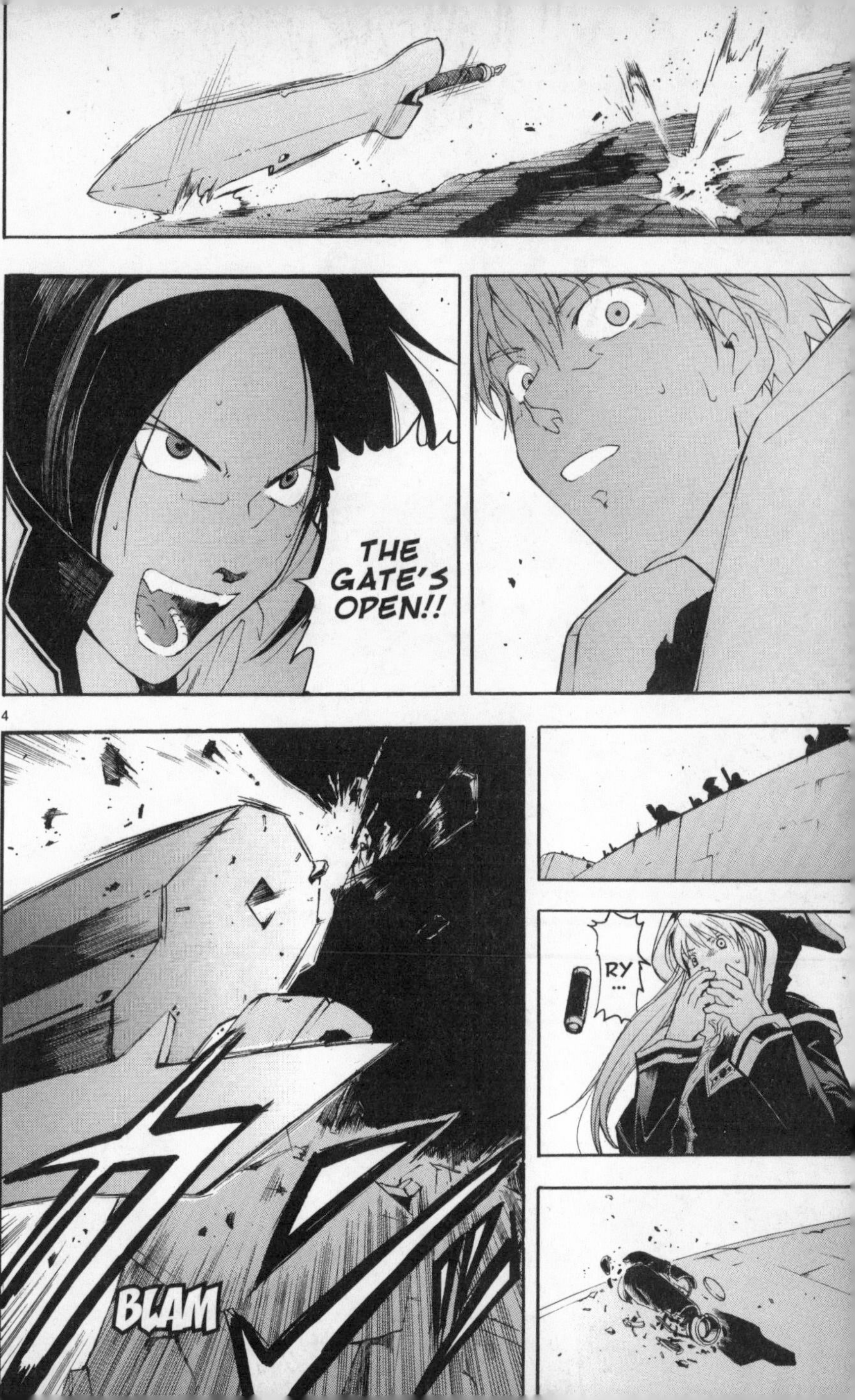
THE GATE'S OPEN!!
RY ...
BLAM

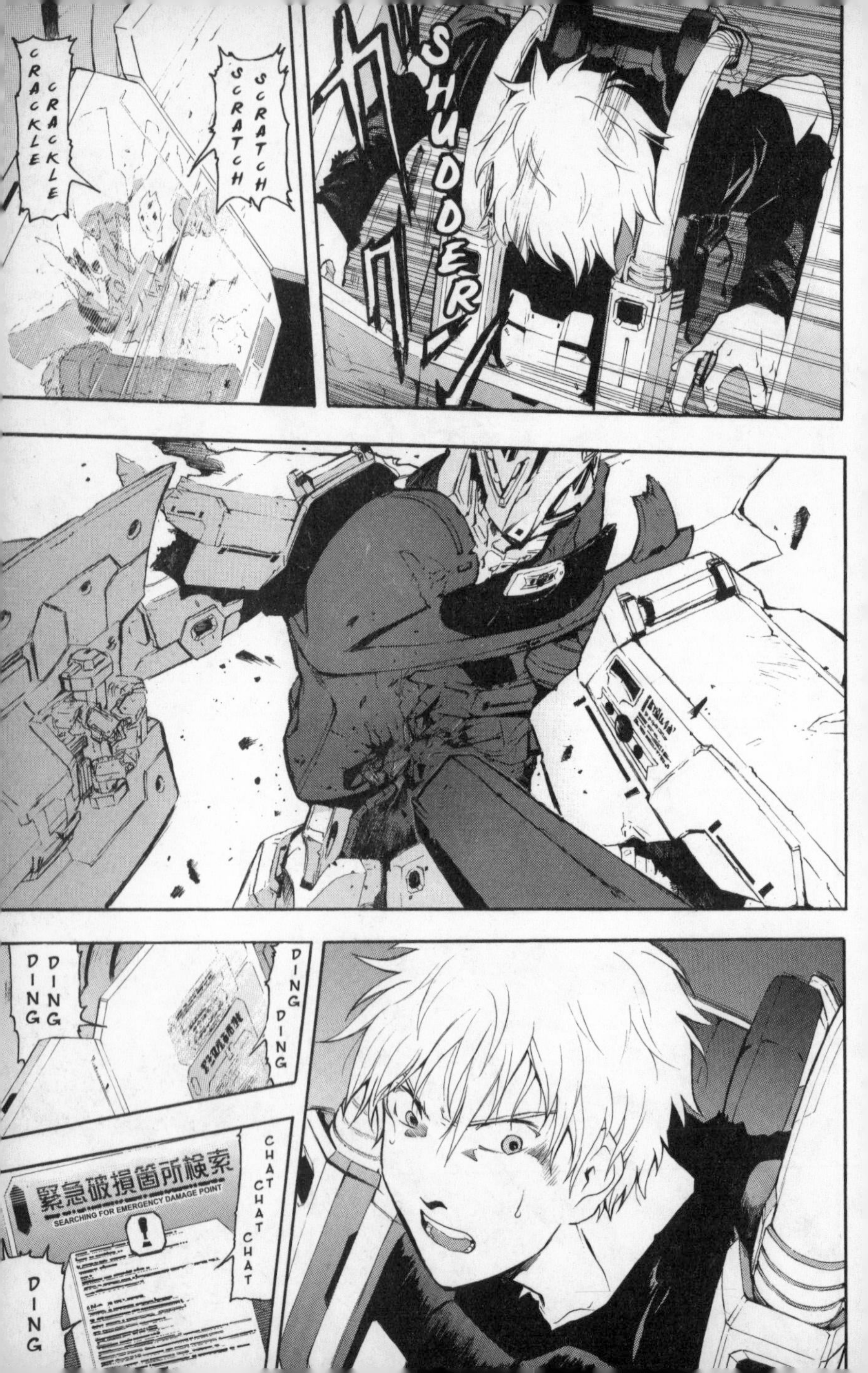
SHUDDER
SCRATCH SCRATCH
CRACKLE CRACKLE
DING DING
DING DING
緊急破損箇所検索
SEARCHING FOR EMERGENCY DAMAGE POINT
CHAT CHAT CHAT CHAT
DING

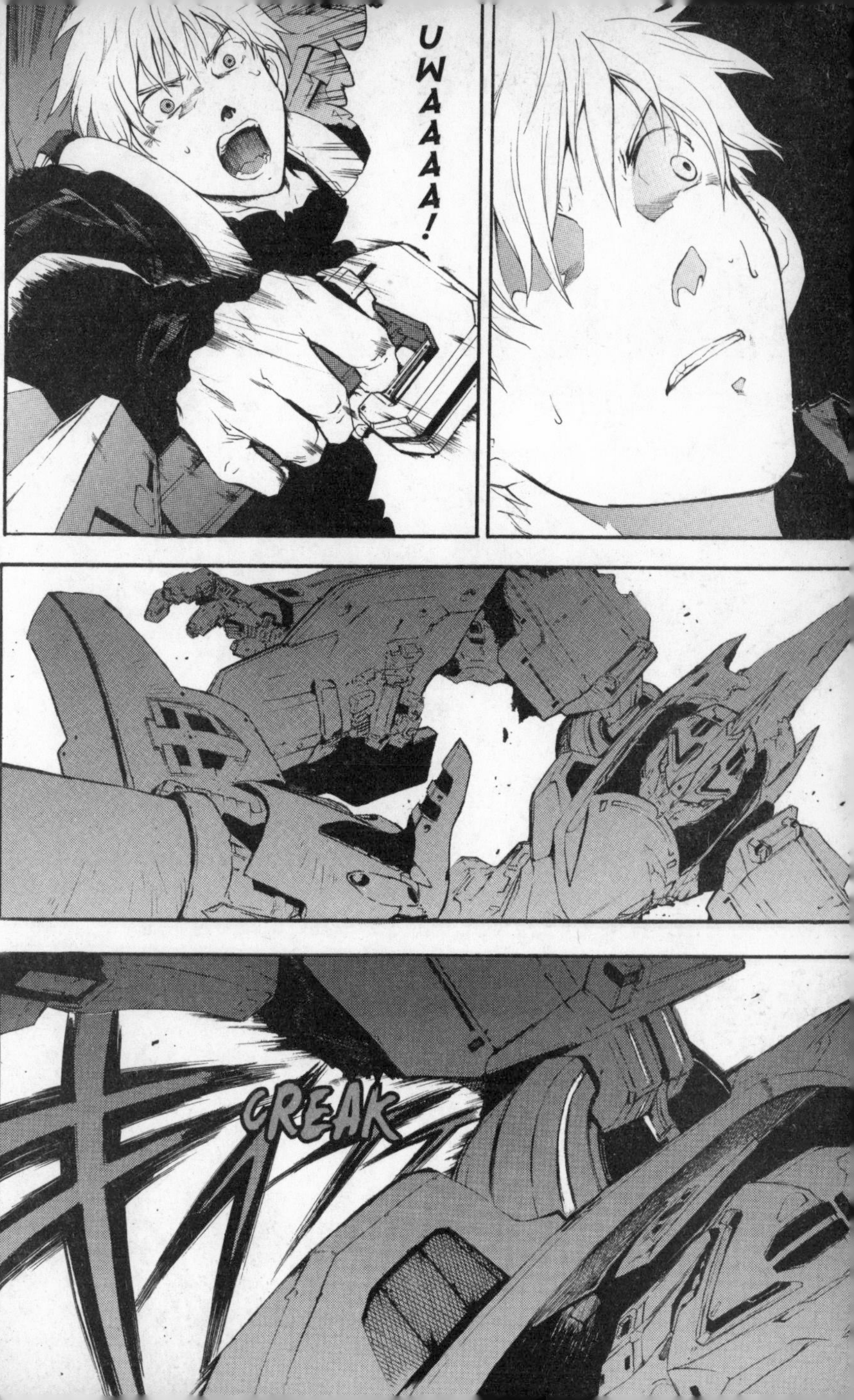
UWAAAAAA!
CREAK

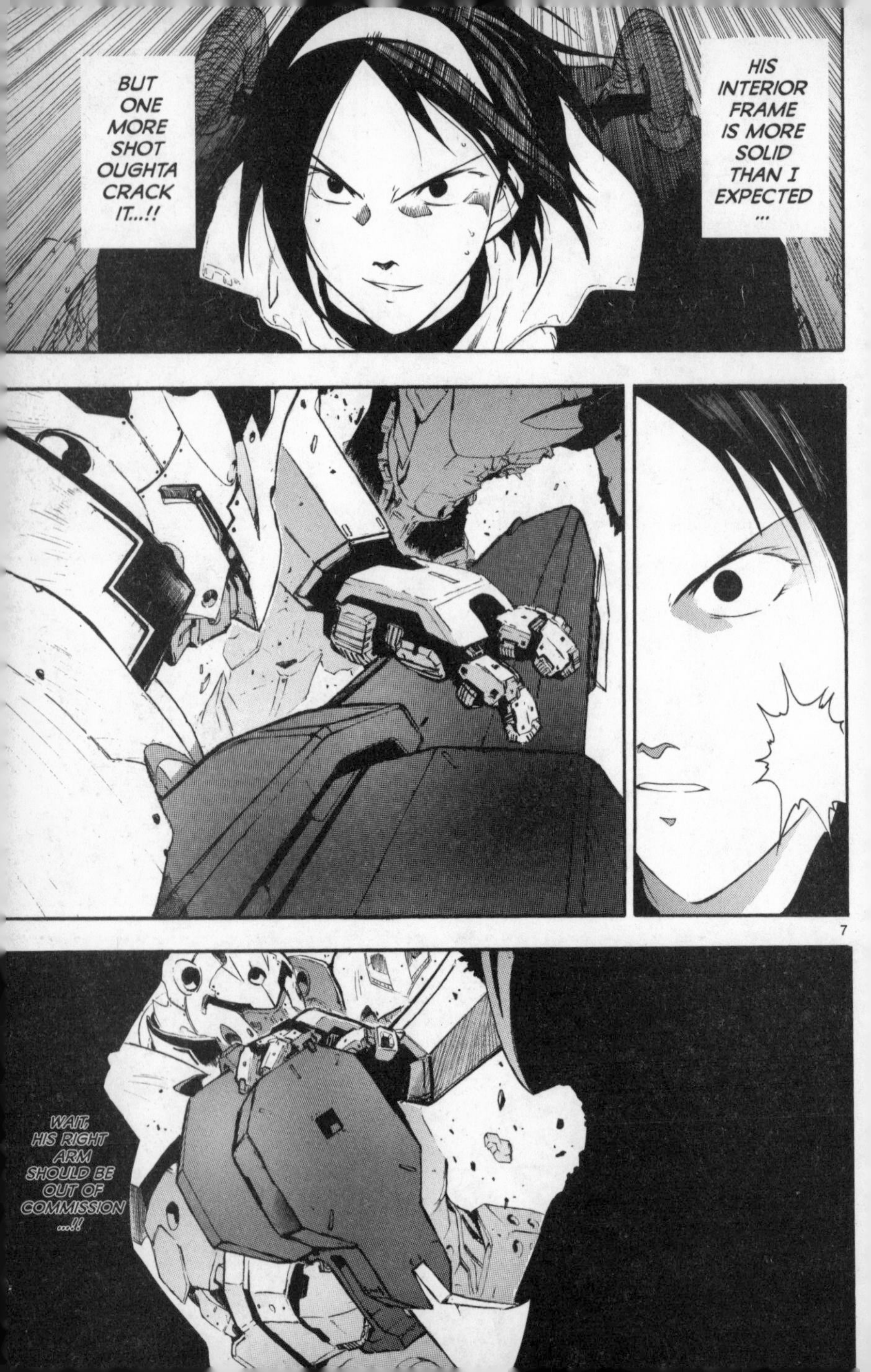
HIS INTERIOR FRAME IS MORE SOLID THAN I EXPECTED ...
BUT ONE MORE SHOT OUGHTA CRACK IT...!!
WAIT, HIS RIGHT ARM SHOULD BE OUT OF COMMISSION ...!!

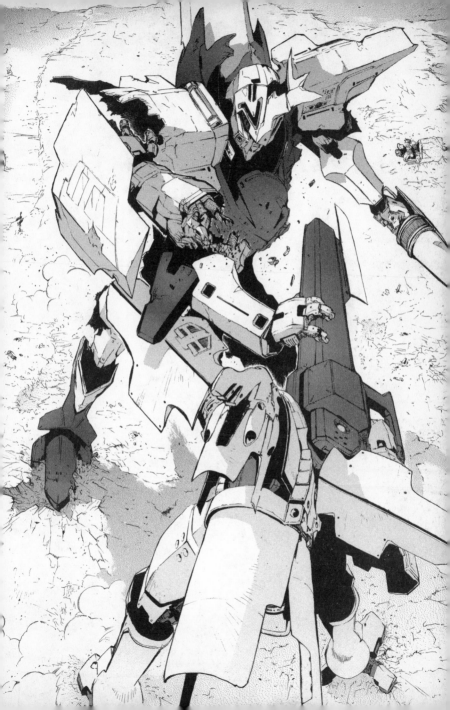

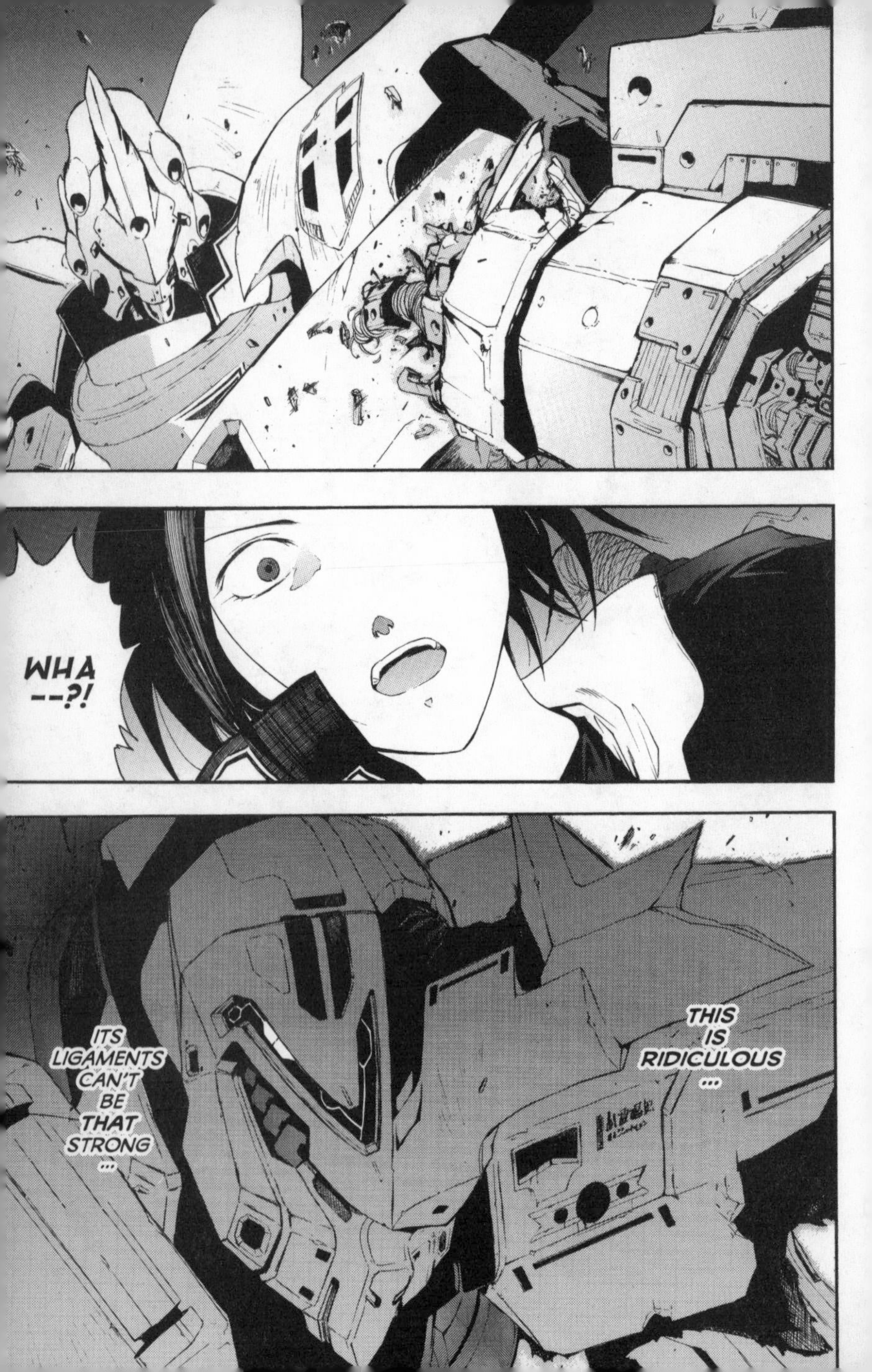
WHA--?!
THIS IS RIDICULOUS...
ITS LIGAMENTS CAN'T BE THAT STRONG...

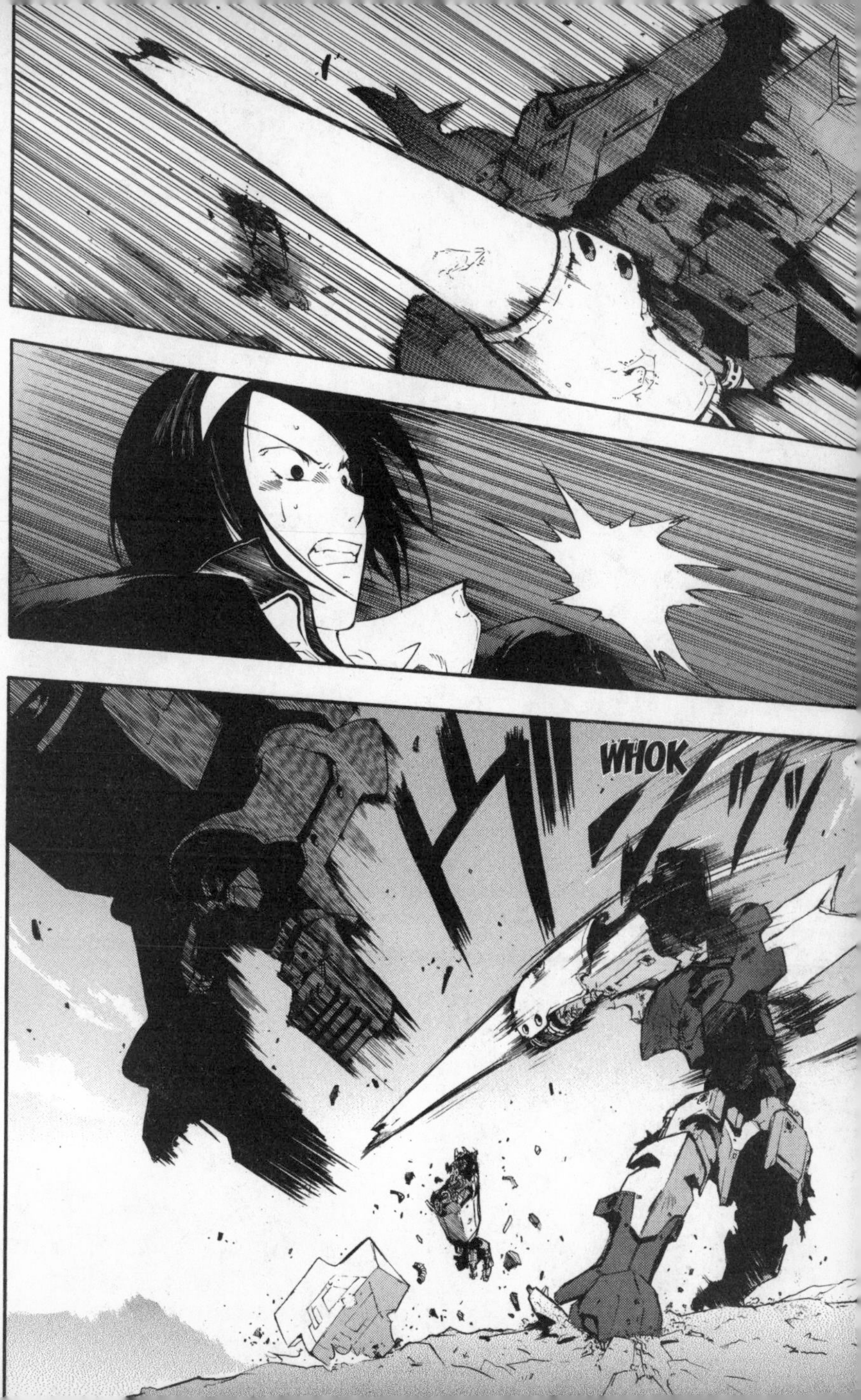
WHOK

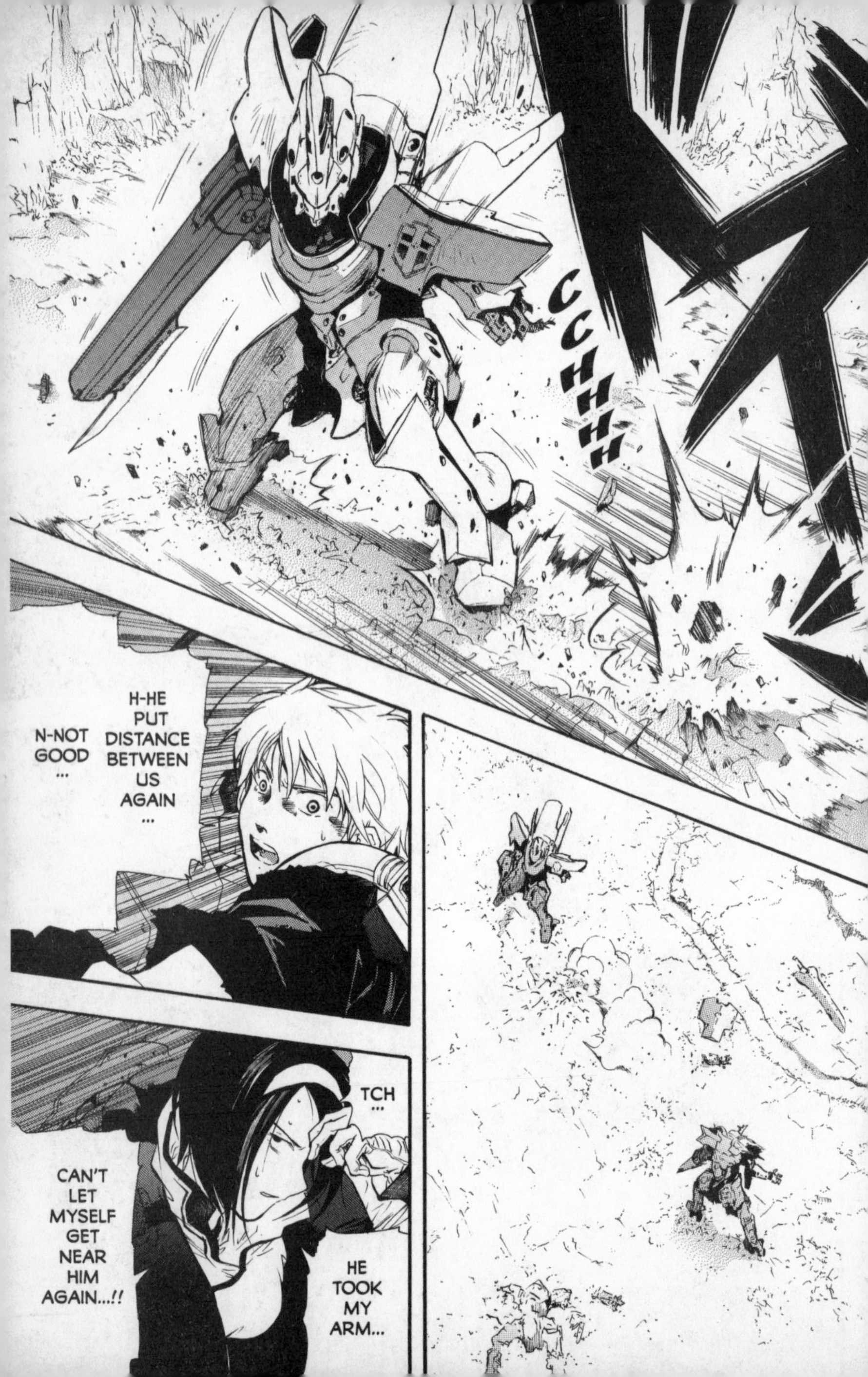
CCHHHH
H-HE PUT DISTANCE BETWEEN US AGAIN...
N-NOT GOOD...
TCH...
HE TOOK MY ARM...
CAN'T LET MYSELF GET NEAR HIM AGAIN...!!

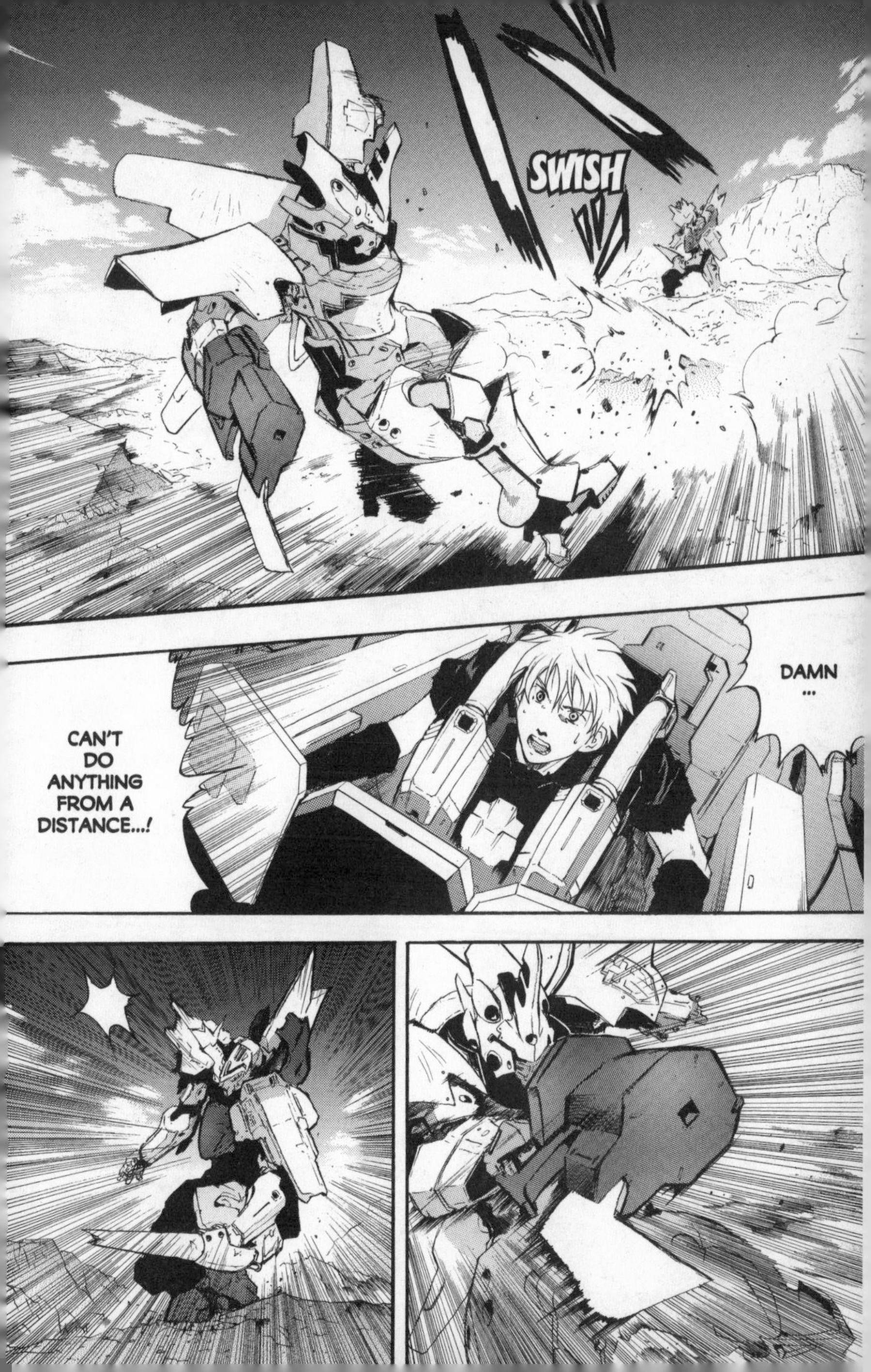
SWISH
DAMN ...
CAN'T DO ANYTHING FROM A DISTANCE...!

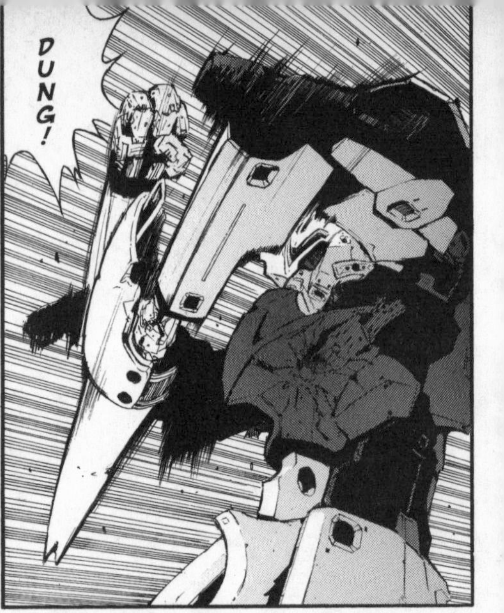
DUNG!
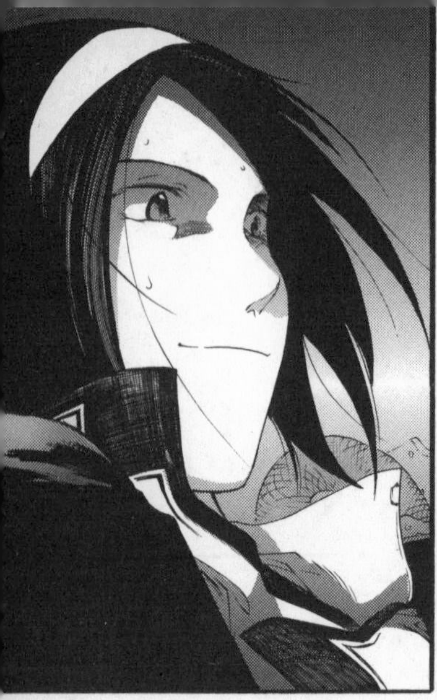
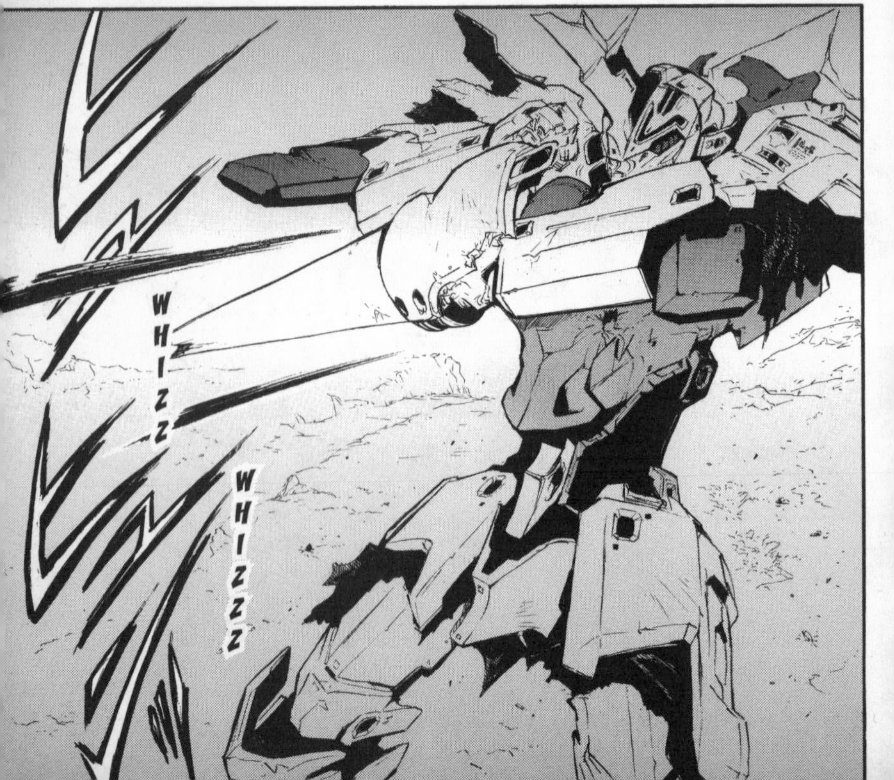
WHIZZ
WHIZZZ

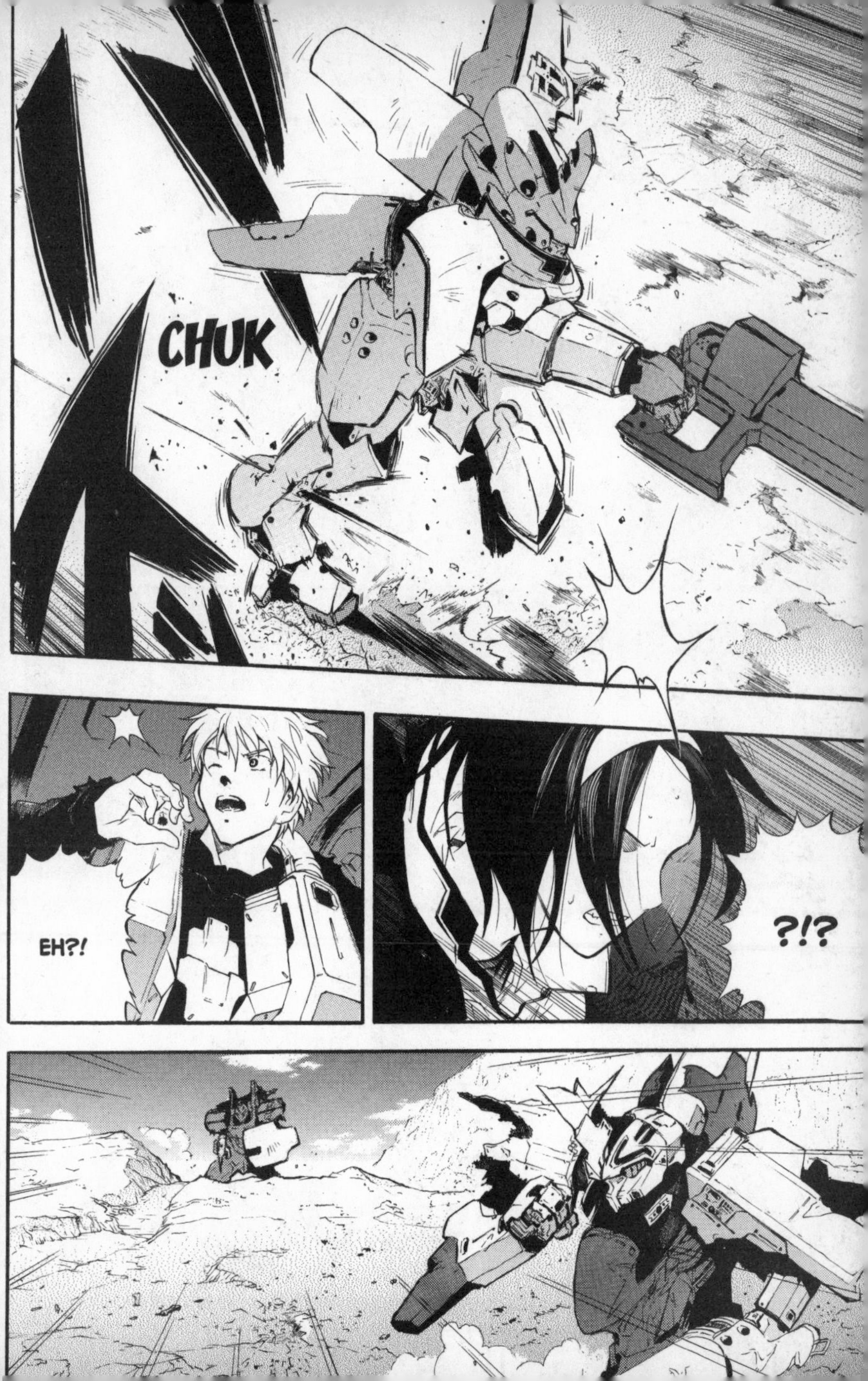
CHUK
?!?
EH?!

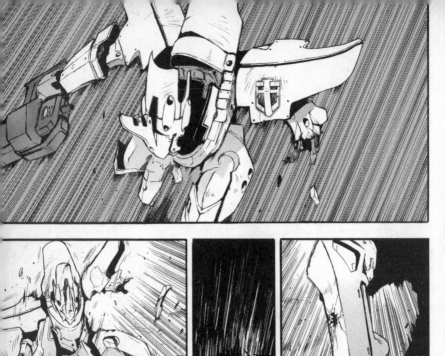

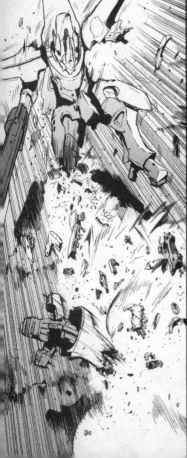

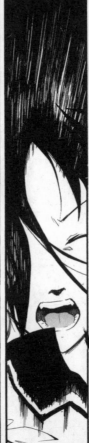

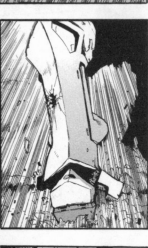

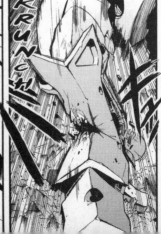

KRUNCH

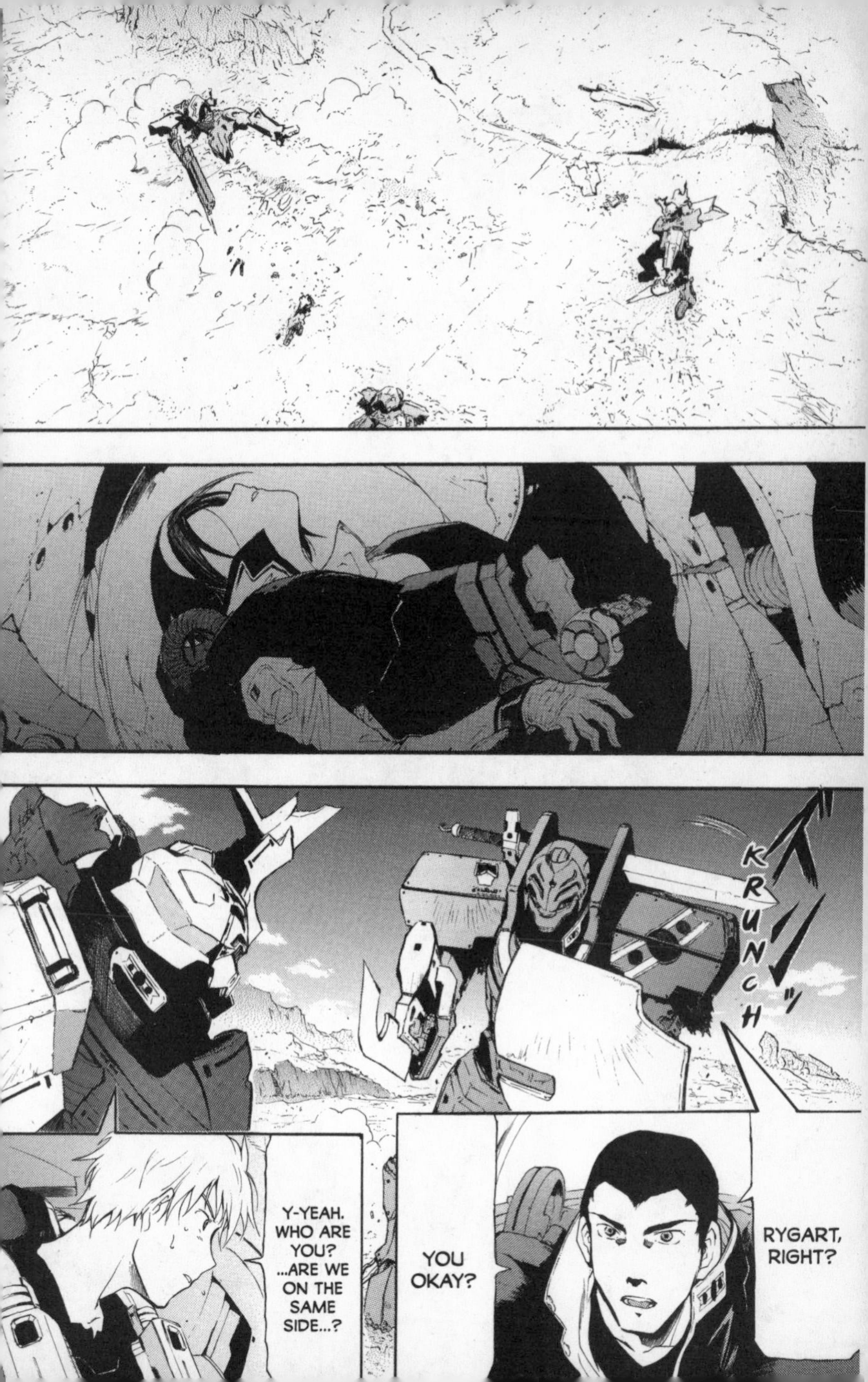
KRUNCH
RYGART, RIGHT?
YOU OKAY?
Y-YEAH. WHO ARE YOU? ...ARE WE ON THE SAME SIDE...?

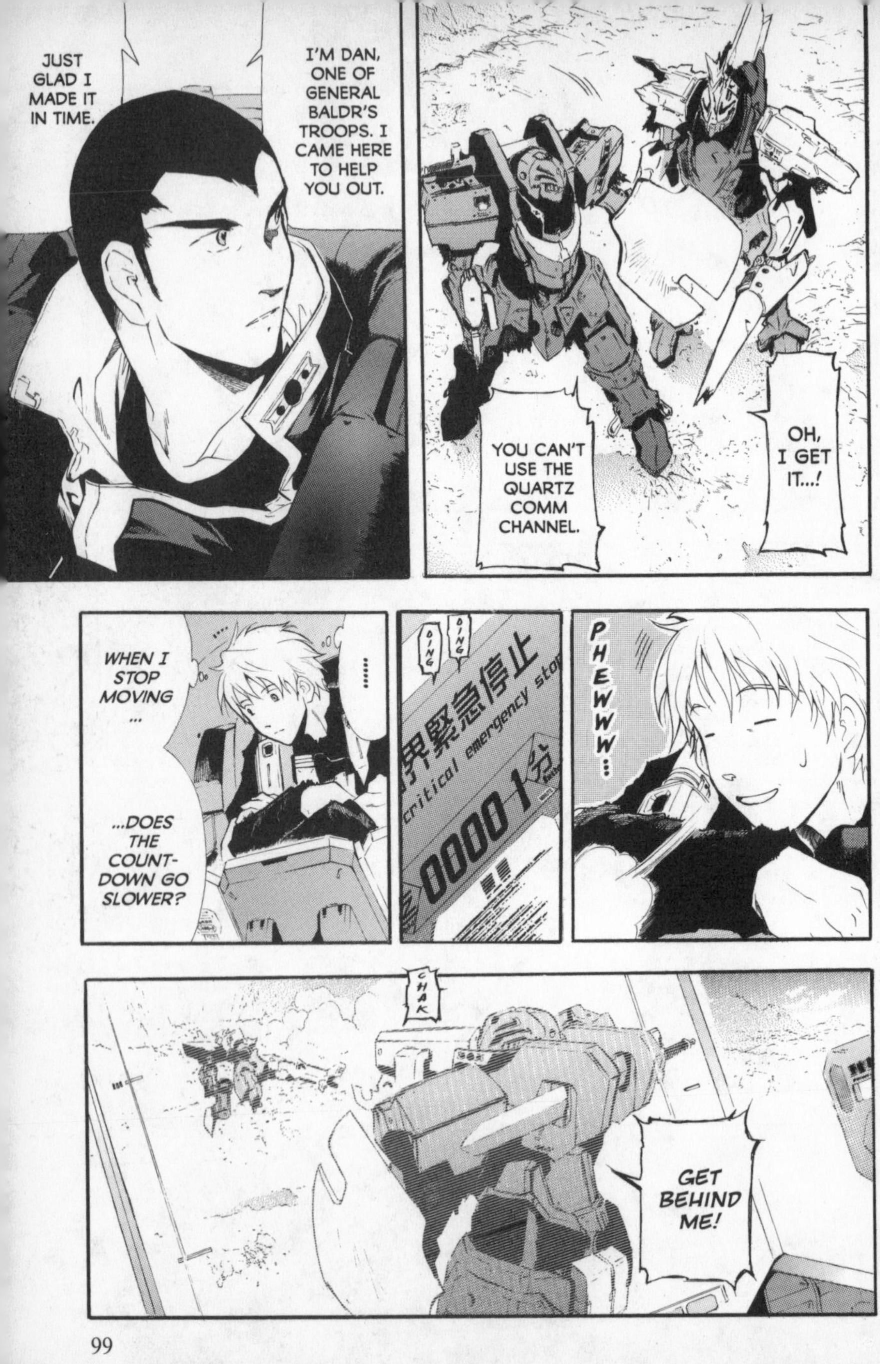
OH, I GET IT...!
YOU CAN'T USE THE QUARTZ COMM CHANNEL.
I'M DAN, ONE OF GENERAL BALDR'S TROOPS. I CAME HERE TO HELP YOU OUT.
JUST GLAD I MADE IT IN TIME.
PHEWWW...
DING
DING
界緊急停止
critical emergency stop
0000
1分
......
WHEN I STOP MOVING...
...DOES THE COUNT-DOWN GO SLOWER?
CHAK
GET BEHIND ME!

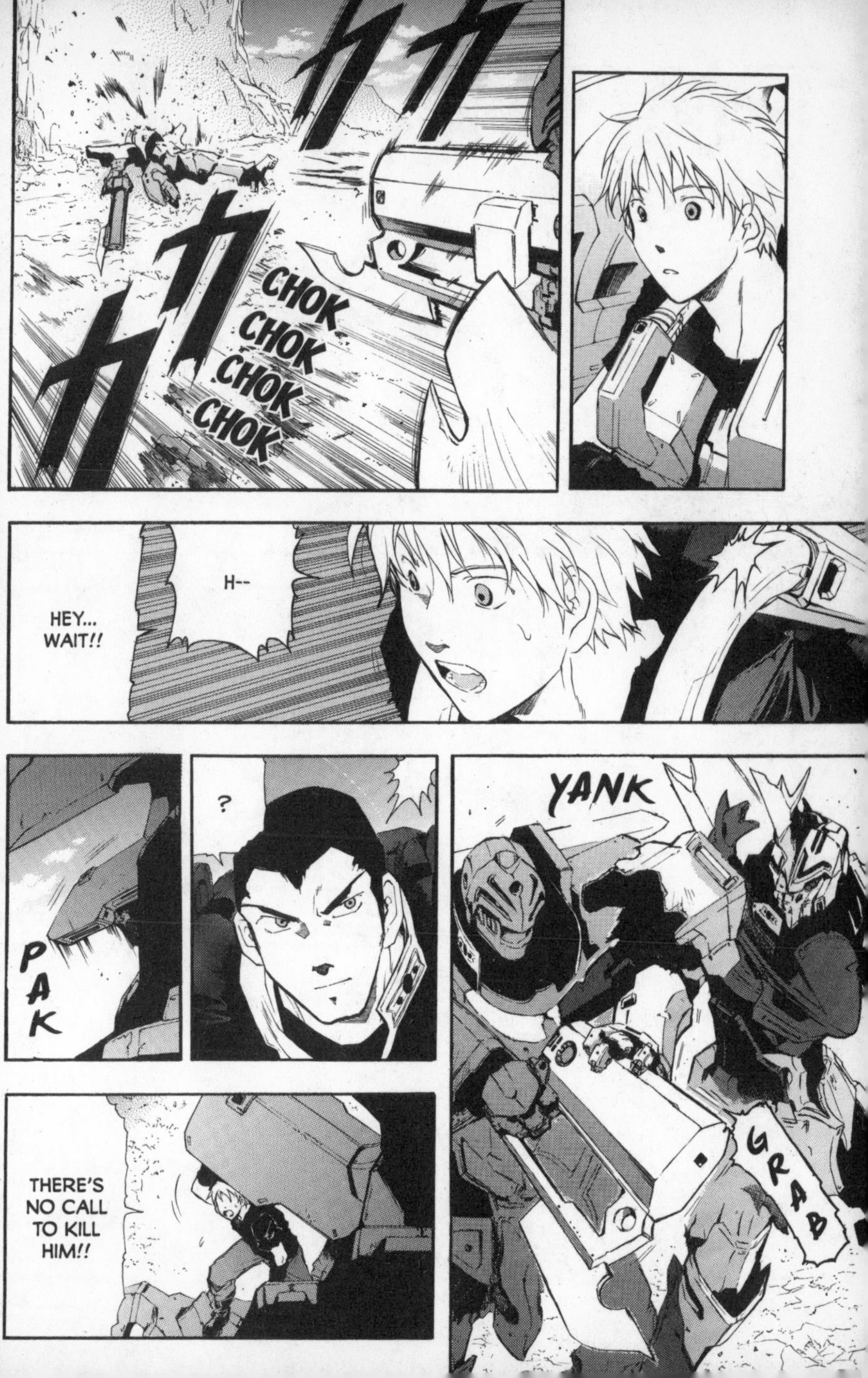
カカカカ
CHOK CHOK CHOK CHOK
H--
HEY... WAIT!!
YANK
GRAB
?
PAK
THERE'S NO CALL TO KILL HIM!!

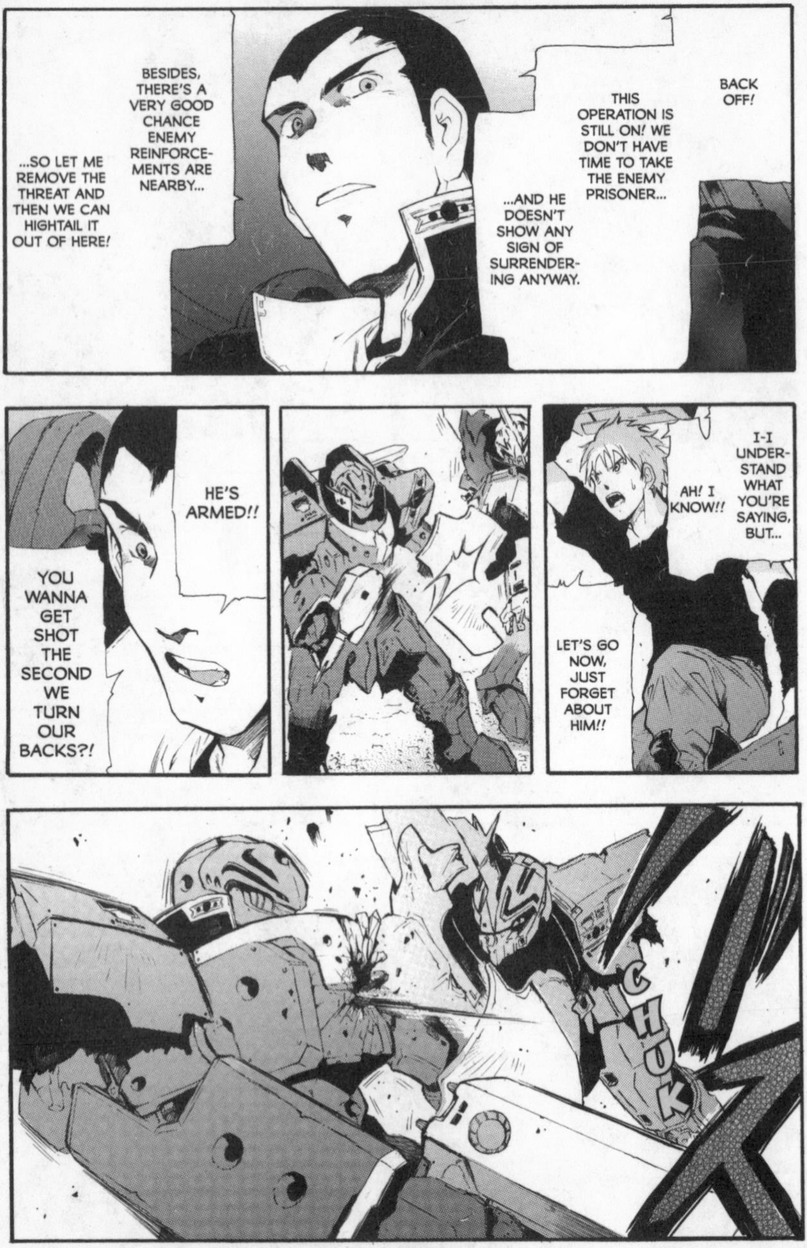
BACK OFF!
THIS OPERATION IS STILL ON! WE DON'T HAVE TIME TO TAKE THE ENEMY PRISONER...
...AND HE DOESN'T SHOW ANY SIGN OF SURRENDERING ANYWAY.
BESIDES, THERE'S A VERY GOOD CHANCE ENEMY REINFORCEMENTS ARE NEARBY...
...SO LET ME REMOVE THE THREAT AND THEN WE CAN HIGHTAIL IT OUT OF HERE!
I-I UNDERSTAND WHAT YOU'RE SAYING, BUT...
AH! I KNOW!!
LET'S GO NOW, JUST FORGET ABOUT HIM!!
HE'S ARMED!!
YOU WANNA GET SHOT THE SECOND WE TURN OUR BACKS?!
CHUK

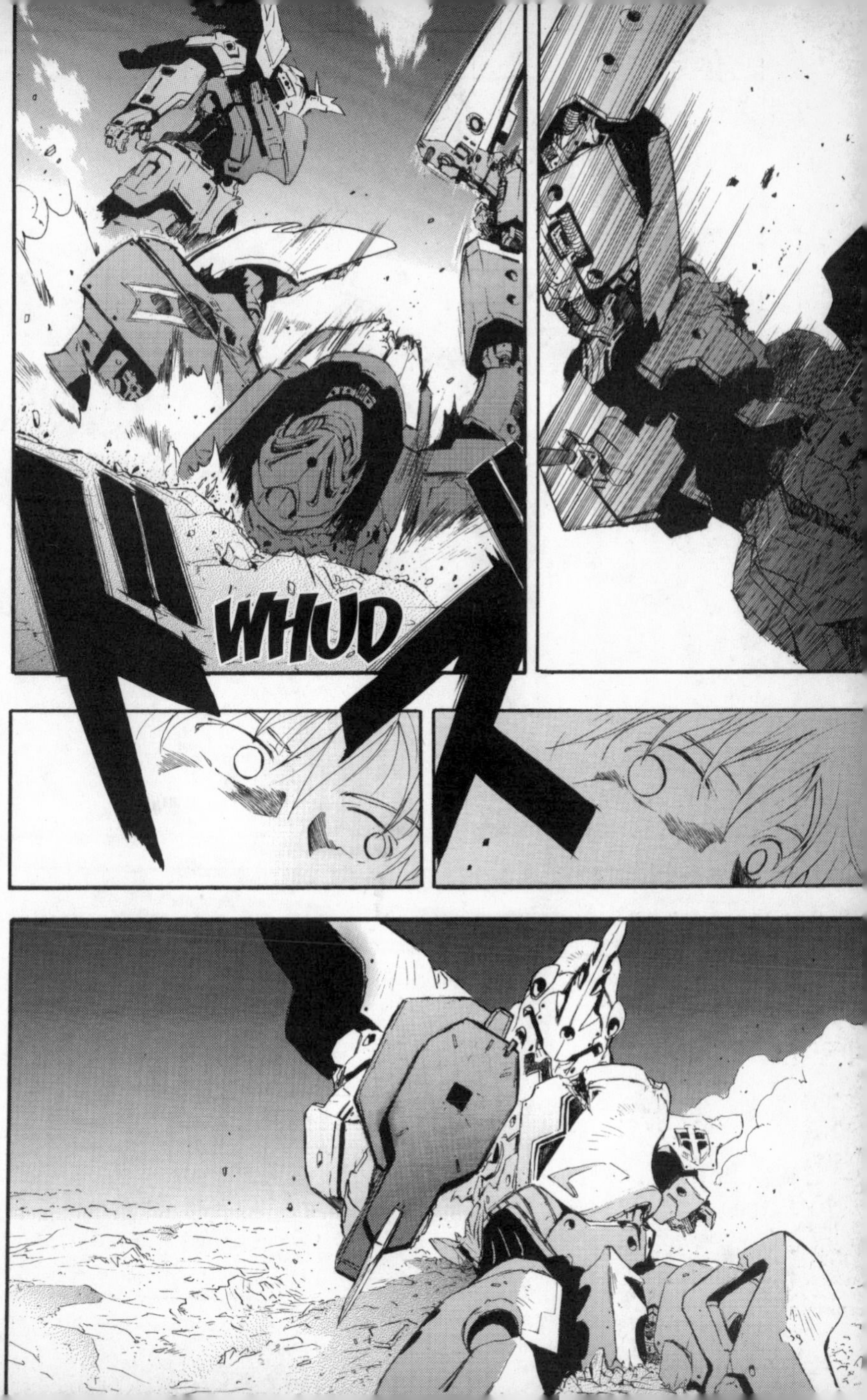
WHUD

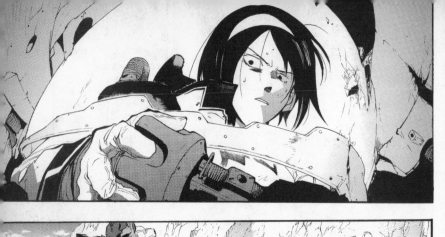

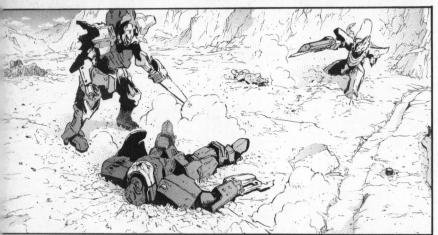

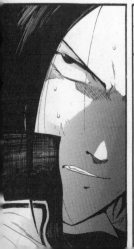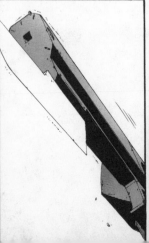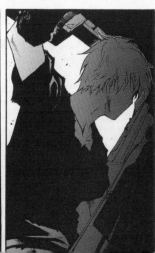

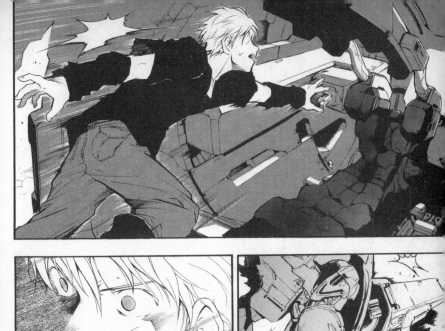

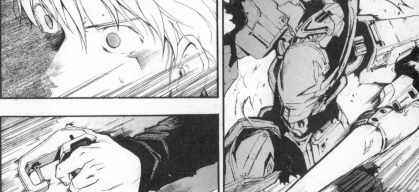

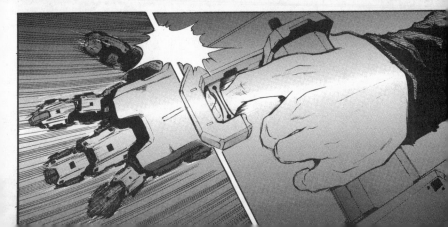

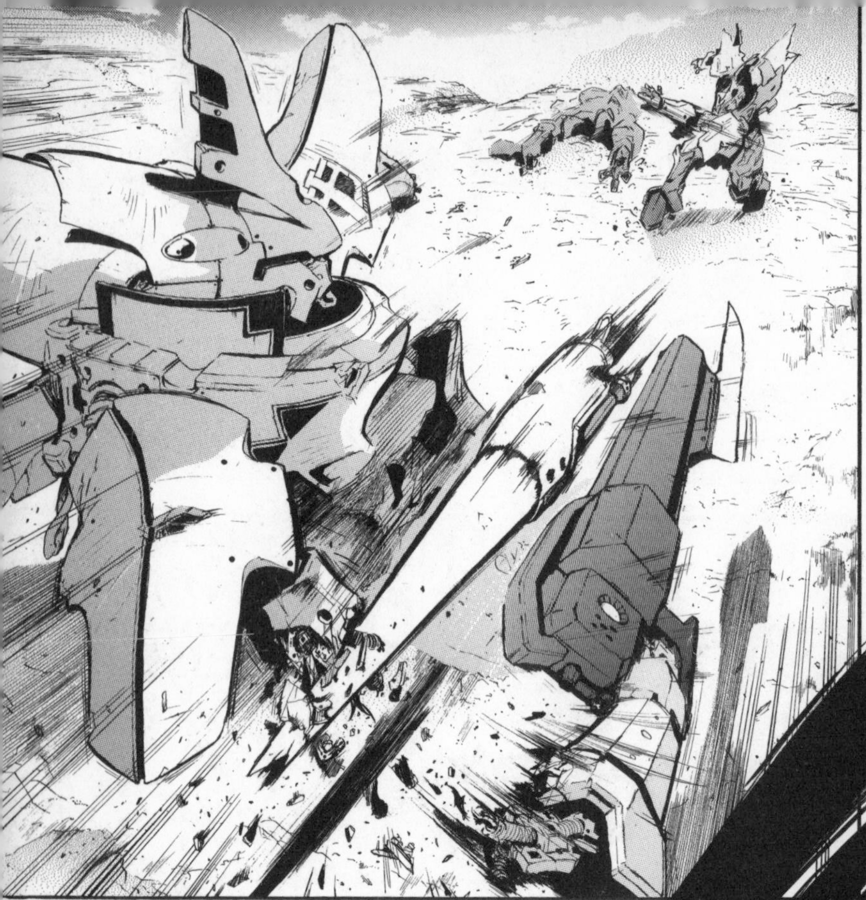
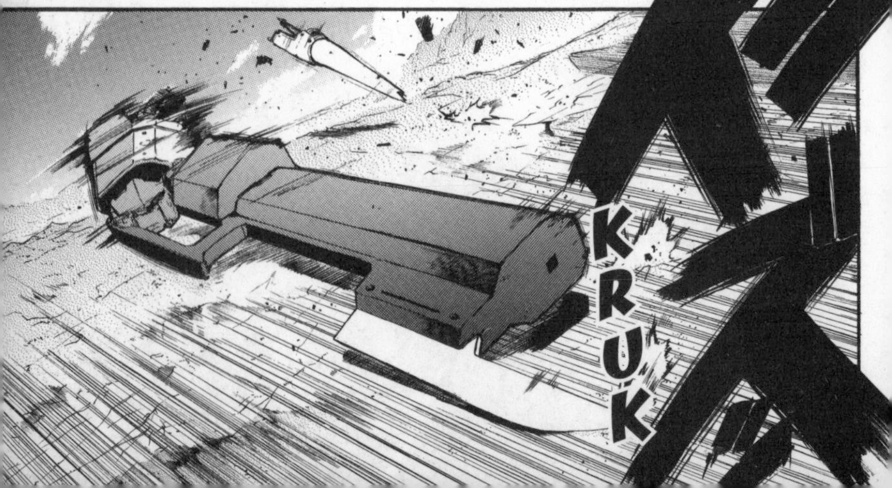
KRUK

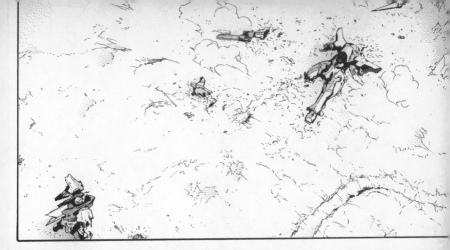

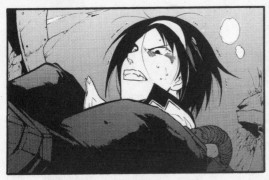

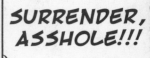
SURRENDER,
ASSHOLE!!!

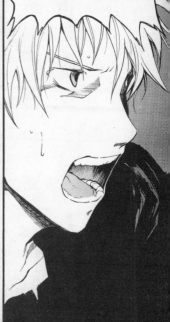

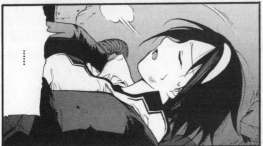

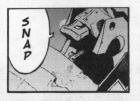
SNAP

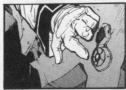

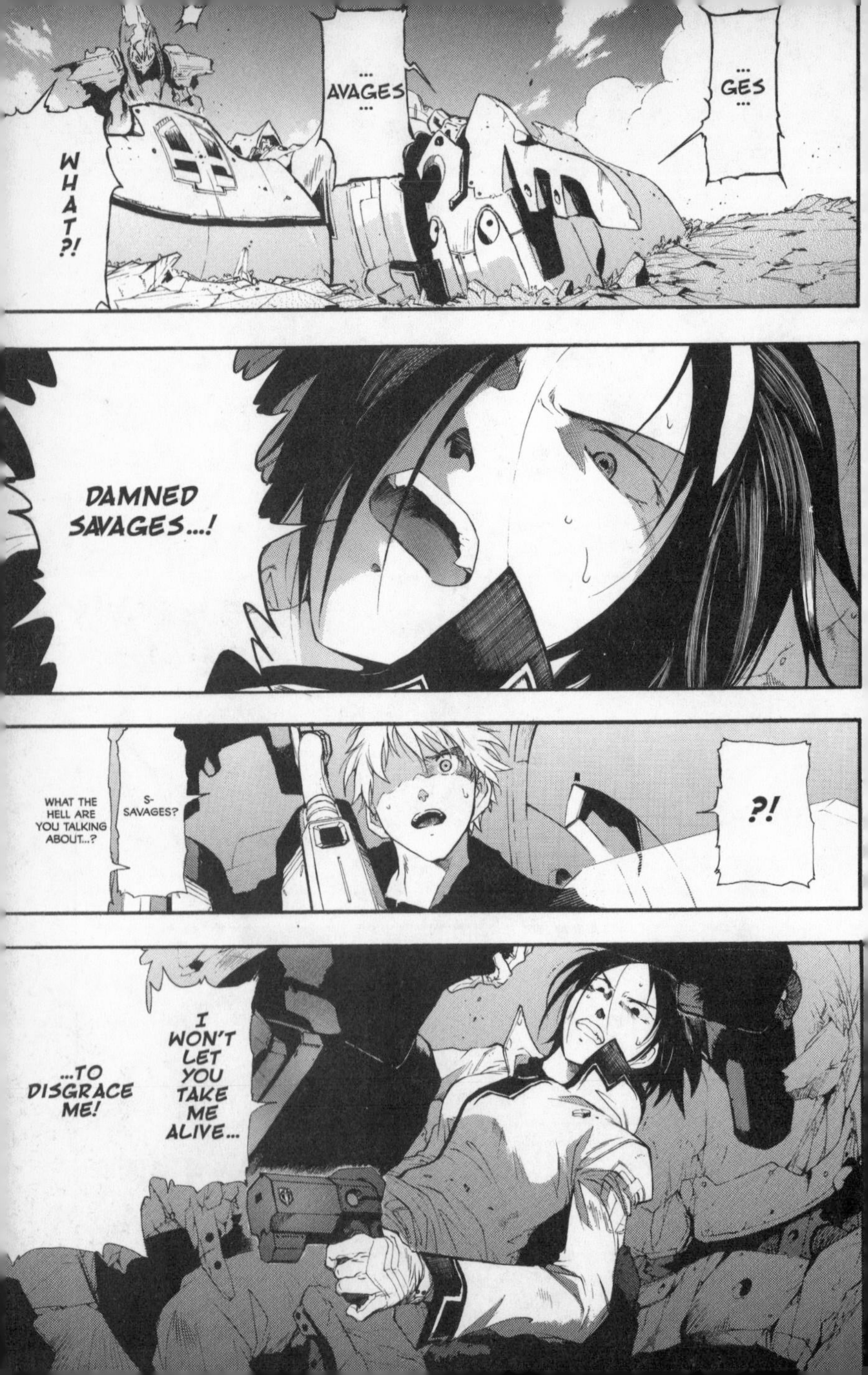
... GES ...
... AVAGES ...
WHAT?!
DAMNED SAVAGES...!
?!
S-SAVAGES?
WHAT THE HELL ARE YOU TALKING ABOUT...?
I WON'T LET YOU TAKE ME ALIVE...
...TO DISGRACE ME!

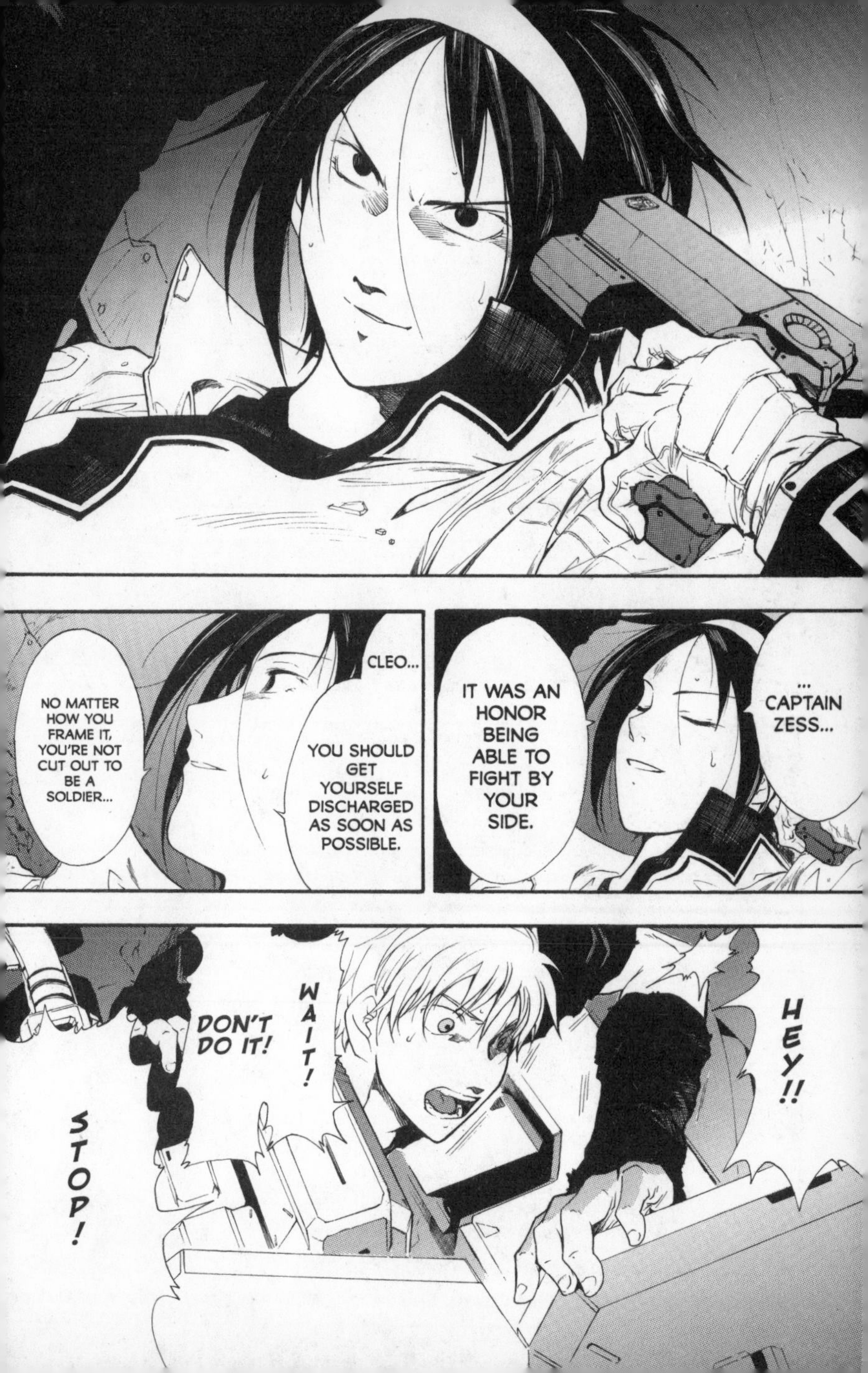
... CAPTAIN ZESS...
IT WAS AN HONOR BEING ABLE TO FIGHT BY YOUR SIDE.
CLEO...
YOU SHOULD GET YOURSELF DISCHARGED AS SOON AS POSSIBLE.
NO MATTER HOW YOU FRAME IT, YOU'RE NOT CUT OUT TO BE A SOLDIER...
HEY!!
WAIT!
DON'T DO IT!
STOP!

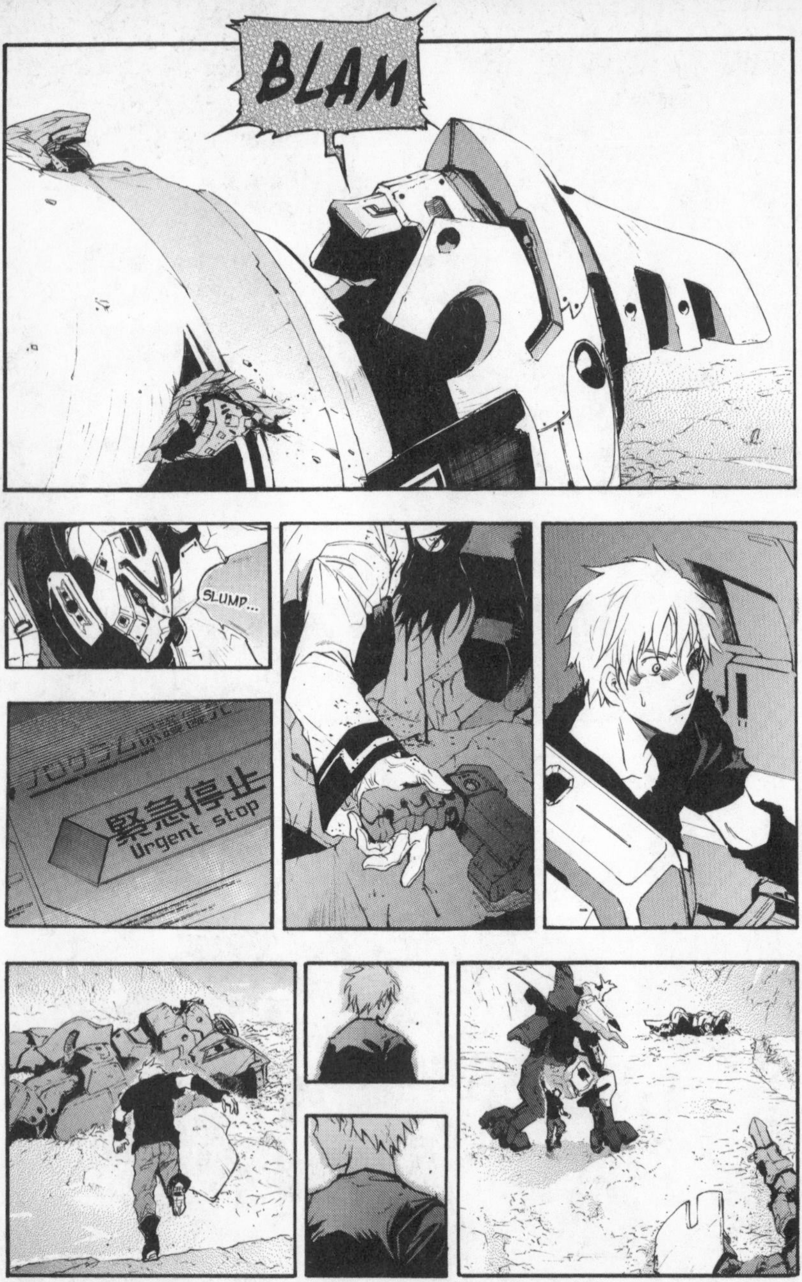
BLAM
SLUMP...
緊急停止
Urgent stop

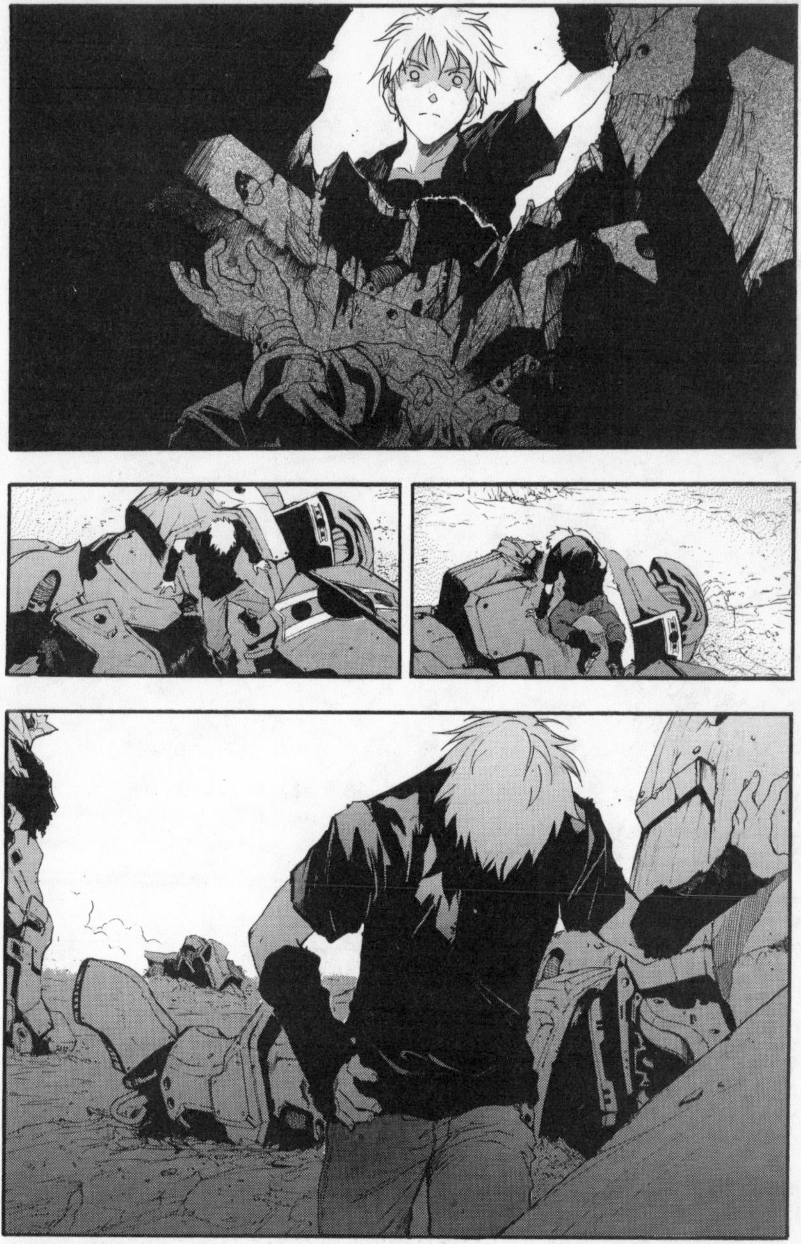

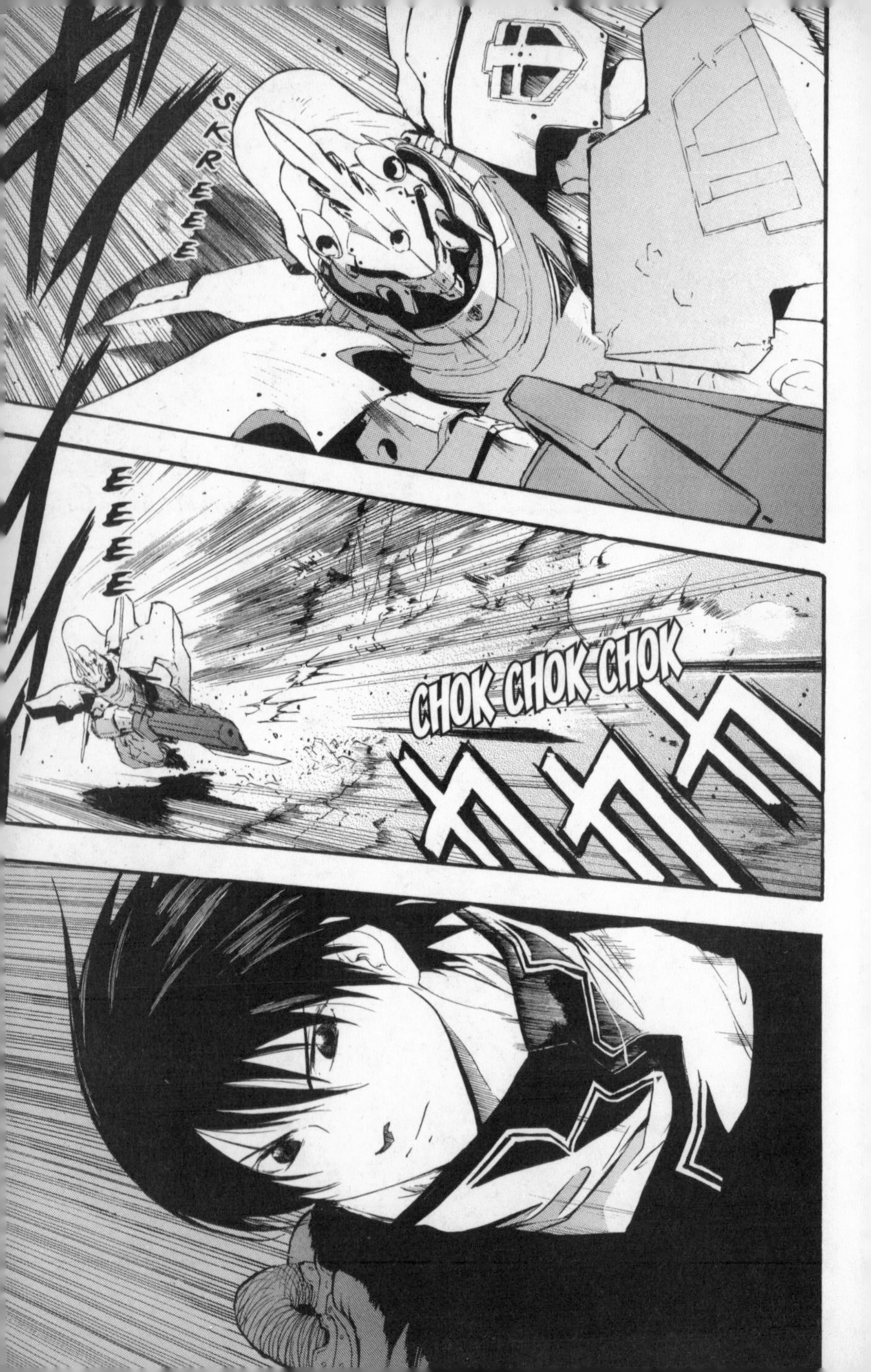
SKREEEE
EEEE
CHOK CHOK CHOK

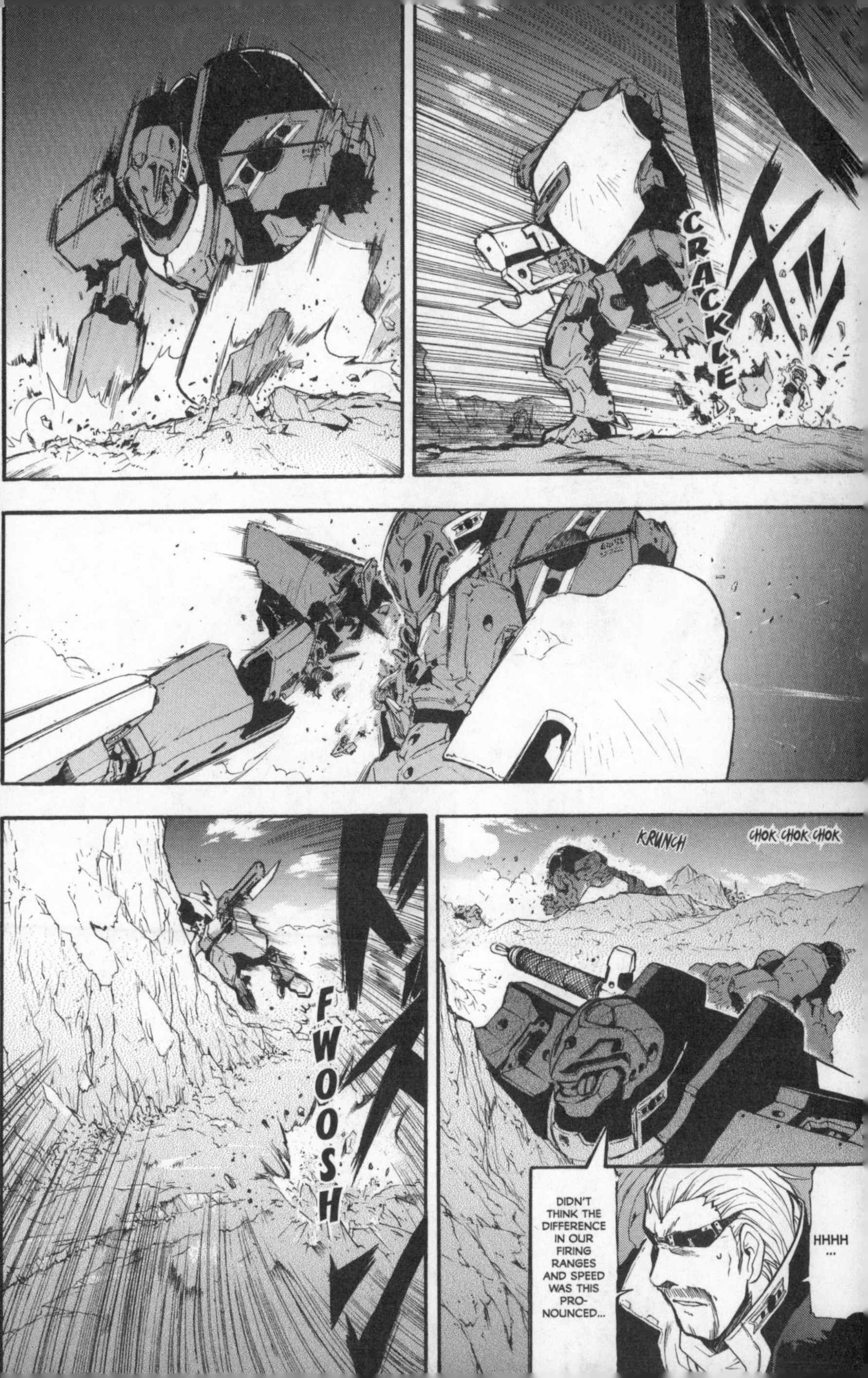
CRACKLE
CHOK CHOK CHOK
KRUNCH
HHHH ...
DIDN'T THINK THE DIFFERENCE IN OUR FIRING RANGES AND SPEED WAS THIS PRO-NOUNCED...
FWOOSH

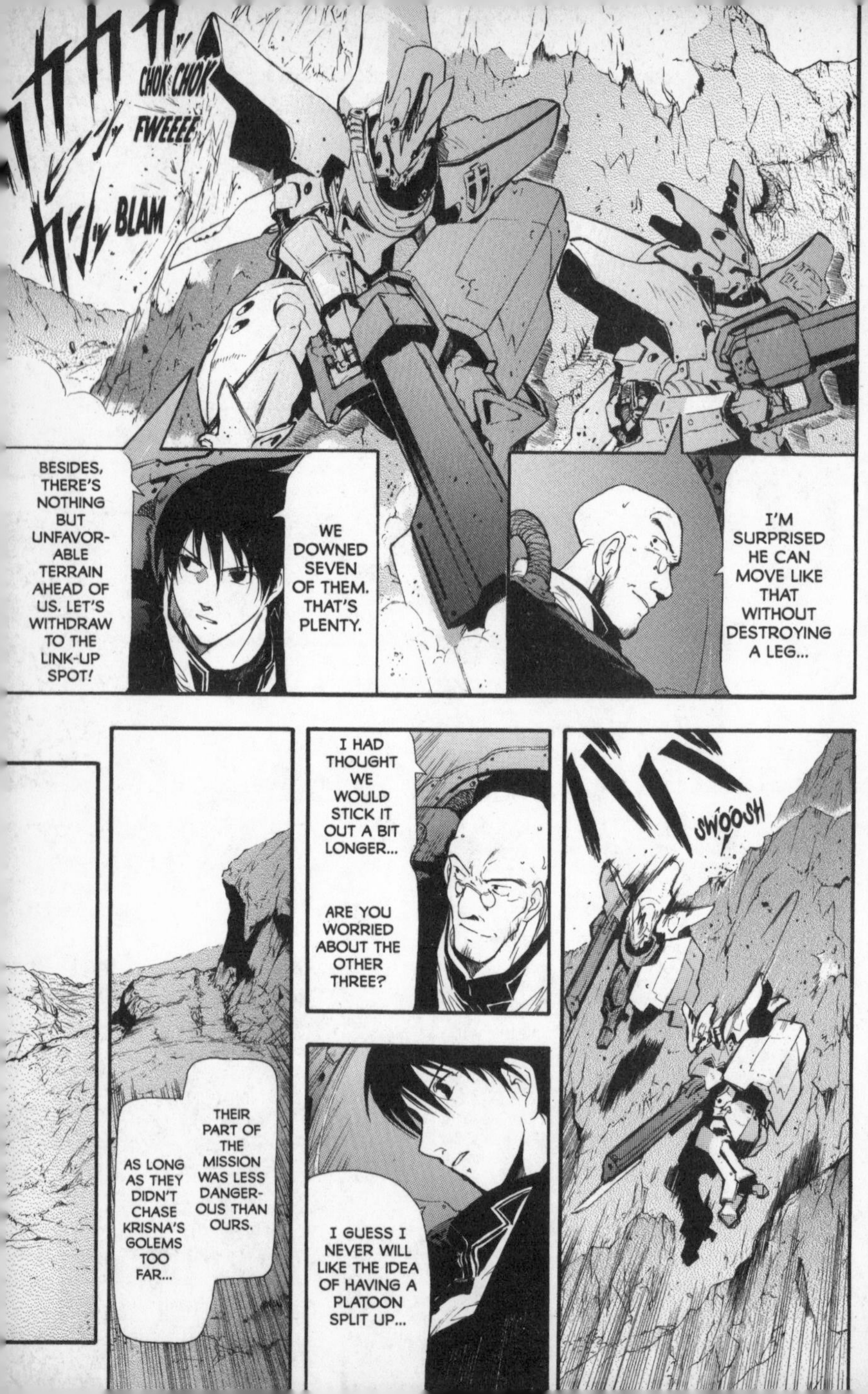
CHOK CHOK
FWEEEE
BLAM
I'M SURPRISED HE CAN MOVE LIKE THAT WITHOUT DESTROYING A LEG...
WE DOWNED SEVEN OF THEM. THAT'S PLENTY.
BESIDES, THERE'S NOTHING BUT UNFAVOR-ABLE TERRAIN AHEAD OF US. LET'S WITHDRAW TO THE LINK-UP SPOT!
SWOOSH
I HAD THOUGHT WE WOULD STICK IT OUT A BIT LONGER...
ARE YOU WORRIED ABOUT THE OTHER THREE?
I GUESS I NEVER WILL LIKE THE IDEA OF HAVING A PLATOON SPLIT UP...
THEIR PART OF THE MISSION WAS LESS DANGER-OUS THAN OURS.
AS LONG AS THEY DIDN'T CHASE KRISNA'S GOLEMS TOO FAR...

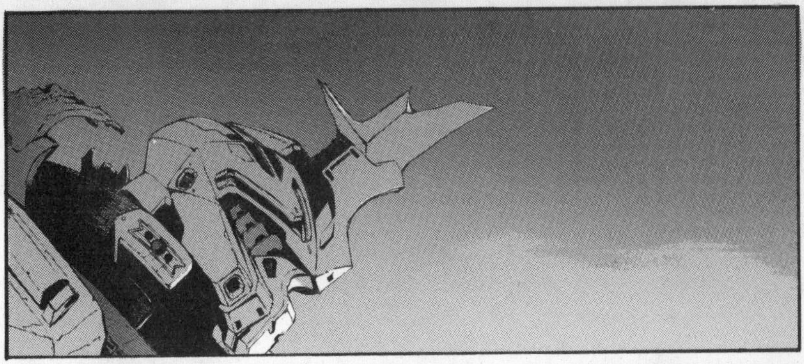

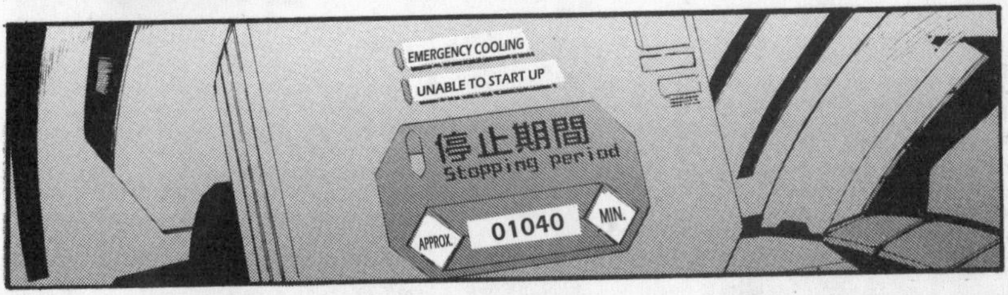
EMERGENCY COOLING
UNABLE TO START UP
停止期間
Stopping period
APPROX.
01040
MIN.

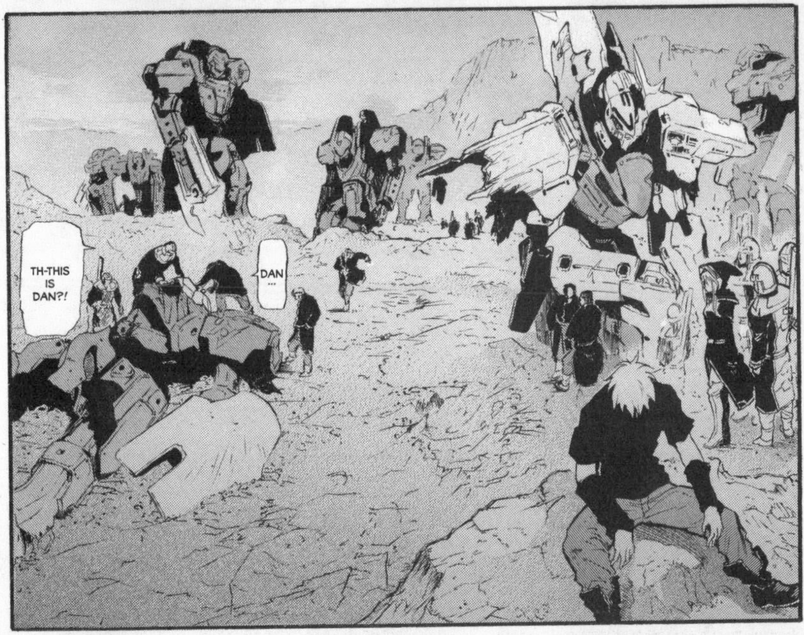
DAN...
TH-THIS IS DAN?!

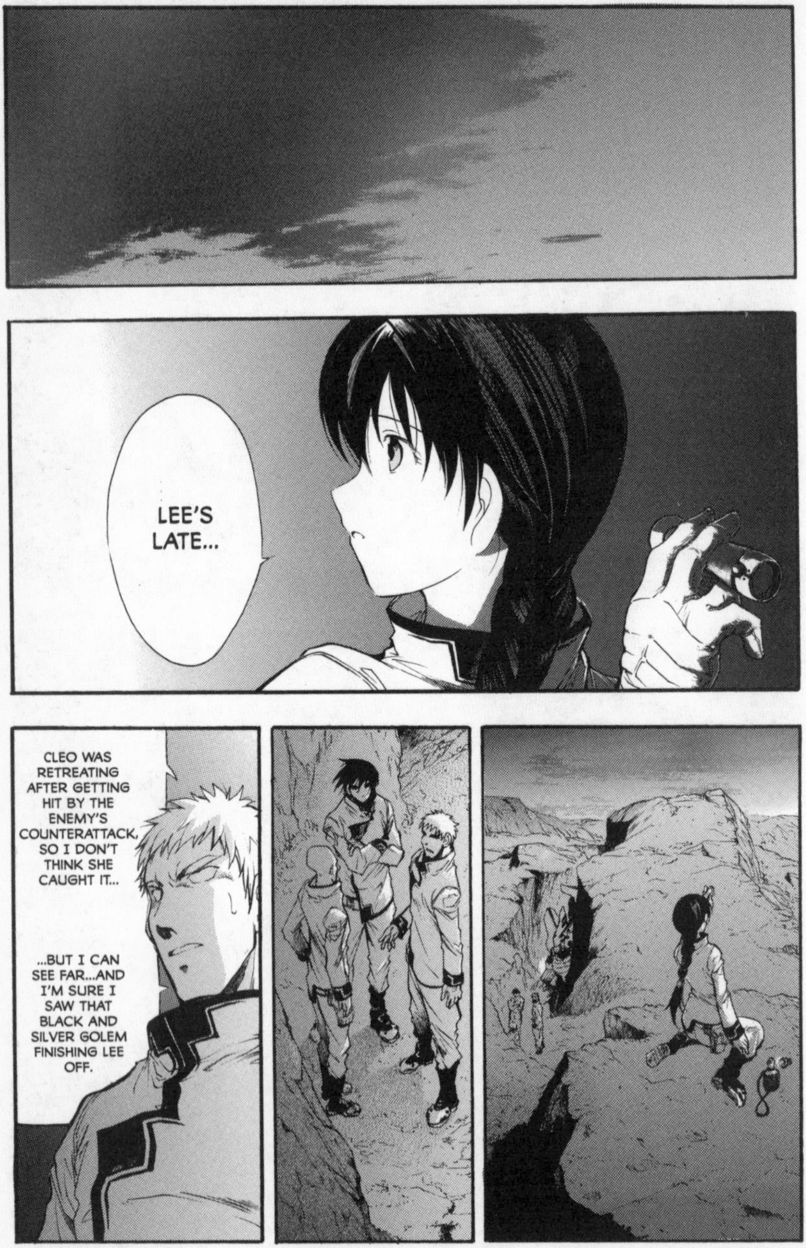
LEE'S LATE...
CLEO WAS RETREATING AFTER GETTING HIT BY THE ENEMY'S COUNTERATTACK, SO I DON'T THINK SHE CAUGHT IT...
...BUT I CAN SEE FAR...AND I'M SURE I SAW THAT BLACK AND SILVER GOLEM FINISHING LEE OFF.

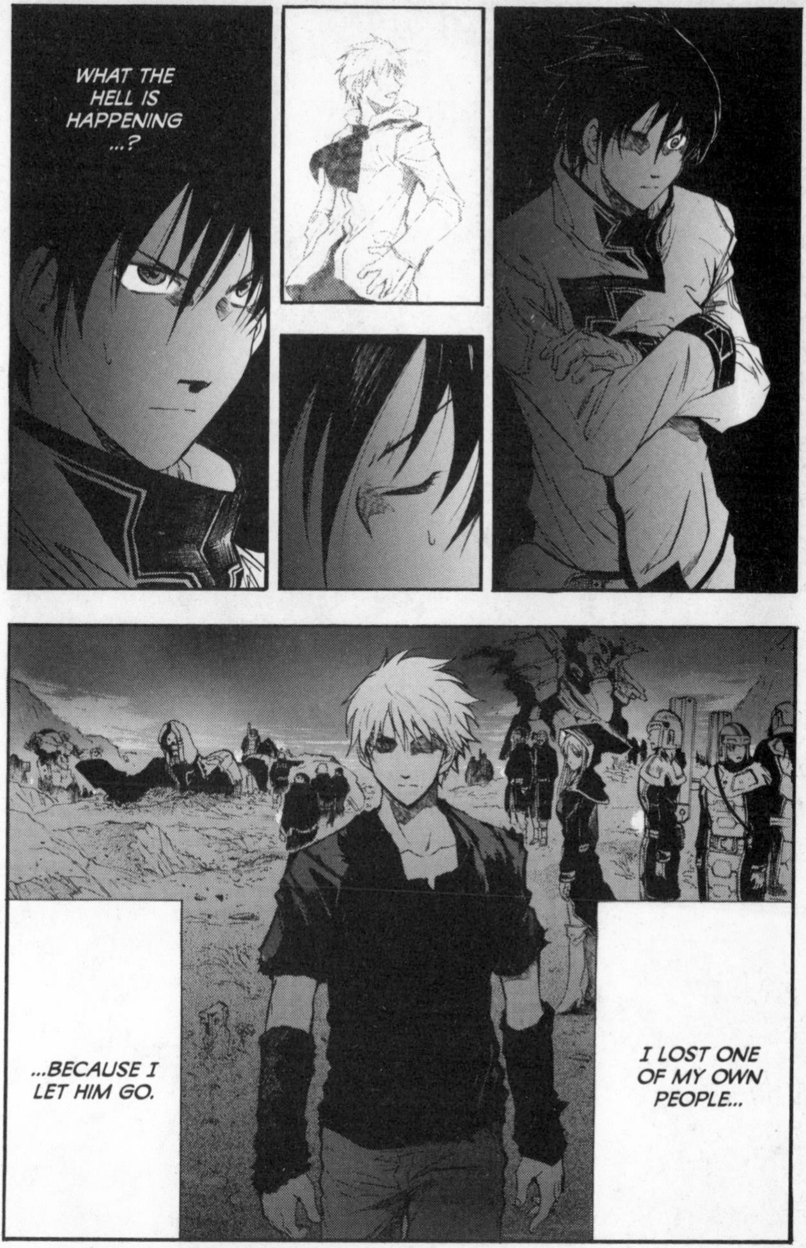
WHAT THE HELL IS HAPPENING ...?
I LOST ONE OF MY OWN PEOPLE...
...BECAUSE I LET HIM GO.

EPISODE 9: DOMESTIC TROUBLES AND EXTERNAL THREATS

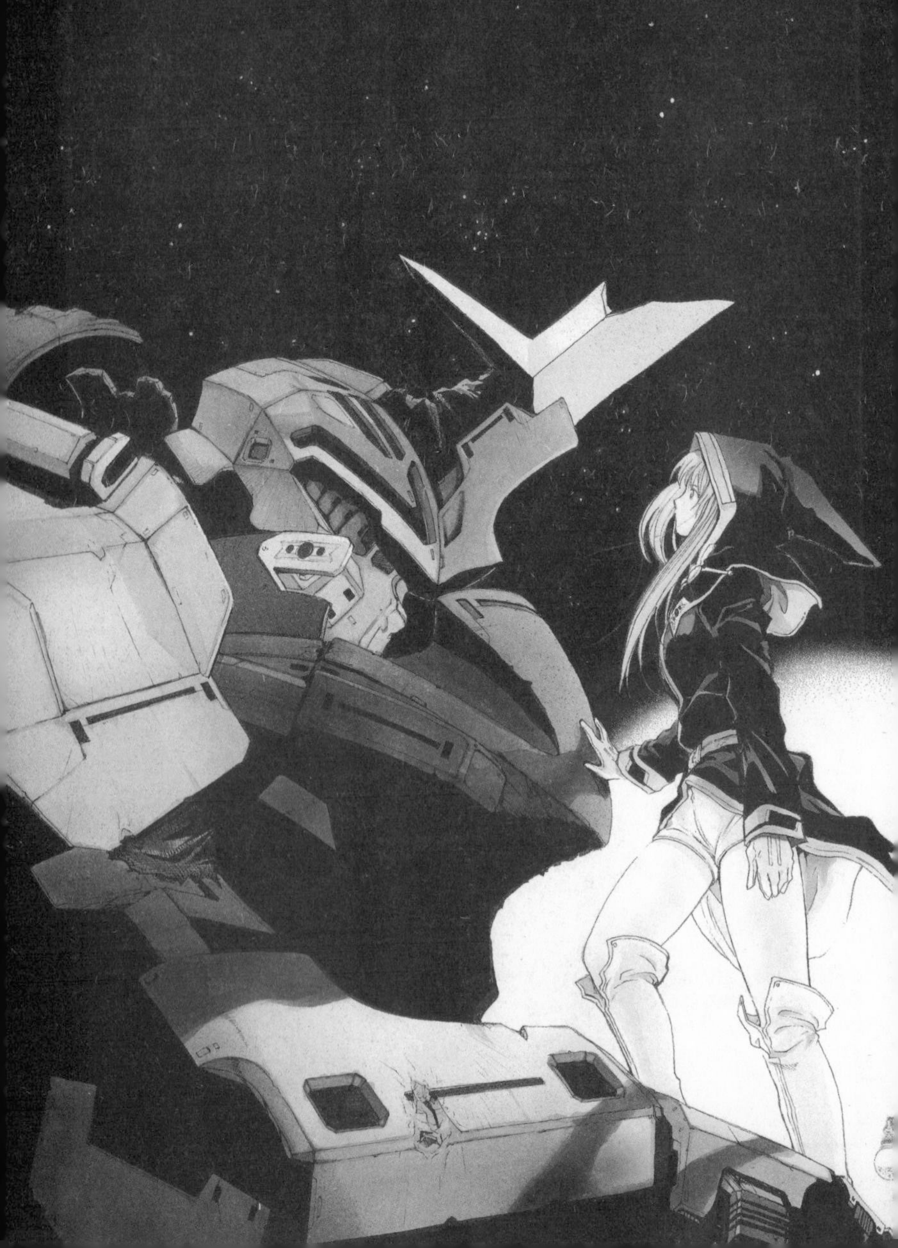

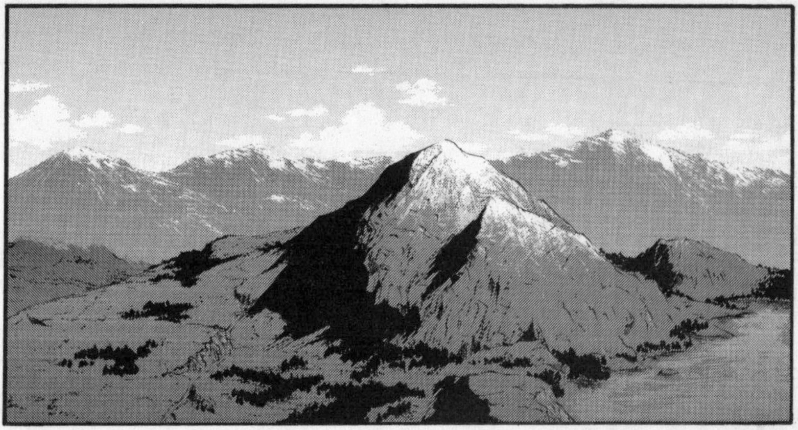

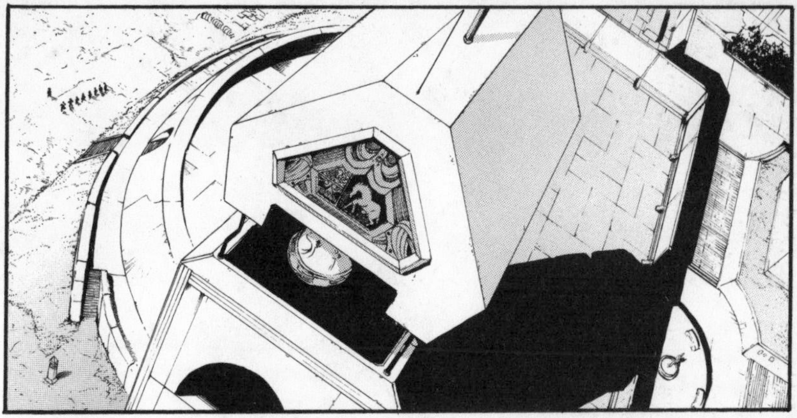

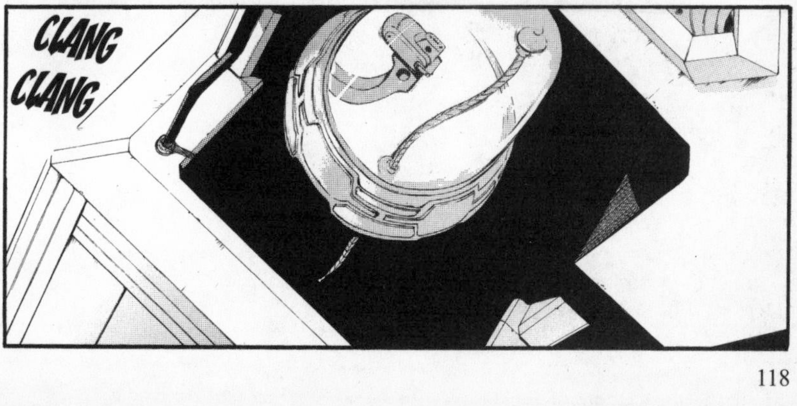
CLANG
CLANG

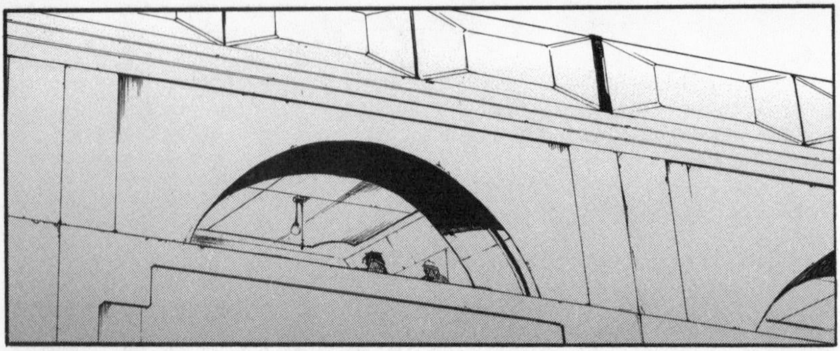

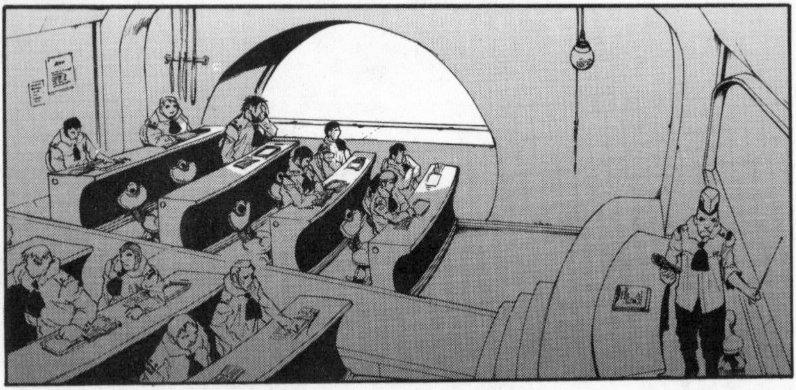

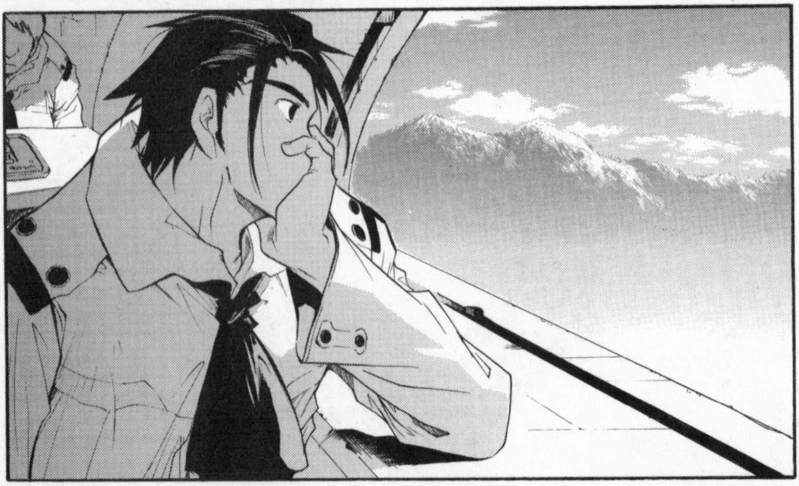

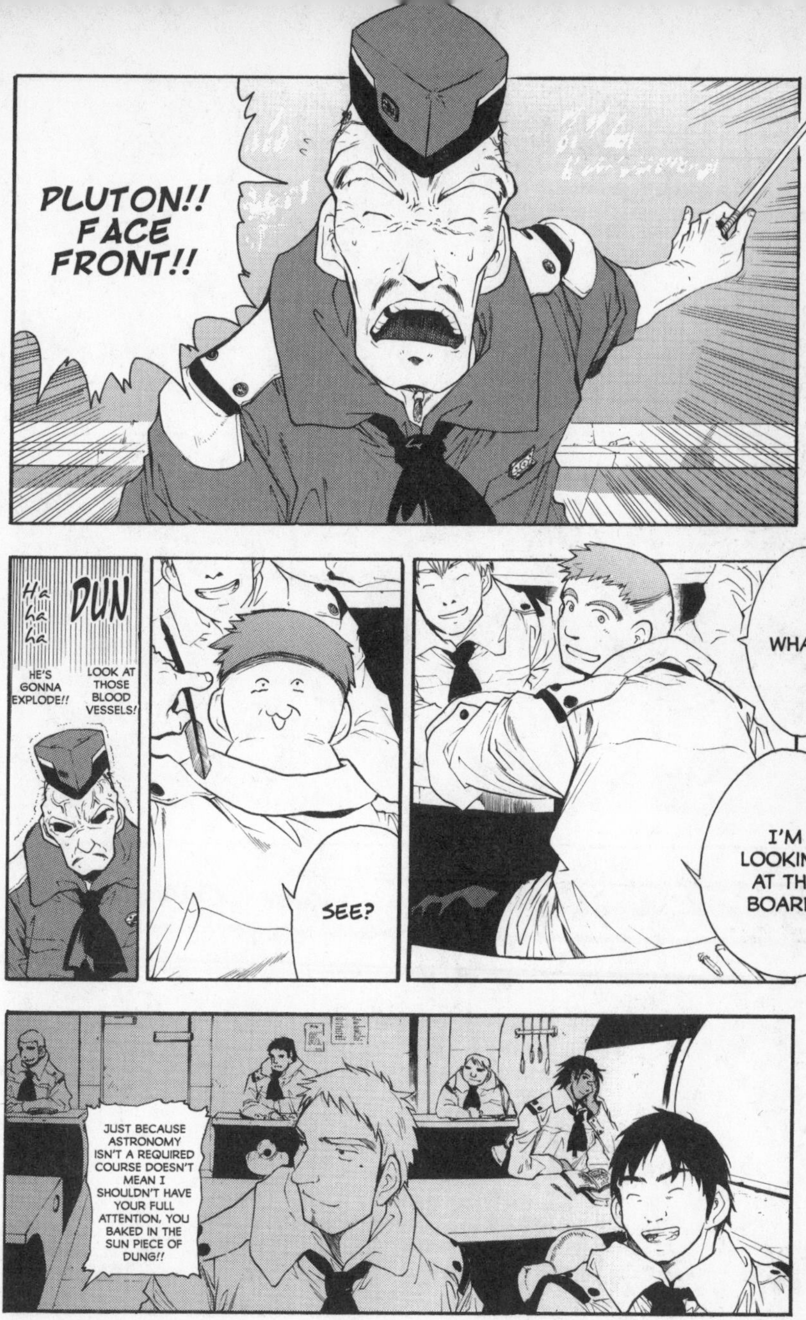
PLUTON!! FACE FRONT!!
WHAT?
I'M LOOKING AT THE BOARD.
SEE?
DUN
Ha ha ha
LOOK AT THOSE BLOOD VESSELS!
HE'S GONNA EXPLODE!!
JUST BECAUSE ASTRONOMY ISN'T A REQUIRED COURSE DOESN'T MEAN I SHOULDN'T HAVE YOUR FULL ATTENTION, YOU BAKED IN THE SUN PIECE OF DUNG!!

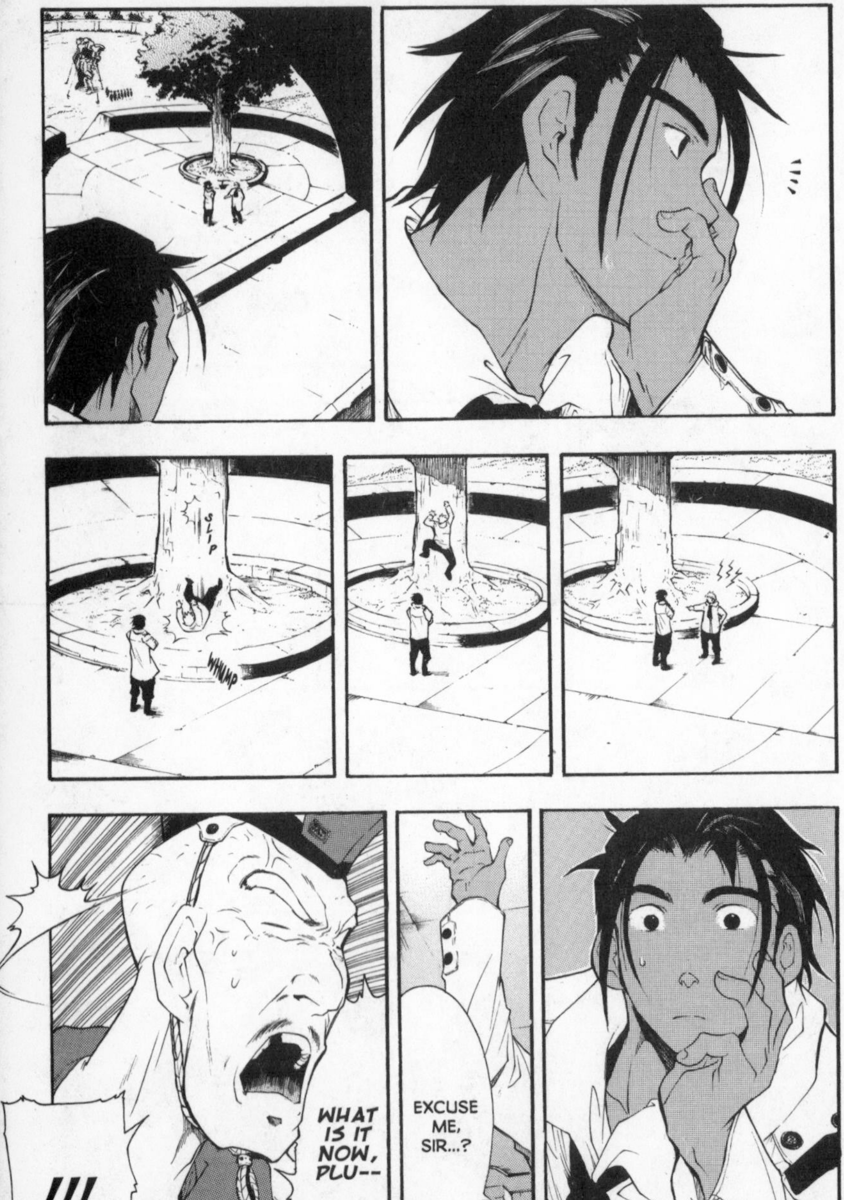
SLIP
WHUMP
EXCUSE ME, SIR...?
WHAT IS IT NOW, PLU--
!!!

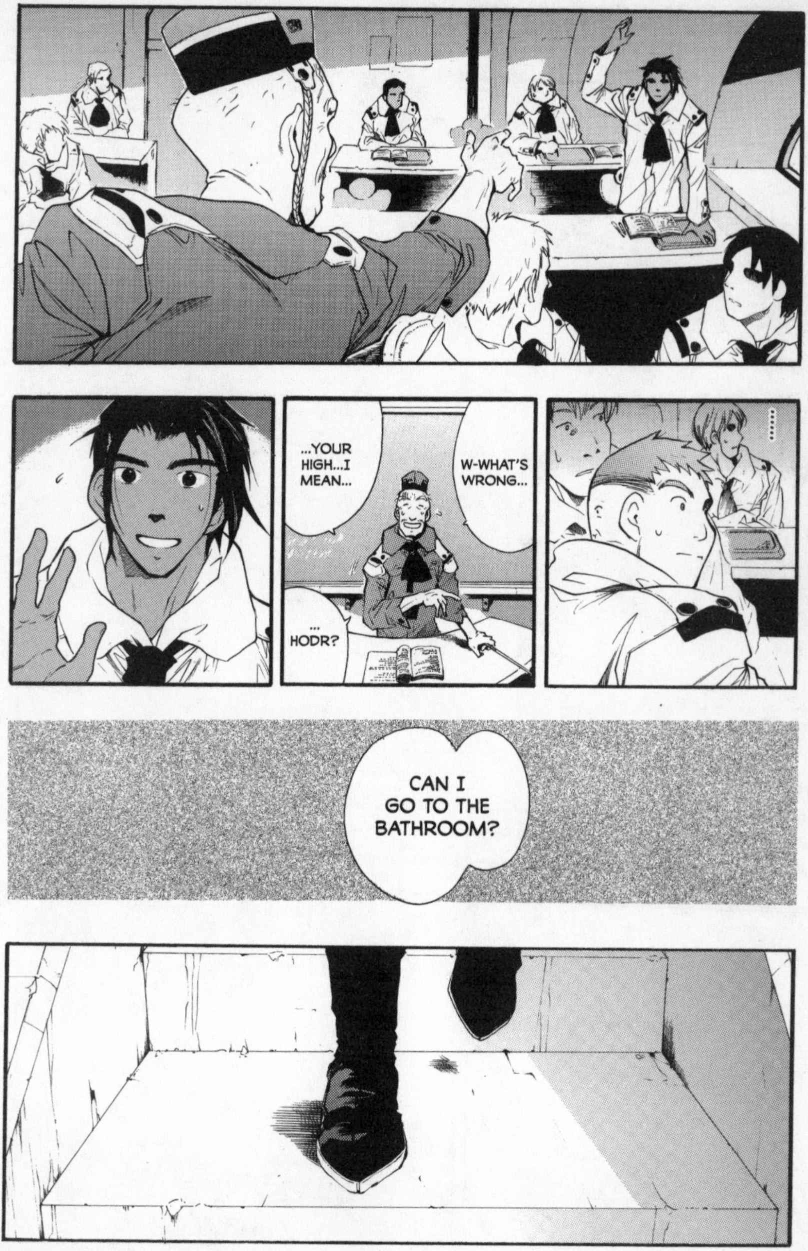
W-WHAT'S WRONG...
...YOUR HIGH...I MEAN...
... HODR?
CAN I GO TO THE BATHROOM?

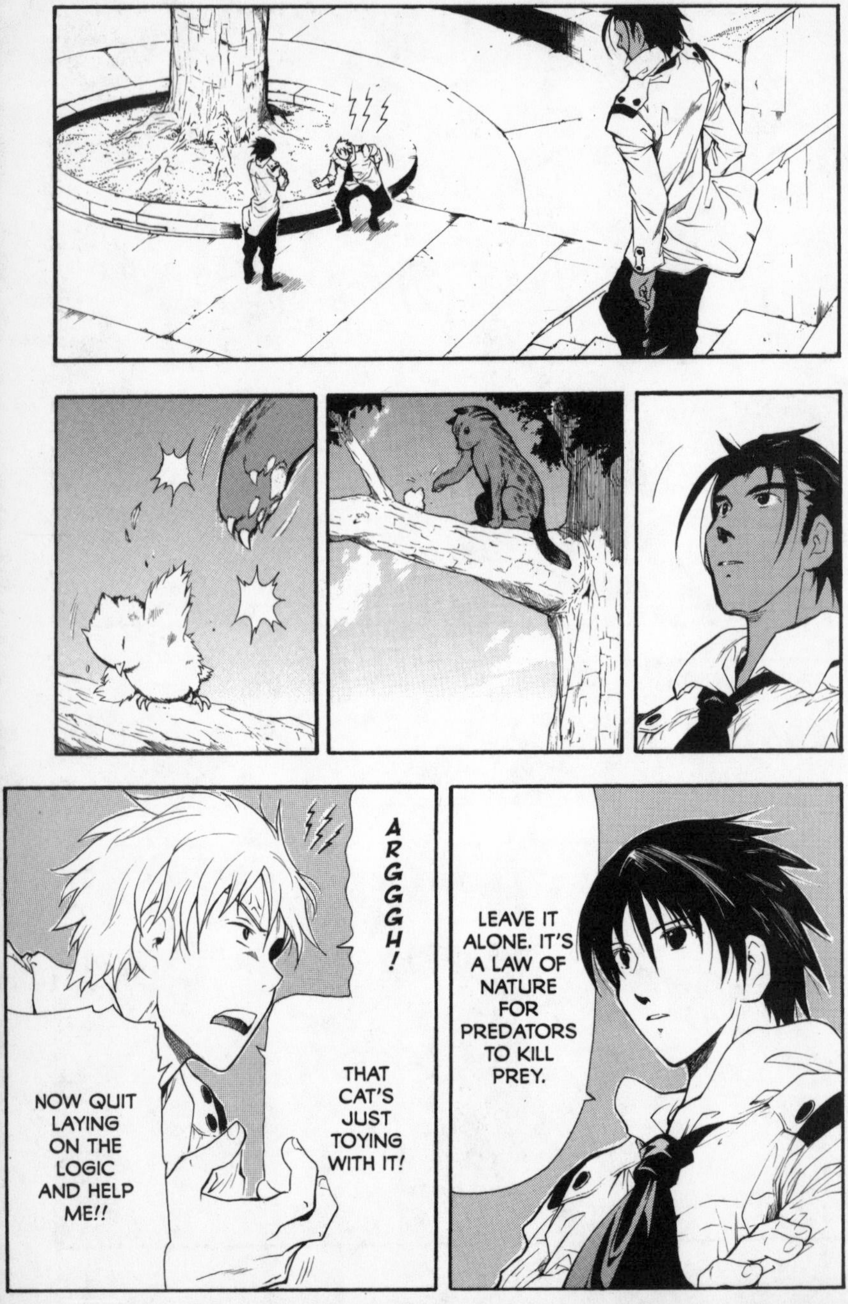
LEAVE IT ALONE. IT'S A LAW OF NATURE FOR PREDATORS TO KILL PREY.
ARGGGH!
THAT CAT'S JUST TOYING WITH IT!
NOW QUIT LAYING ON THE LOGIC AND HELP ME!!

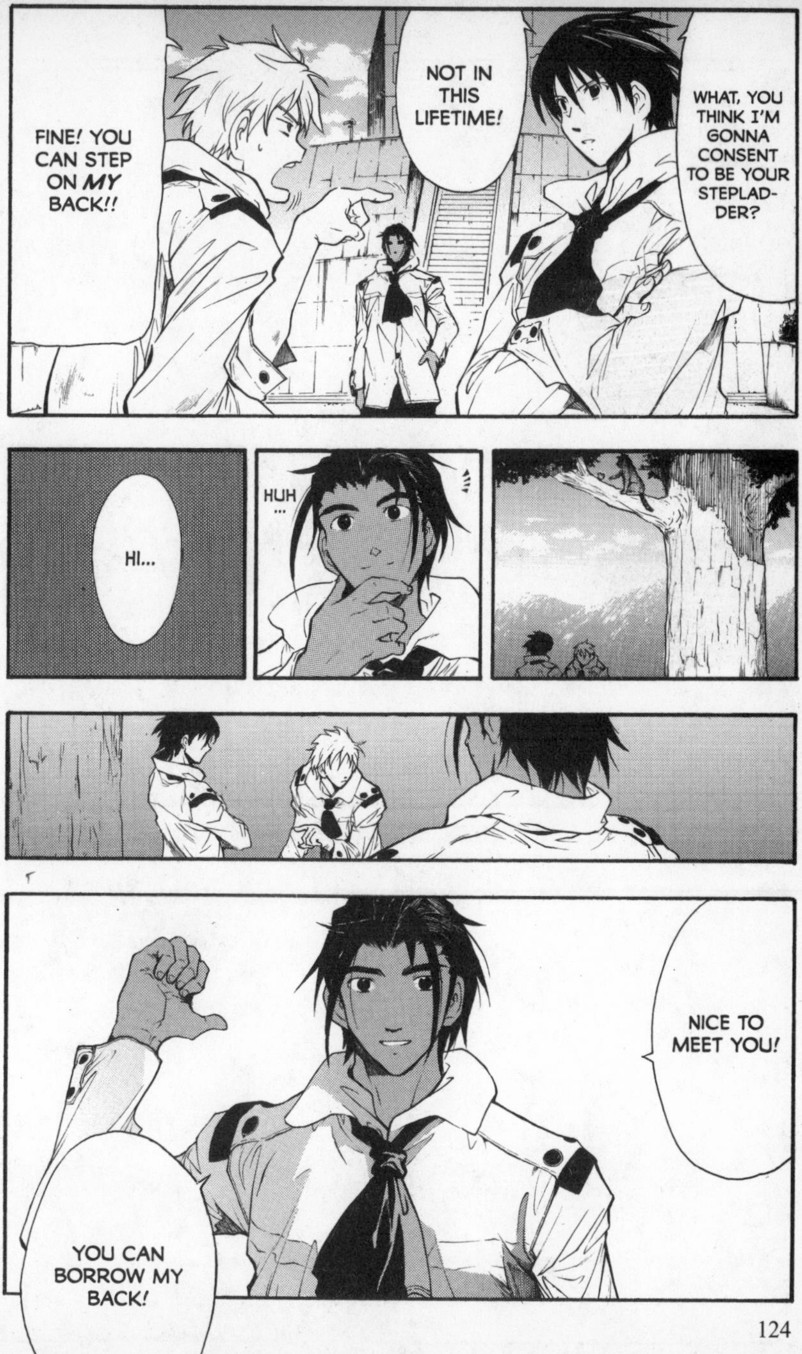
WHAT, YOU THINK I'M GONNA CONSENT TO BE YOUR STEPLAD-DER?
NOT IN THIS LIFETIME!
FINE! YOU CAN STEP ON *MY* BACK!!
HUH ...
HI...
NICE TO MEET YOU!
YOU CAN BORROW MY BACK!

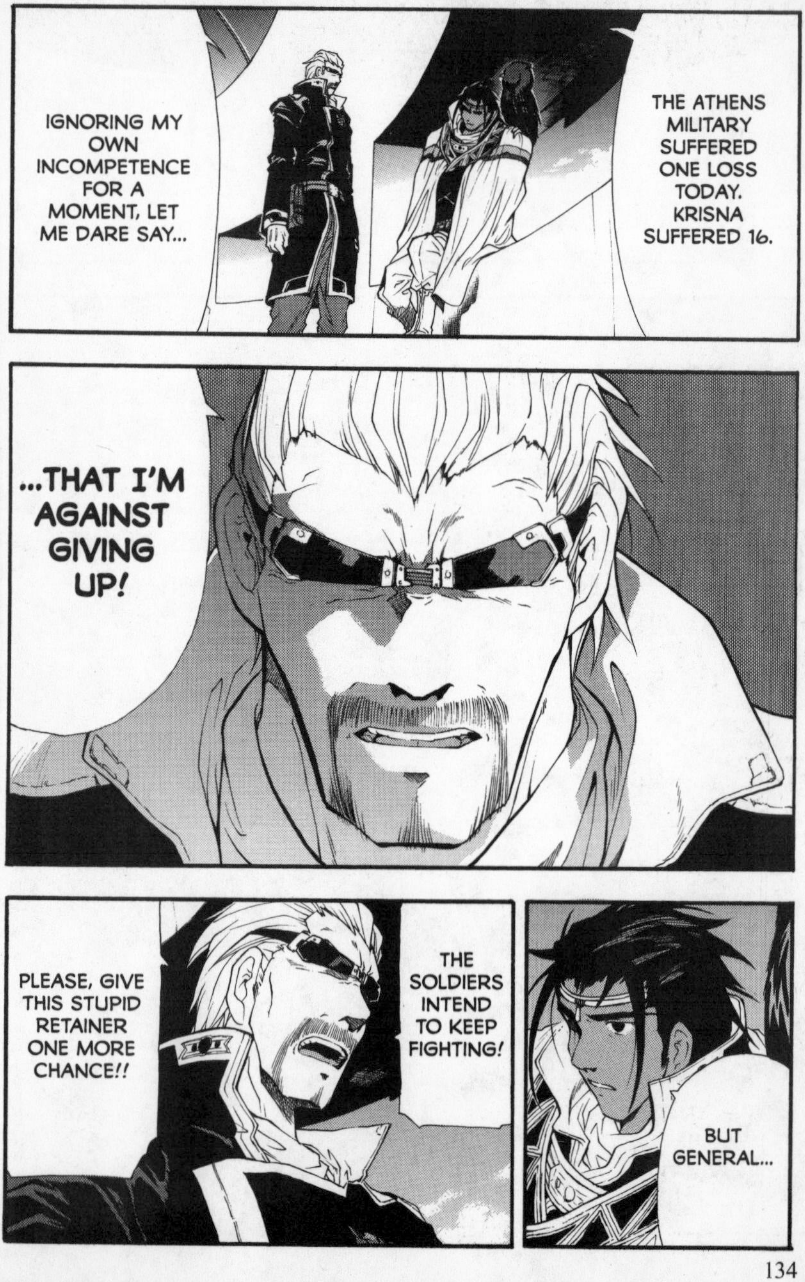
THE ATHENS MILITARY SUFFERED ONE LOSS TODAY. KRISNA SUFFERED 16.
IGNORING MY OWN INCOMPETENCE FOR A MOMENT, LET ME DARE SAY...
...THAT I'M AGAINST GIVING UP!
BUT GENERAL...
THE SOLDIERS INTEND TO KEEP FIGHTING!
PLEASE, GIVE THIS STUPID RETAINER ONE MORE CHANCE!!

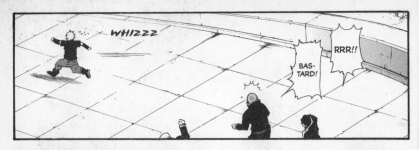

WHIZZZ

RRR!!

BAS-
TARD!

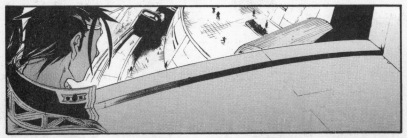

DAN WAS A MAN
OF FEW WORDS,
BUT HE OFTEN
LOOKED AFTER
THE YOUNG
SOLDIERS...SO
OUR PEOPLE ARE
MORE THAN A
LITTLE UNHAPPY
ABOUT THE
SITUATION.

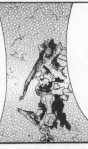

UNFORTU-
NATELY, A
LARGE
PORTION OF
THE CASTLE
GARRISON
WITNESSED
RYGART
STOPPING
DAN...

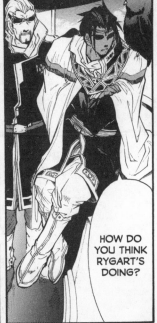

HOW DO
YOU THINK
RYGART'S
DOING?

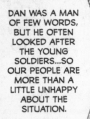

YOUR
HIGHNESS
...!

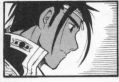

......

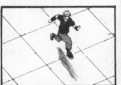

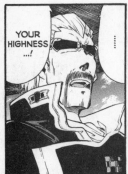

133

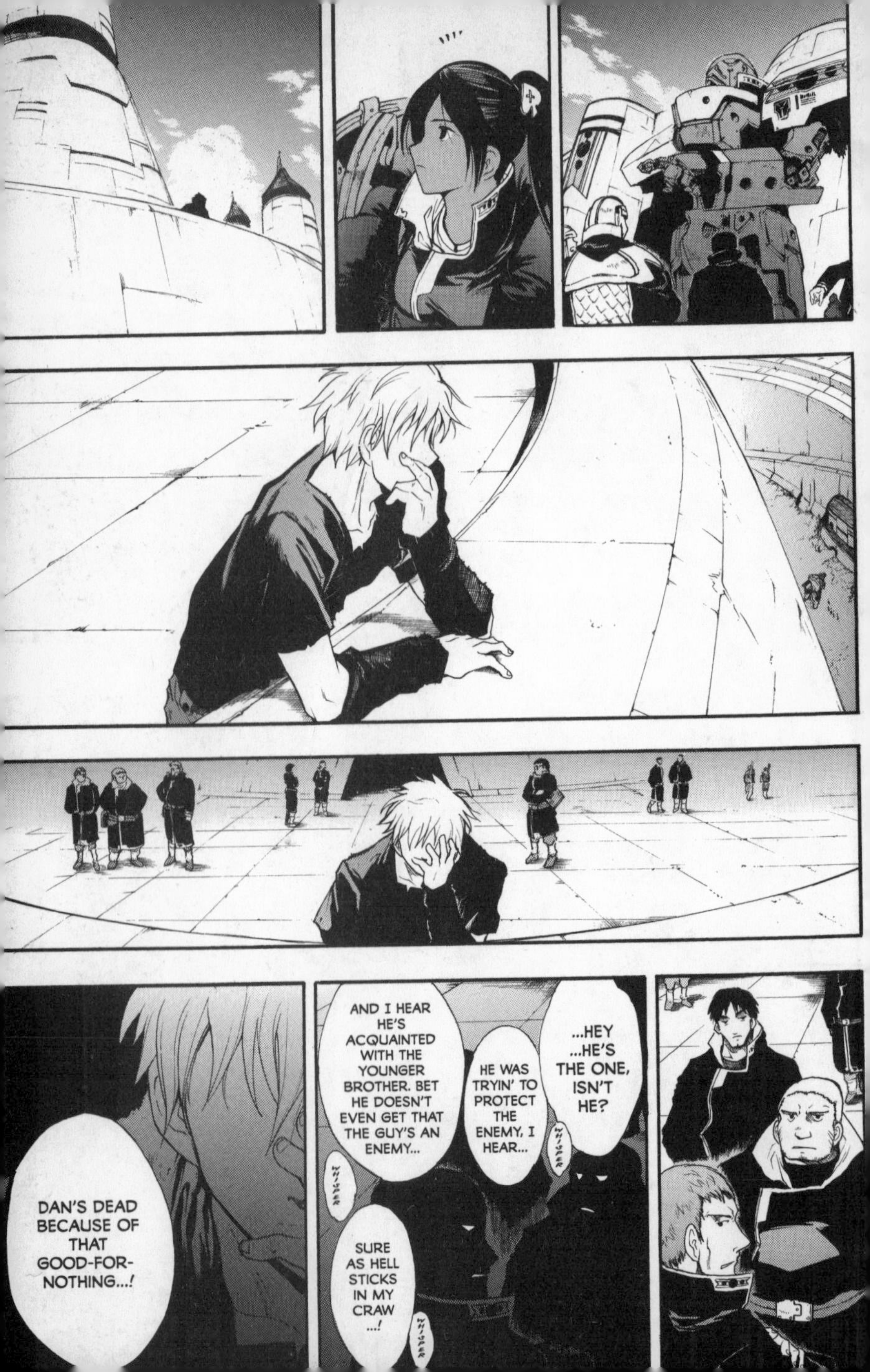
...HEY ...HE'S THE ONE, ISN'T HE?
HE WAS TRYIN' TO PROTECT THE ENEMY, I HEAR...
AND I HEAR HE'S ACQUAINTED WITH THE YOUNGER BROTHER. BET HE DOESN'T EVEN GET THAT THE GUY'S AN ENEMY...
SURE AS HELL STICKS IN MY CRAW ...!
DAN'S DEAD BECAUSE OF THAT GOOD-FOR-NOTHING...!

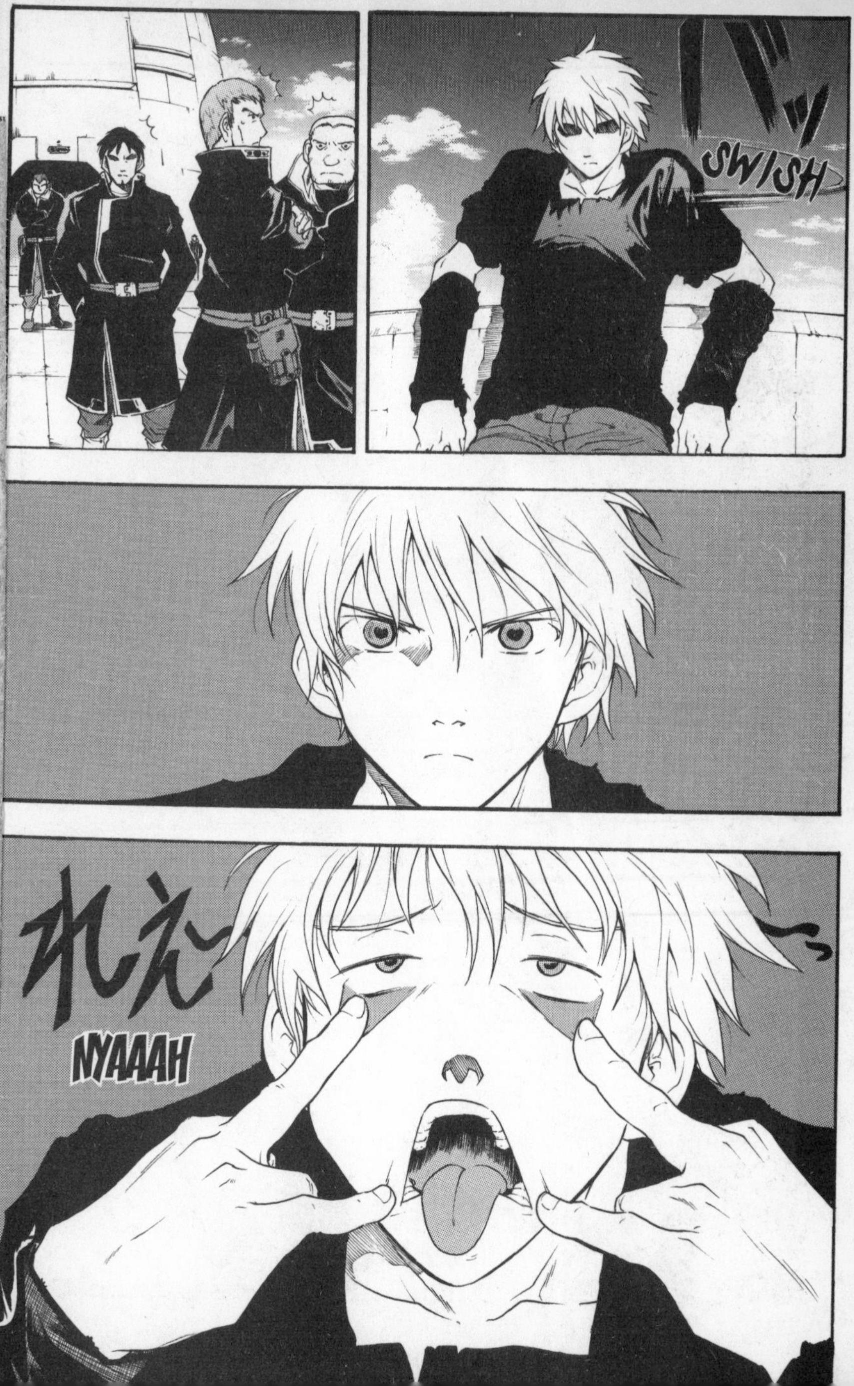
SWISH
NYAAAH

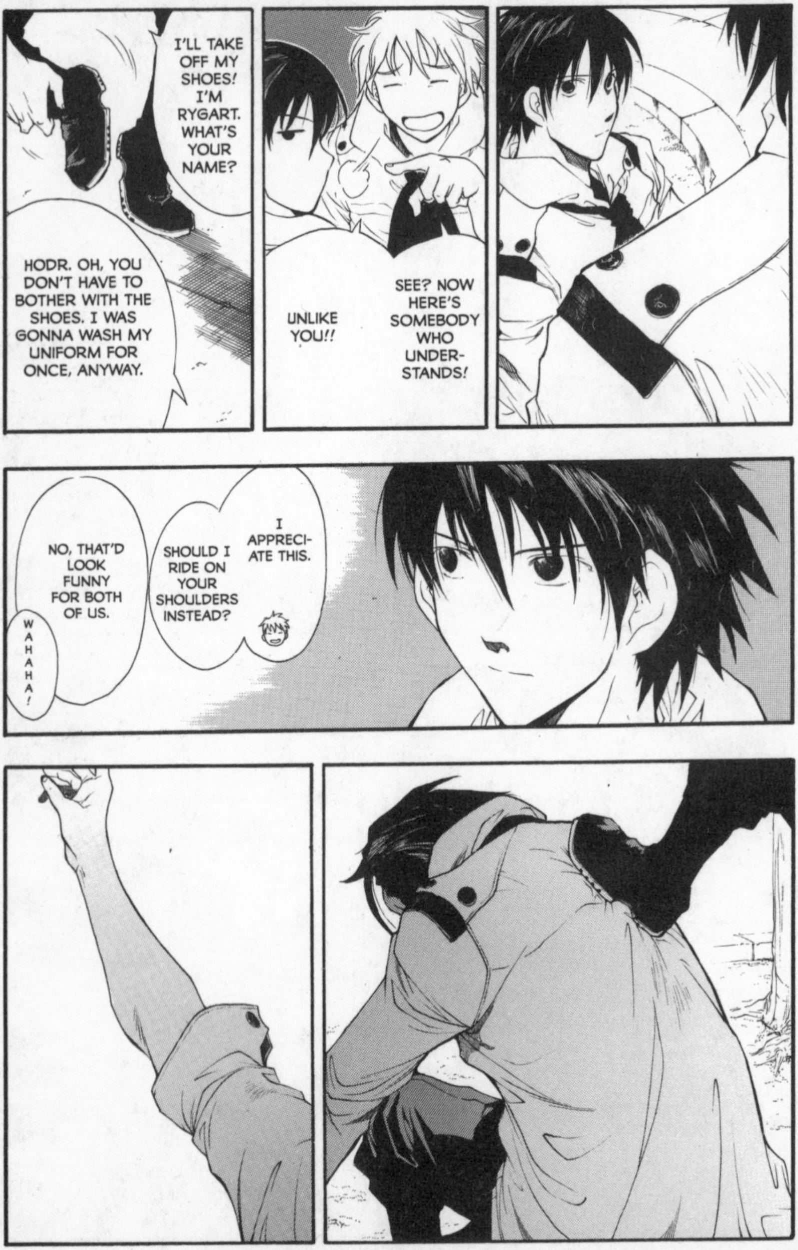
SEE? NOW HERE'S SOMEBODY WHO UNDER-STANDS!
UNLIKE YOU!!
I'LL TAKE OFF MY SHOES! I'M RYGART. WHAT'S YOUR NAME?
HODR. OH, YOU DON'T HAVE TO BOTHER WITH THE SHOES. I WAS GONNA WASH MY UNIFORM FOR ONCE, ANYWAY.
I APPRECI-ATE THIS.
SHOULD I RIDE ON YOUR SHOULDERS INSTEAD?
NO, THAT'D LOOK FUNNY FOR BOTH OF US.
WAHAHA!

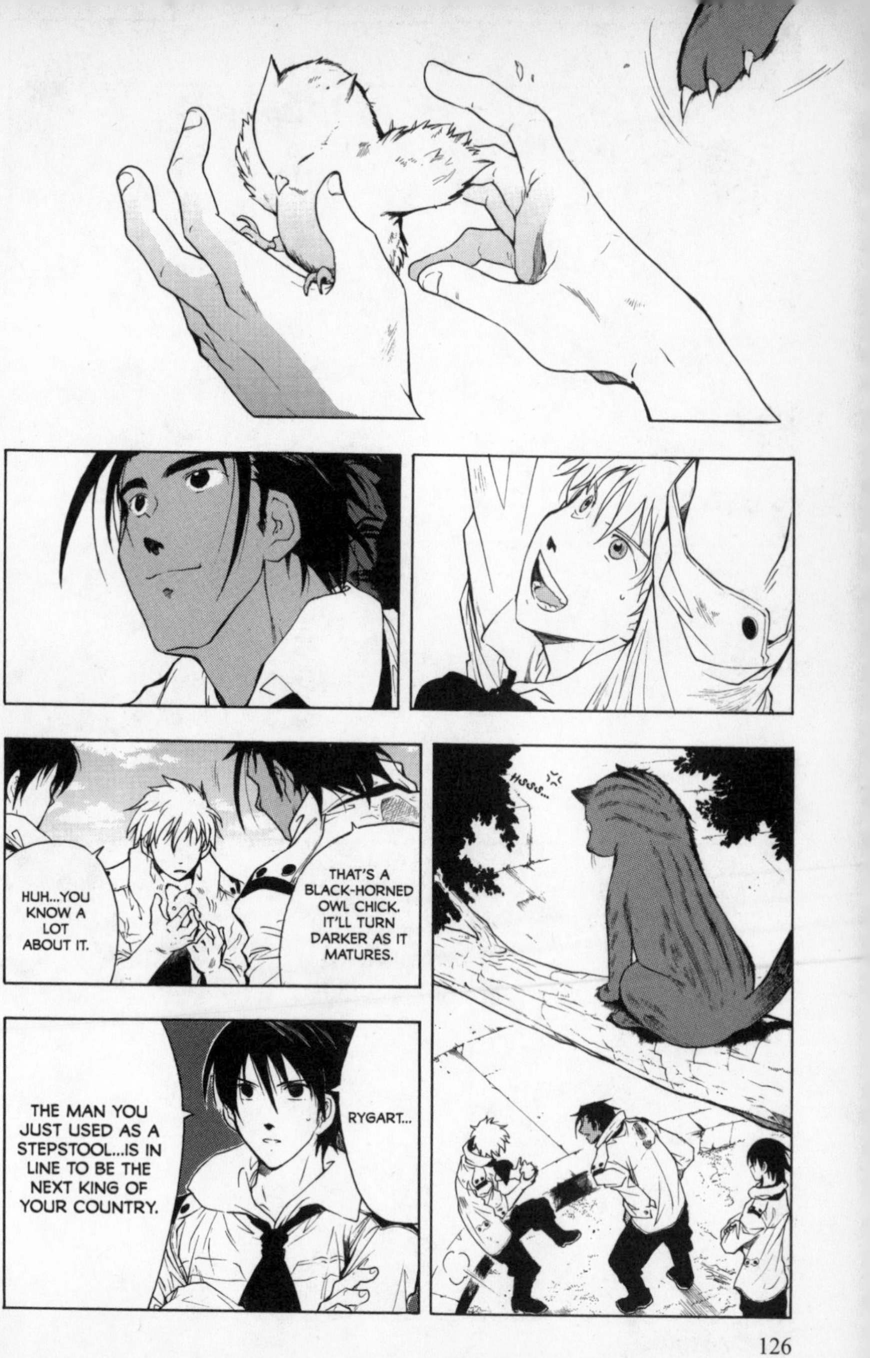
HSSS...
THAT'S A BLACK-HORNED OWL CHICK. IT'LL TURN DARKER AS IT MATURES.
HUH...YOU KNOW A LOT ABOUT IT.
RYGART...
THE MAN YOU JUST USED AS A STEPSTOOL...IS IN LINE TO BE THE NEXT KING OF YOUR COUNTRY.

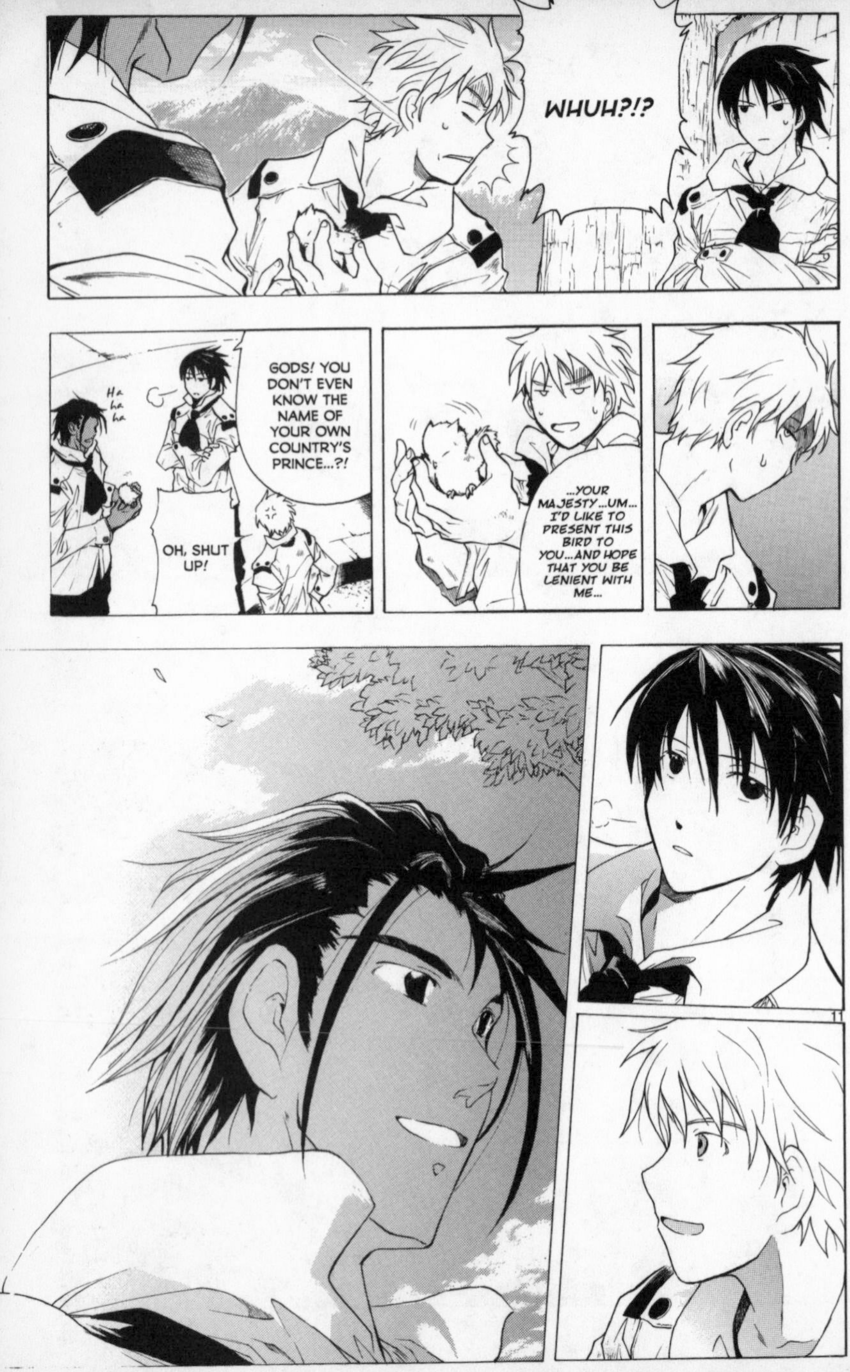
WHUH?!?
...YOUR MAJESTY...UM... I'D LIKE TO PRESENT THIS BIRD TO YOU...AND HOPE THAT YOU BE LENIENT WITH ME...
GODS! YOU DON'T EVEN KNOW THE NAME OF YOUR OWN COUNTRY'S PRINCE...?!
Ha ha ha
OH, SHUT UP!

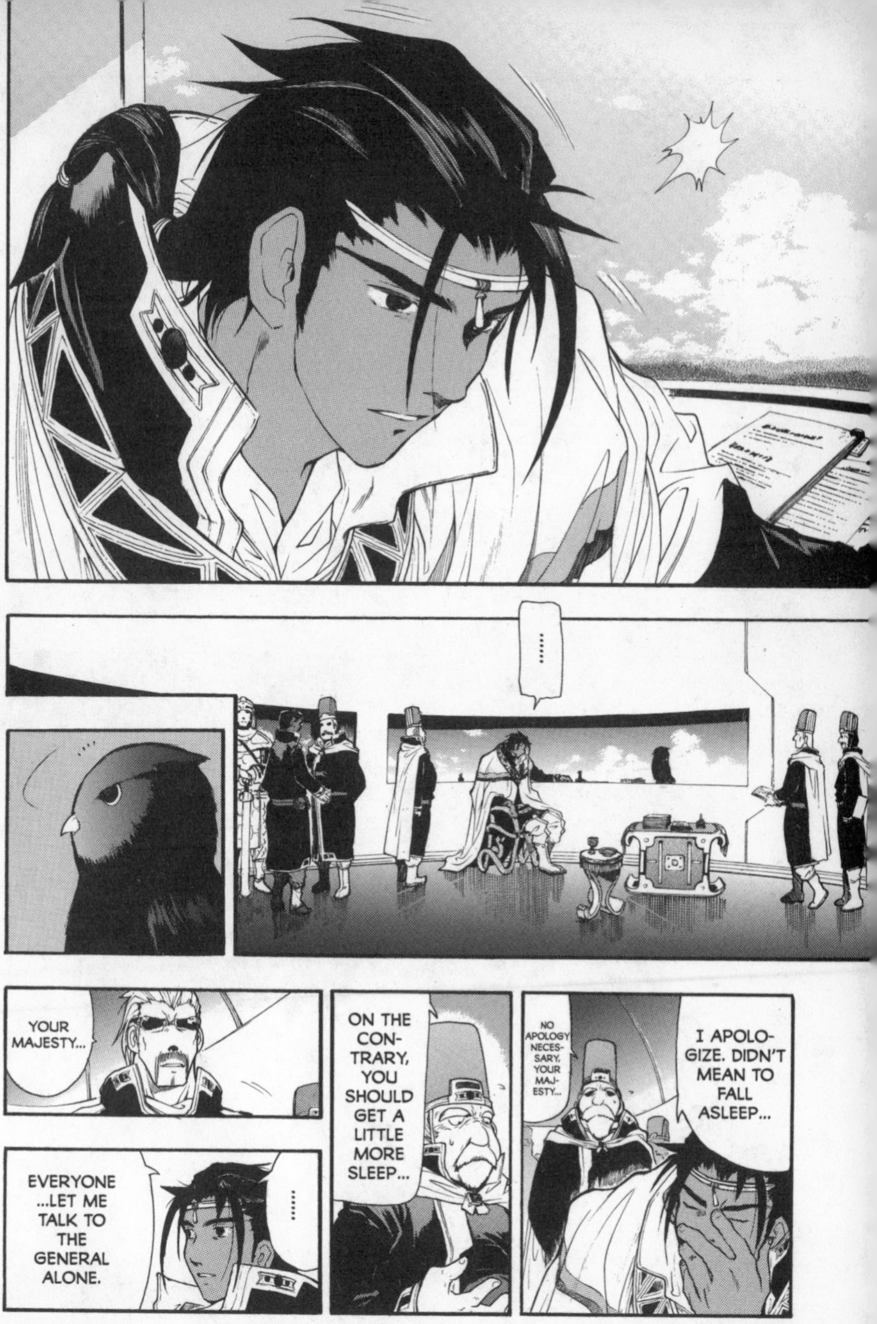
......
...
I APOLO-GIZE. DIDN'T MEAN TO FALL ASLEEP...
NO APOLOGY NECES-SARY, YOUR MAJ-ESTY...
ON THE CON-TRARY, YOU SHOULD GET A LITTLE MORE SLEEP...
YOUR MAJESTY...
......
EVERYONE ...LET ME TALK TO THE GENERAL ALONE.

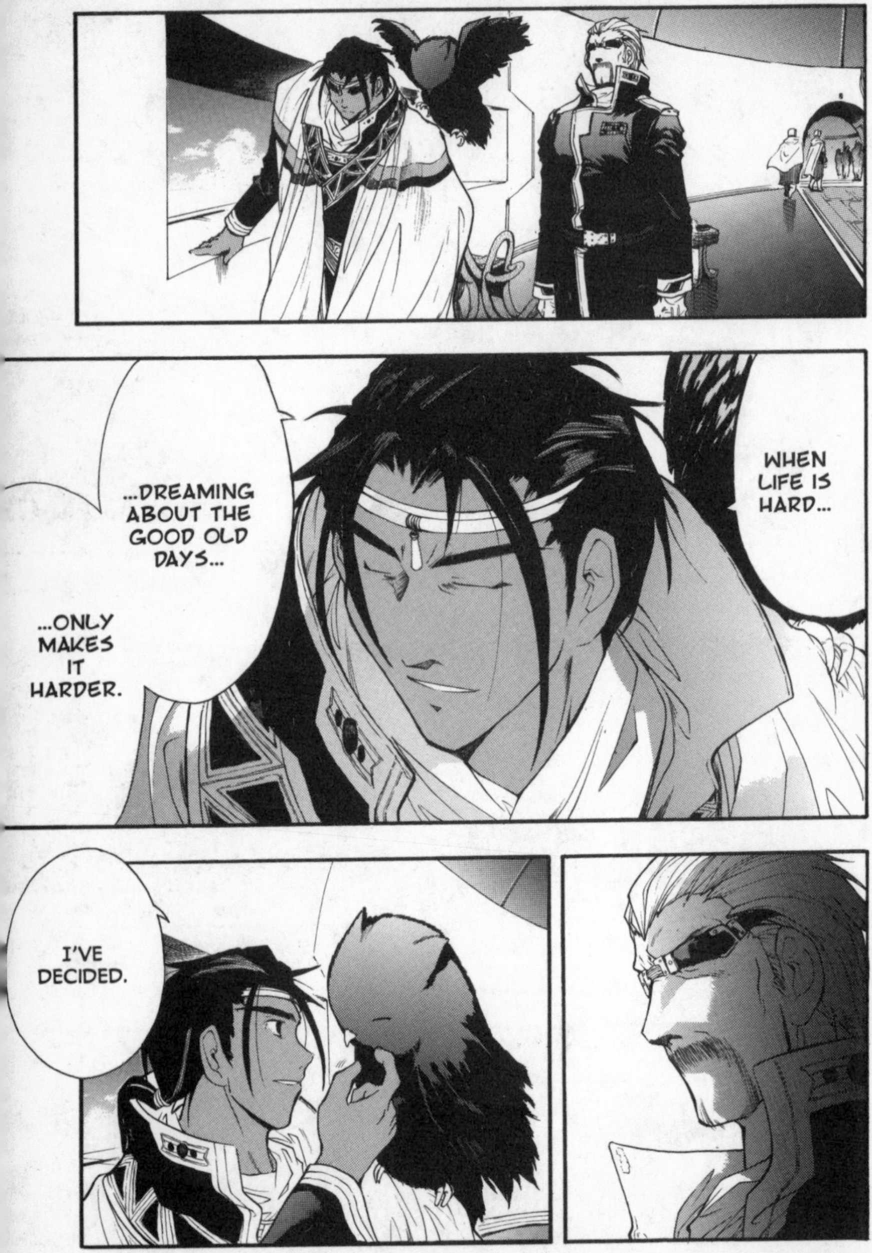
WHEN LIFE IS HARD...
...DREAMING ABOUT THE GOOD OLD DAYS...
...ONLY MAKES IT HARDER.
I'VE DECIDED.

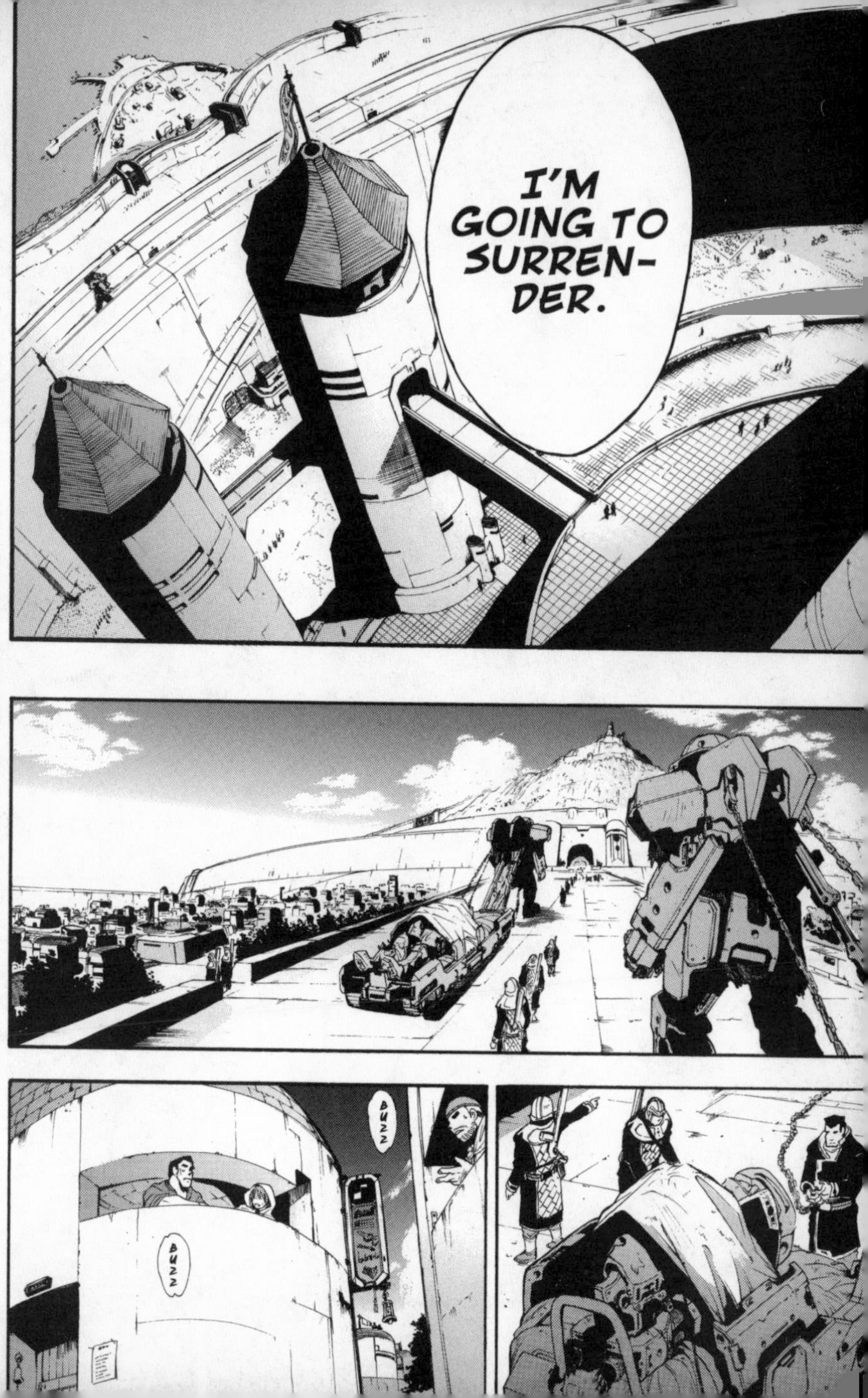
I'M GOING TO SURREN-DER.
BUZZ
BUZZ

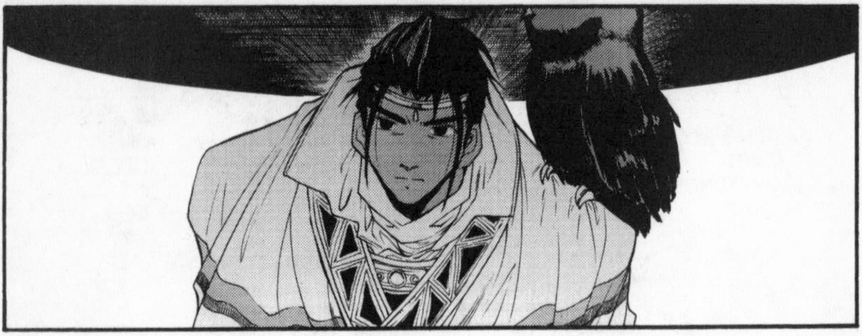
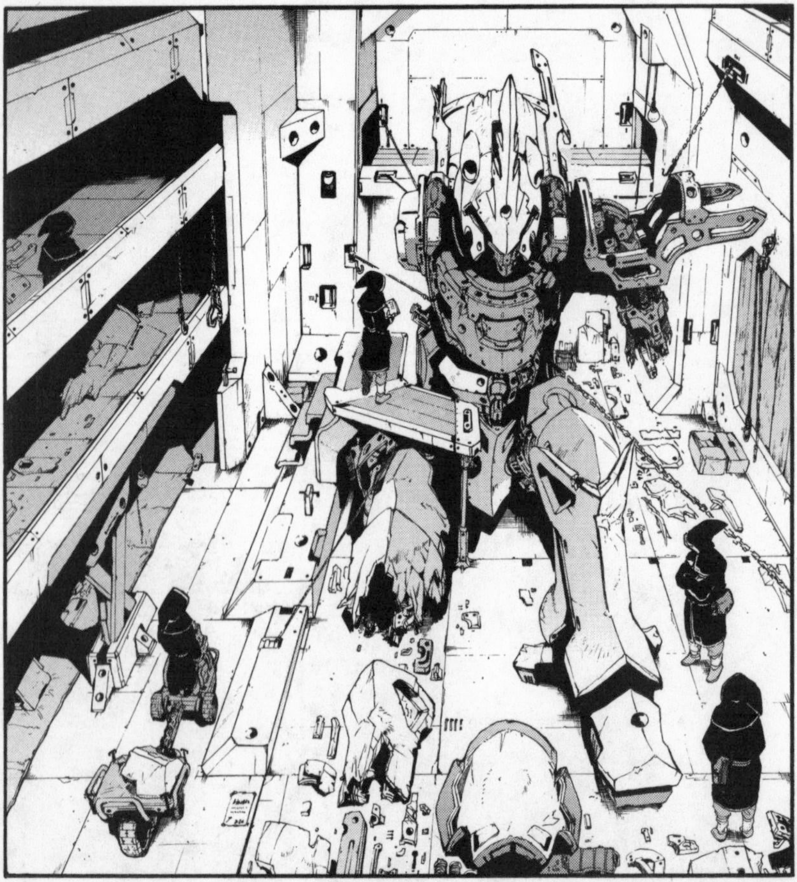

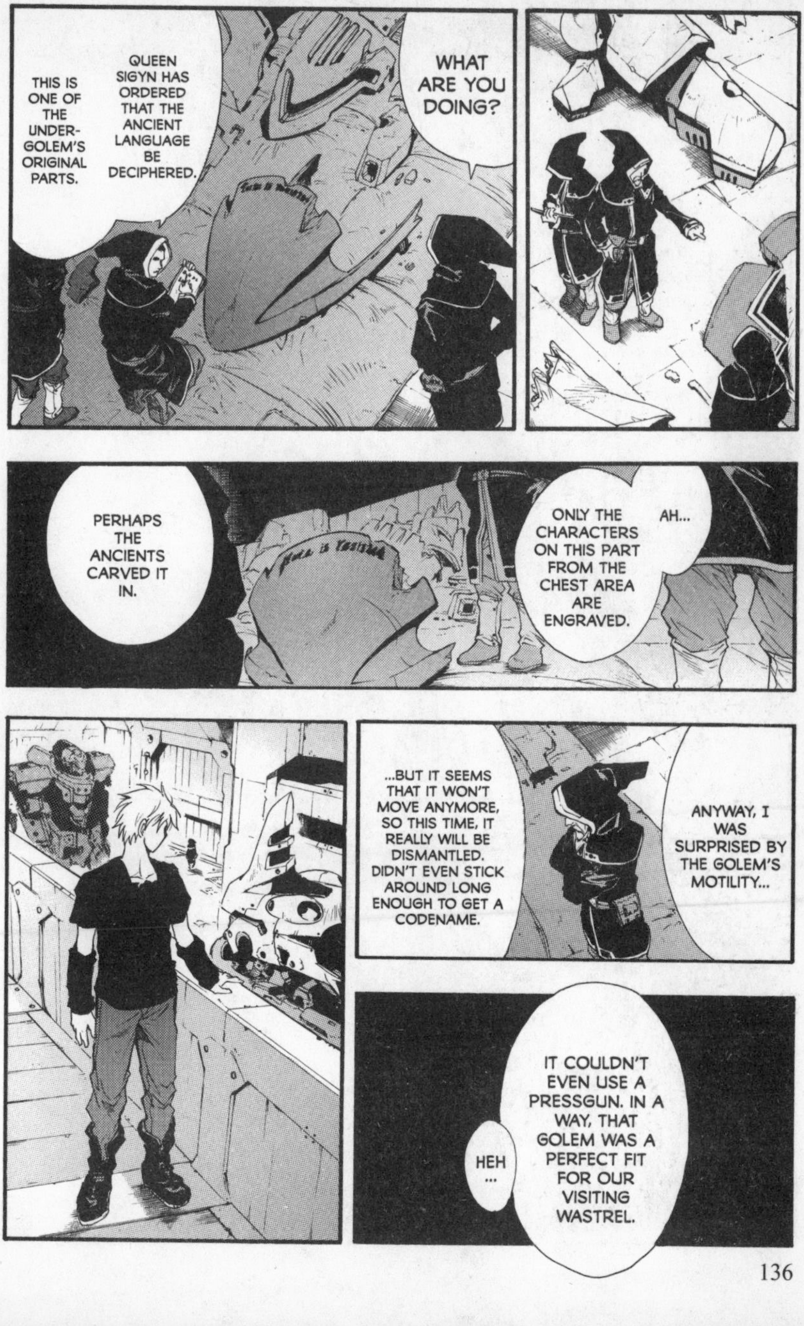
WHAT ARE YOU DOING?
QUEEN SIGYN HAS ORDERED THAT THE ANCIENT LANGUAGE BE DECIPHERED.
THIS IS ONE OF THE UNDER-GOLEM'S ORIGINAL PARTS.
AH...
ONLY THE CHARACTERS ON THIS PART FROM THE CHEST AREA ARE ENGRAVED.
PERHAPS THE ANCIENTS CARVED IT IN.
ANYWAY, I WAS SURPRISED BY THE GOLEM'S MOTILITY...
...BUT IT SEEMS THAT IT WON'T MOVE ANYMORE, SO THIS TIME, IT REALLY WILL BE DISMANTLED. DIDN'T EVEN STICK AROUND LONG ENOUGH TO GET A CODENAME.
IT COULDN'T EVEN USE A PRESSGUN. IN A WAY, THAT GOLEM WAS A PERFECT FIT FOR OUR VISITING WASTREL.
HEH...

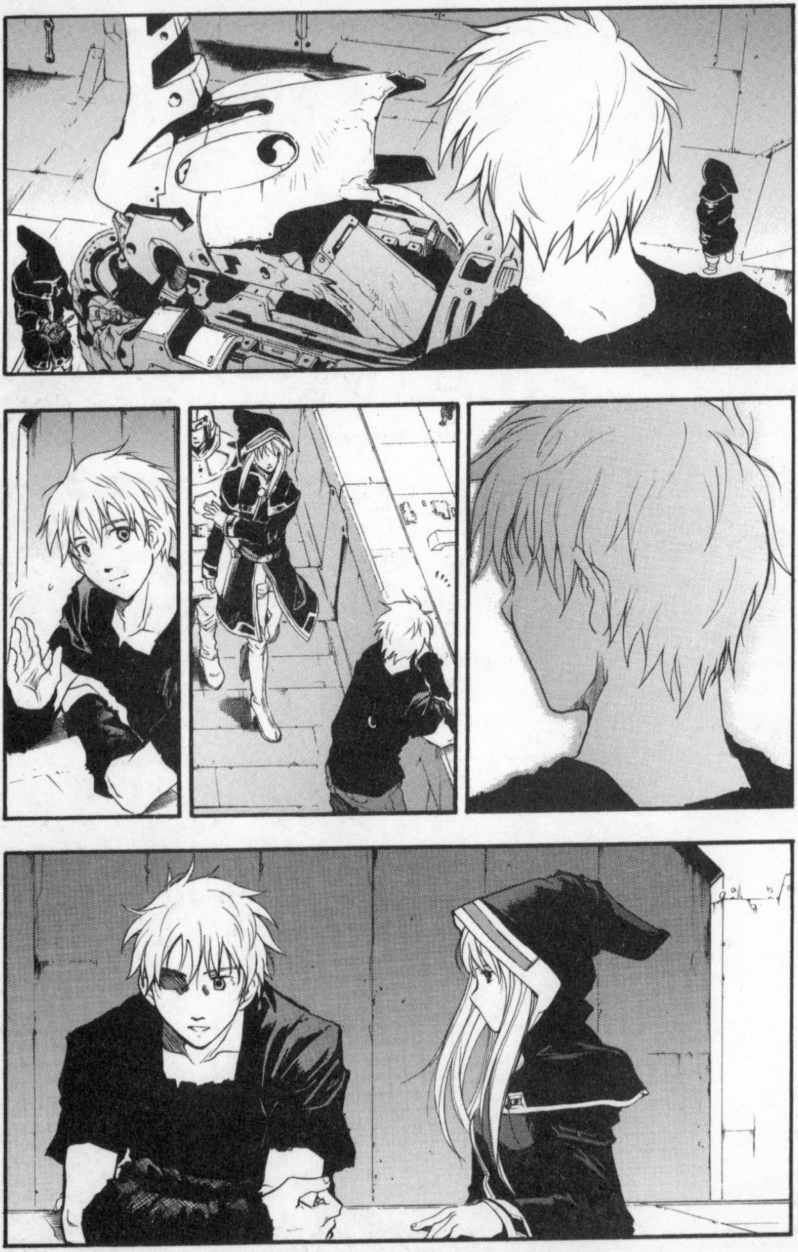

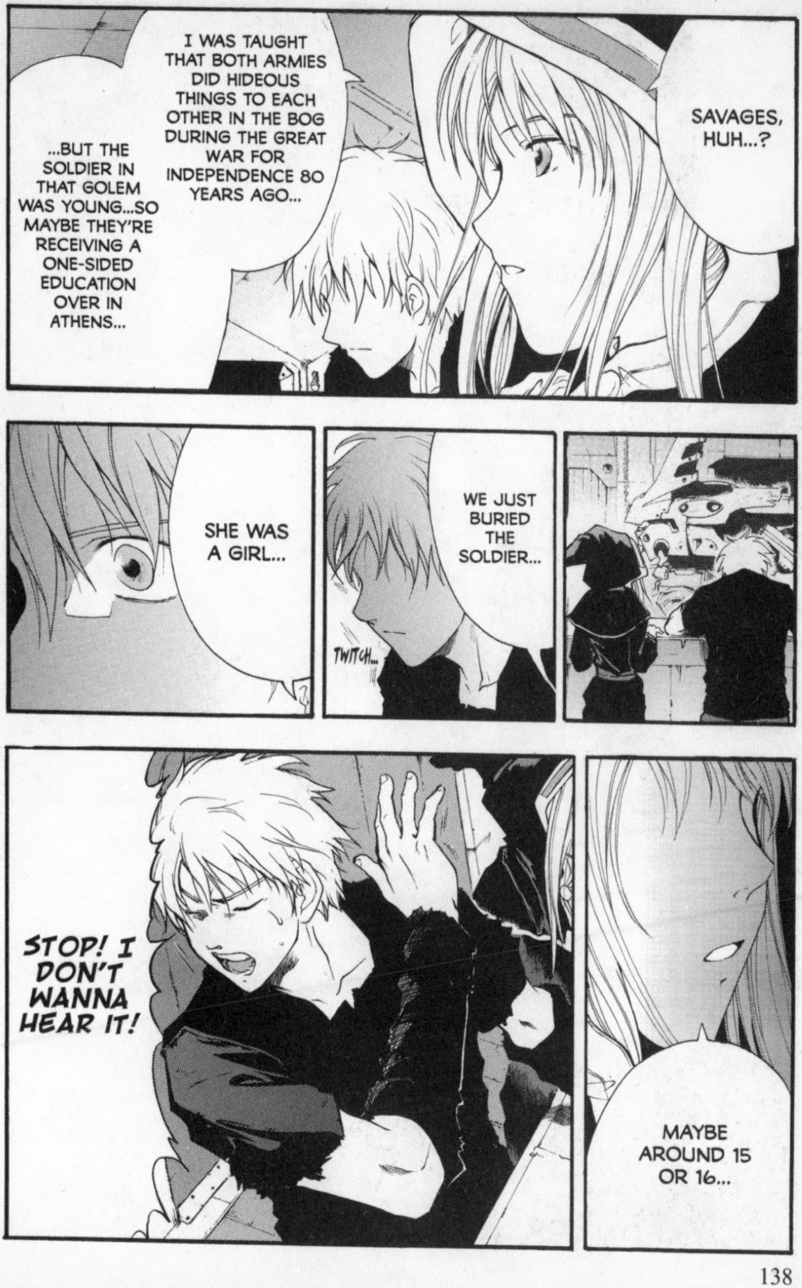
SAVAGES, HUH...?
I WAS TAUGHT THAT BOTH ARMIES DID HIDEOUS THINGS TO EACH OTHER IN THE BOG DURING THE GREAT WAR FOR INDEPENDENCE 80 YEARS AGO...
...BUT THE SOLDIER IN THAT GOLEM WAS YOUNG...SO MAYBE THEY'RE RECEIVING A ONE-SIDED EDUCATION OVER IN ATHENS...
WE JUST BURIED THE SOLDIER...
TWITCH...
SHE WAS A GIRL...
MAYBE AROUND 15 OR 16...
STOP! I DON'T WANNA HEAR IT!

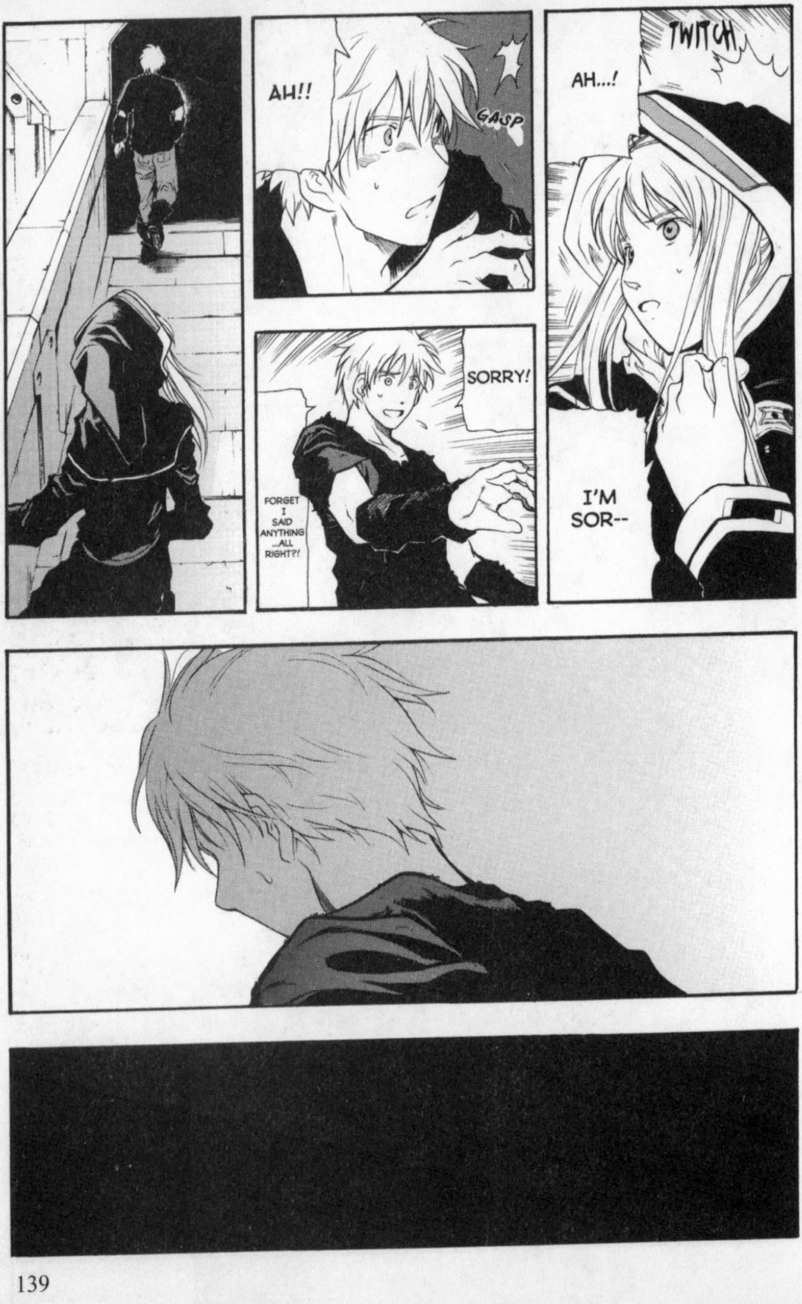
TWITCH
AH...!
I'M SOR--
AH!!
GASP
SORRY!
FORGET I SAID ANYTHING ...ALL RIGHT?!

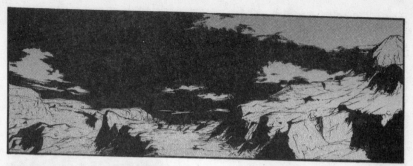

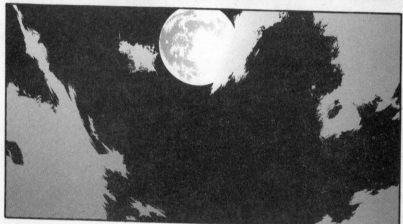

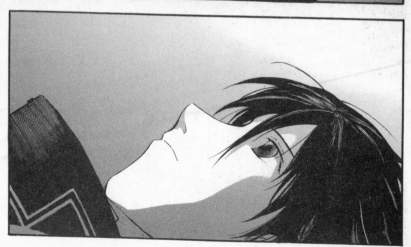

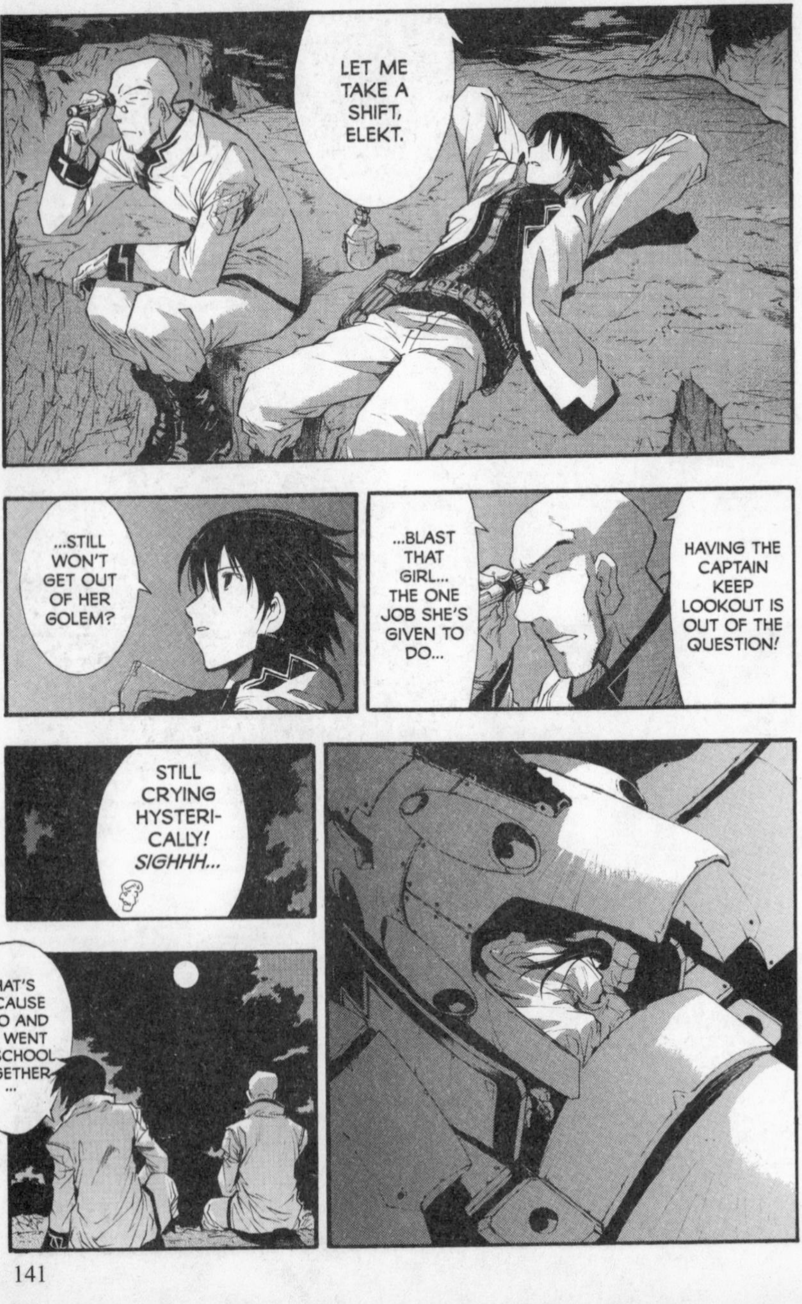
LET ME TAKE A SHIFT, ELEKT.
HAVING THE CAPTAIN KEEP LOOKOUT IS OUT OF THE QUESTION!
...BLAST THAT GIRL... THE ONE JOB SHE'S GIVEN TO DO...
...STILL WON'T GET OUT OF HER GOLEM?
STILL CRYING HYSTERI-CALLY! *SIGHHH...*
THAT'S BECAUSE CLEO AND LEE WENT TO SCHOOL TOGETHER ...

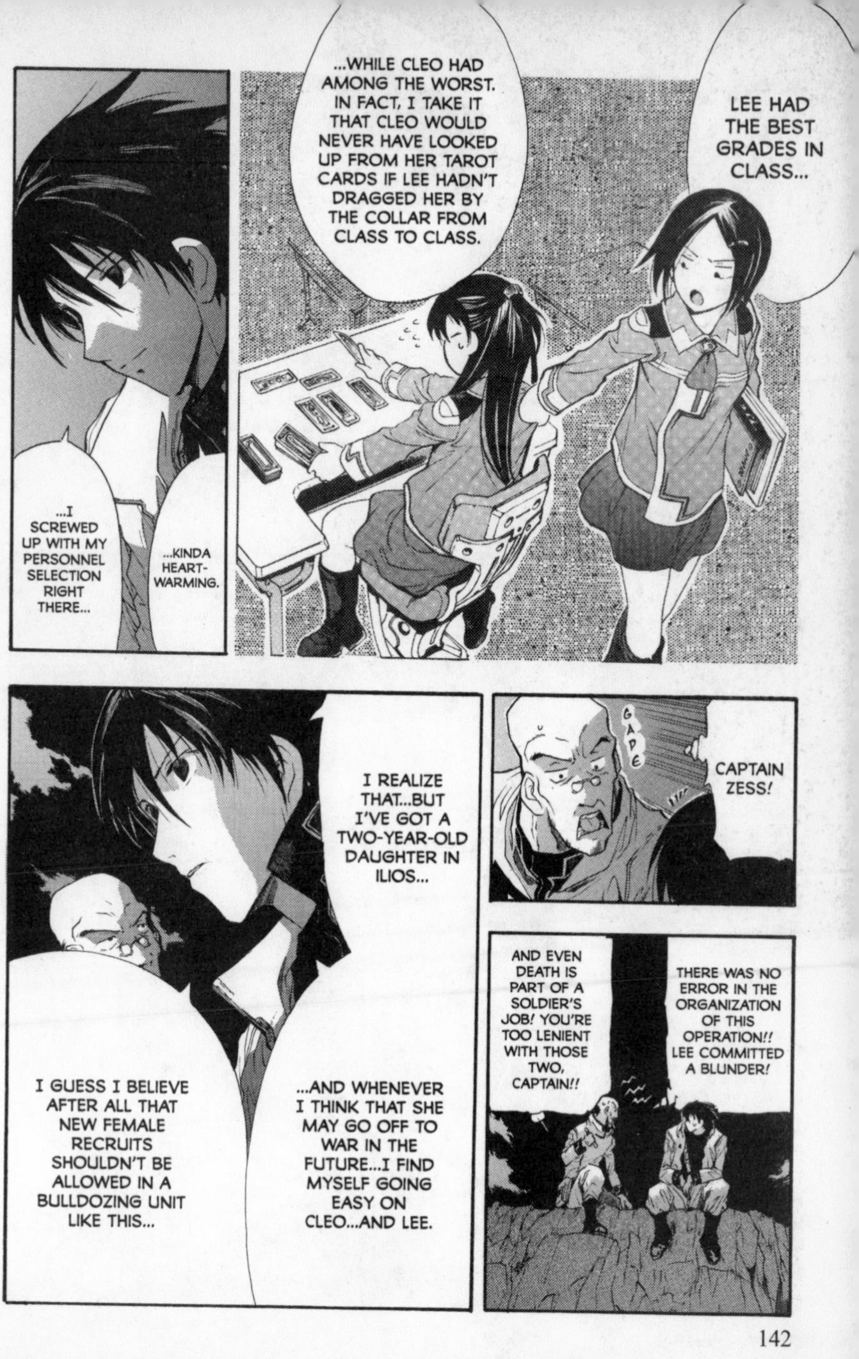
LEE HAD THE BEST GRADES IN CLASS...
...WHILE CLEO HAD AMONG THE WORST. IN FACT, I TAKE IT THAT CLEO WOULD NEVER HAVE LOOKED UP FROM HER TAROT CARDS IF LEE HADN'T DRAGGED HER BY THE COLLAR FROM CLASS TO CLASS.
...KINDA HEART-WARMING.
...I SCREWED UP WITH MY PERSONNEL SELECTION RIGHT THERE...
GADE
CAPTAIN ZESS!
THERE WAS NO ERROR IN THE ORGANIZATION OF THIS OPERATION!! LEE COMMITTED A BLUNDER!
AND EVEN DEATH IS PART OF A SOLDIER'S JOB! YOU'RE TOO LENIENT WITH THOSE TWO, CAPTAIN!!
I REALIZE THAT...BUT I'VE GOT A TWO-YEAR-OLD DAUGHTER IN ILIOS...
...AND WHENEVER I THINK THAT SHE MAY GO OFF TO WAR IN THE FUTURE...I FIND MYSELF GOING EASY ON CLEO...AND LEE.
I GUESS I BELIEVE AFTER ALL THAT NEW FEMALE RECRUITS SHOULDN'T BE ALLOWED IN A BULLDOZING UNIT LIKE THIS...

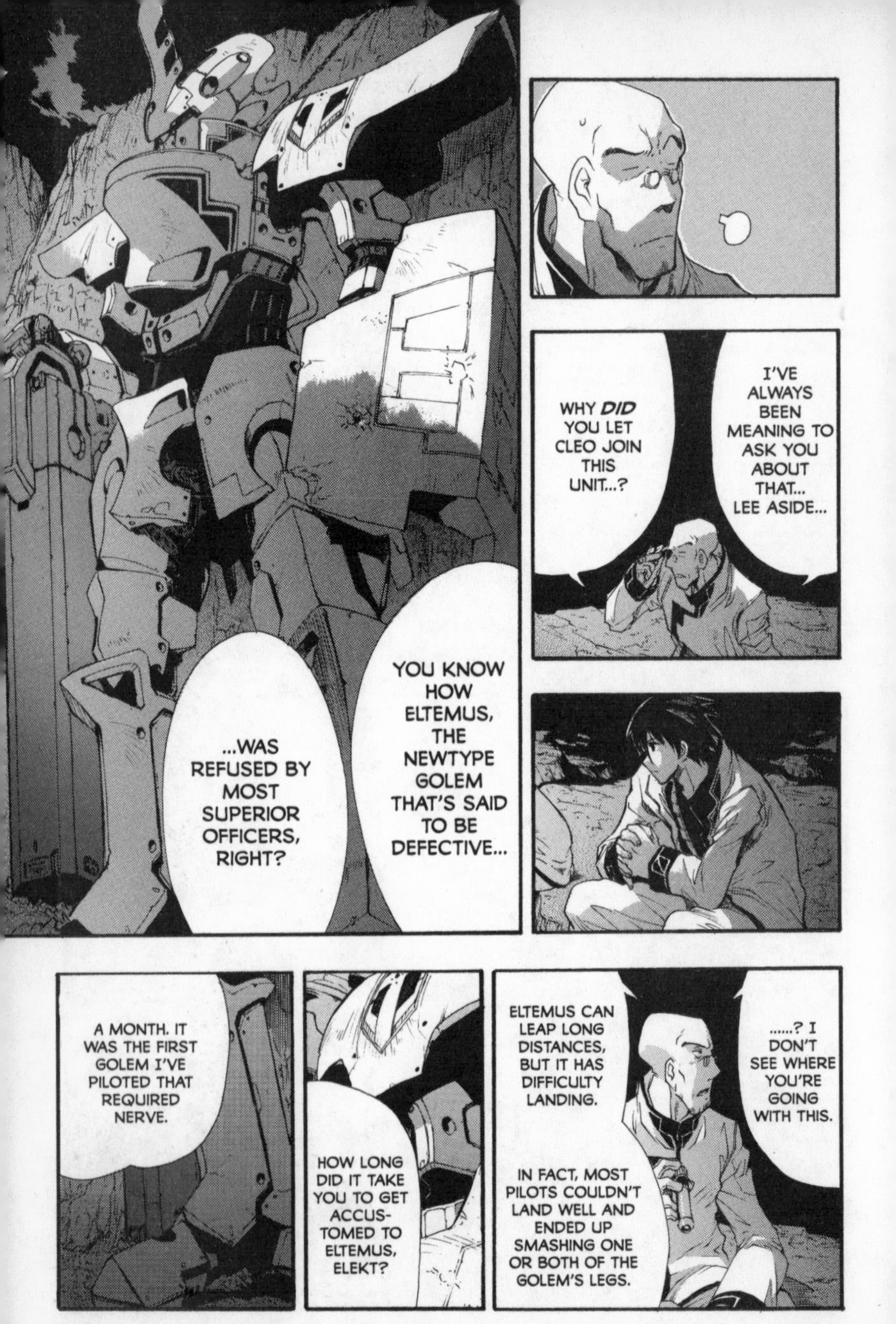
I'VE ALWAYS BEEN MEANING TO ASK YOU ABOUT THAT... LEE ASIDE...
WHY *DID* YOU LET CLEO JOIN THIS UNIT...?
YOU KNOW HOW ELTEMUS, THE NEWTYPE GOLEM THAT'S SAID TO BE DEFECTIVE...
...WAS REFUSED BY MOST SUPERIOR OFFICERS, RIGHT?
......? I DON'T SEE WHERE YOU'RE GOING WITH THIS.
ELTEMUS CAN LEAP LONG DISTANCES, BUT IT HAS DIFFICULTY LANDING.
IN FACT, MOST PILOTS COULDN'T LAND WELL AND ENDED UP SMASHING ONE OR BOTH OF THE GOLEM'S LEGS.
HOW LONG DID IT TAKE YOU TO GET ACCUS-TOMED TO ELTEMUS, ELEKT?
A MONTH. IT WAS THE FIRST GOLEM I'VE PILOTED THAT REQUIRED NERVE.

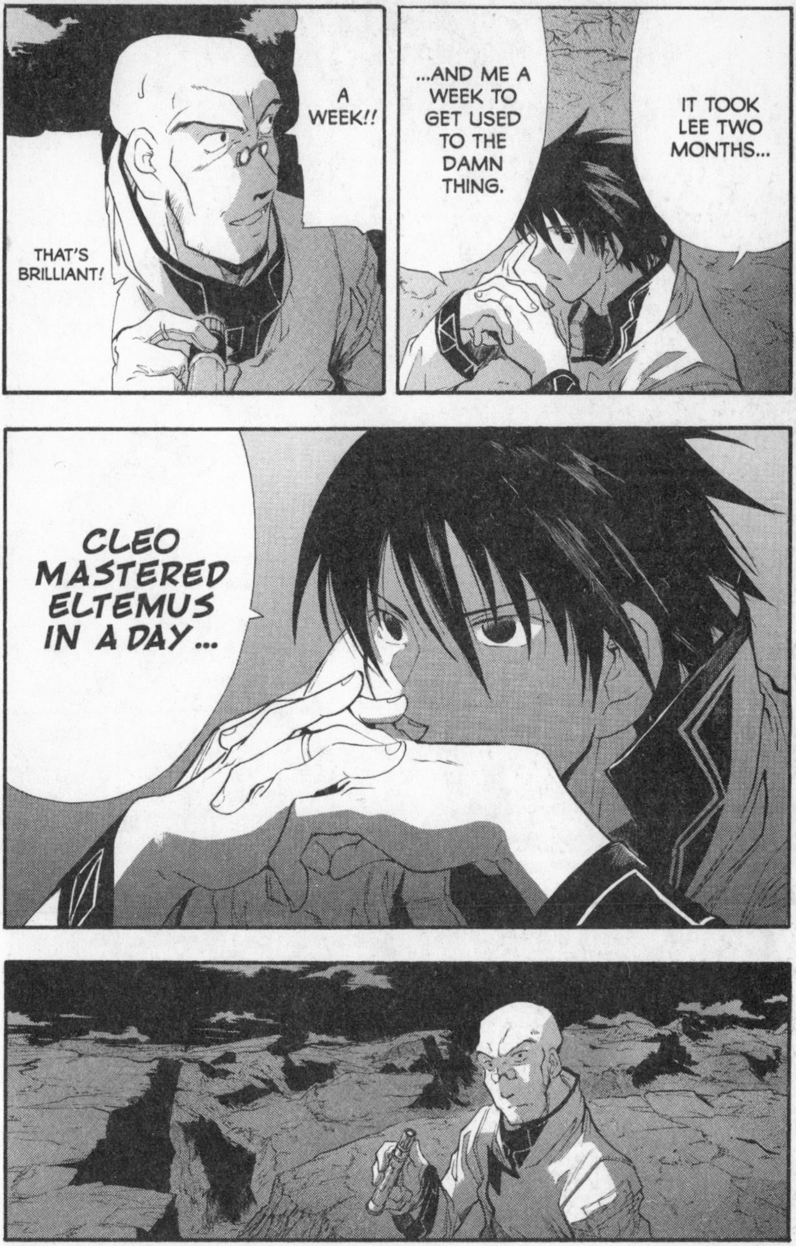
IT TOOK LEE TWO MONTHS...
...AND ME A WEEK TO GET USED TO THE DAMN THING.
A WEEK!!
THAT'S BRILLIANT!
CLEO MASTERED ELTEMUS IN A DAY...

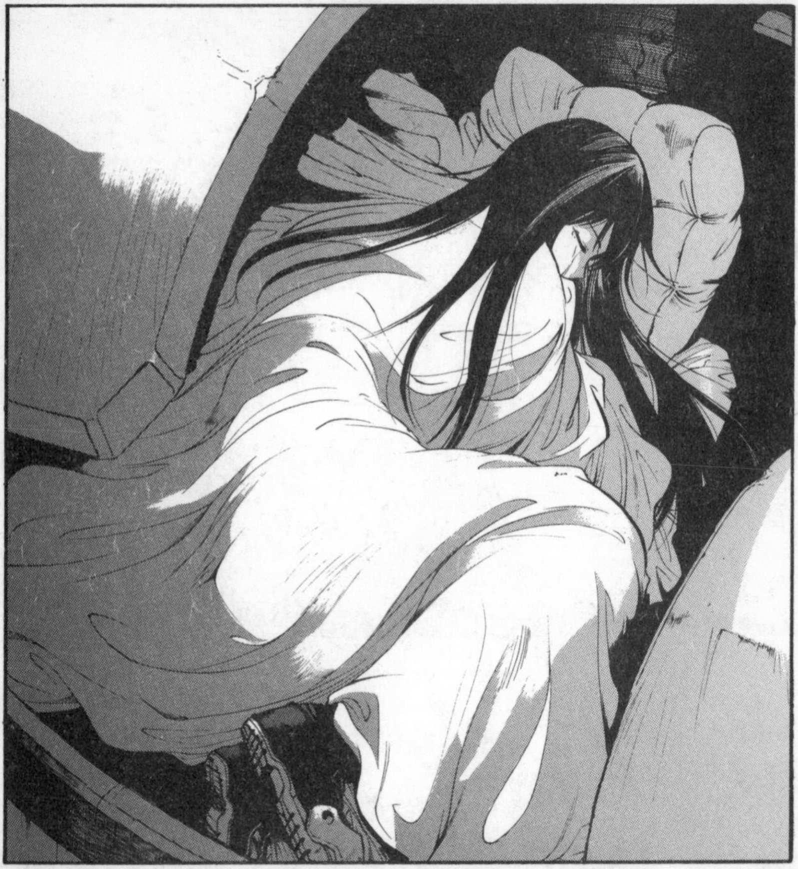
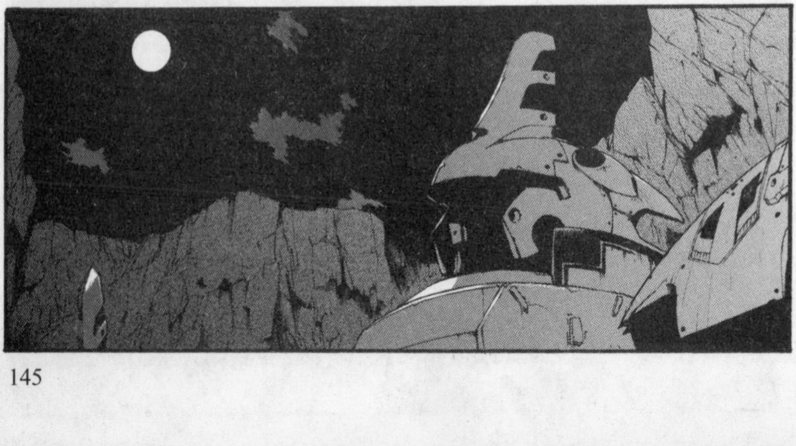

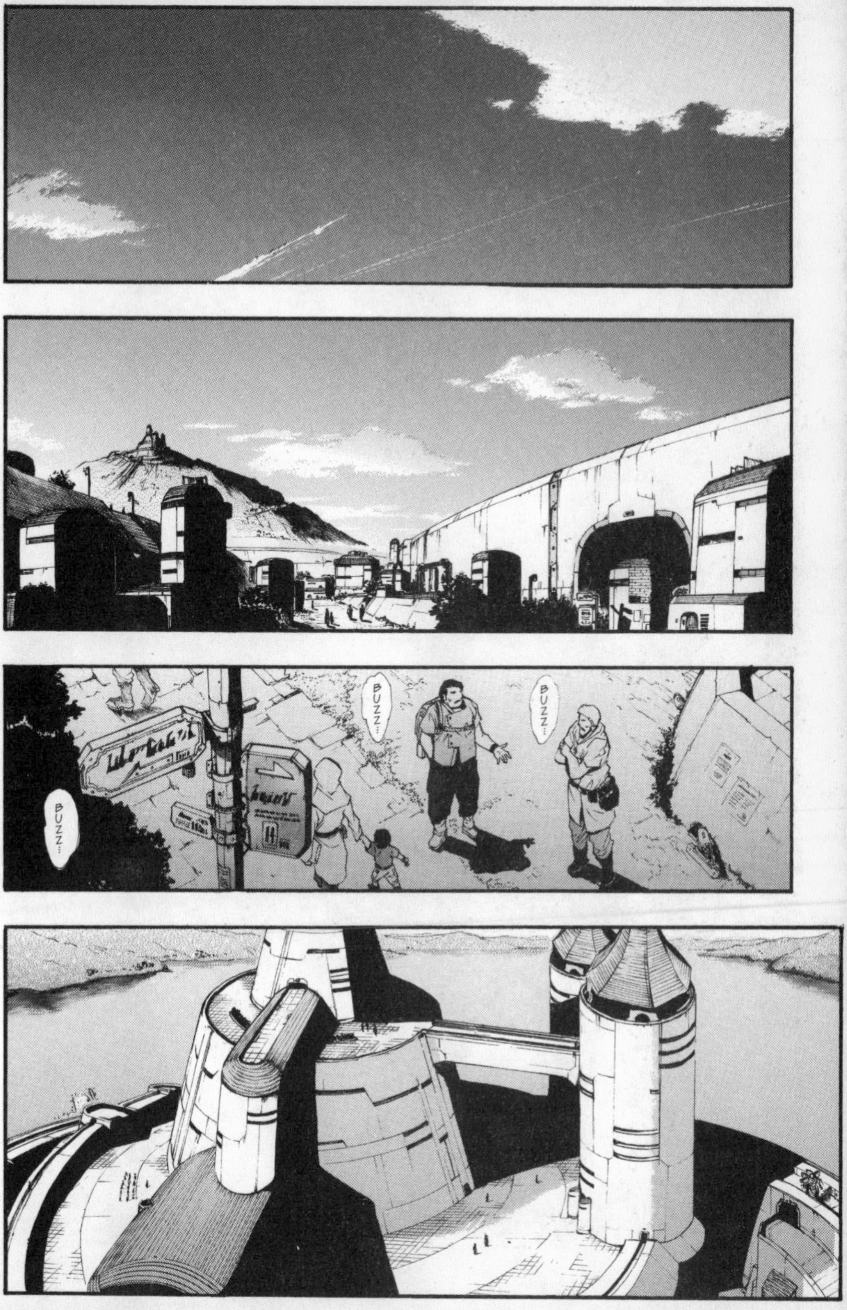
BUZZ...
BUZZ...
BUZZ...

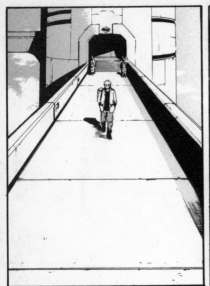

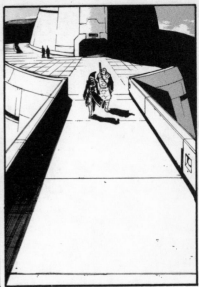

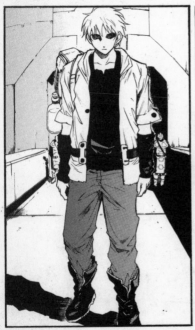

MEET ME
IN THE
HANGAR
AFTER
BREAKFA--

......!

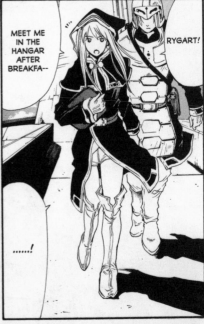

RYGART!

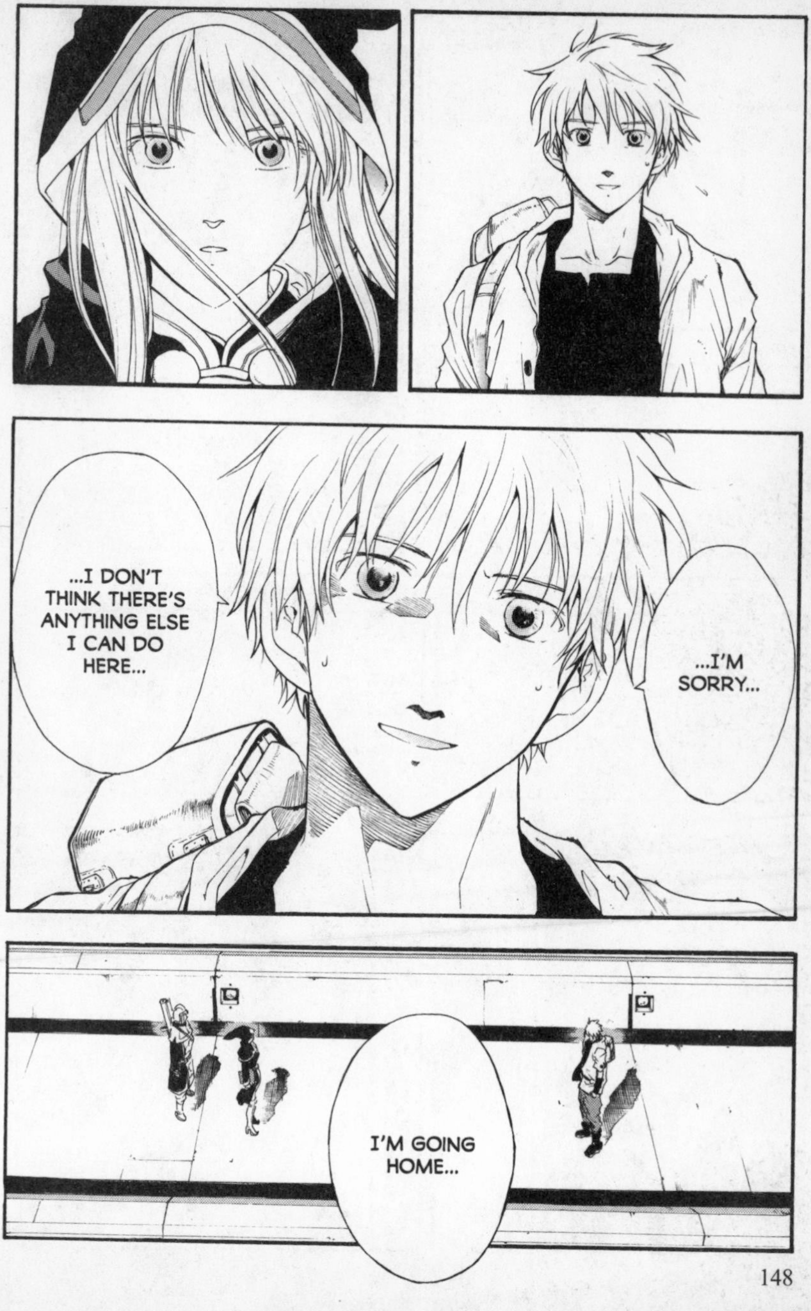
...I'M SORRY...
...I DON'T THINK THERE'S ANYTHING ELSE I CAN DO HERE...
I'M GOING HOME...

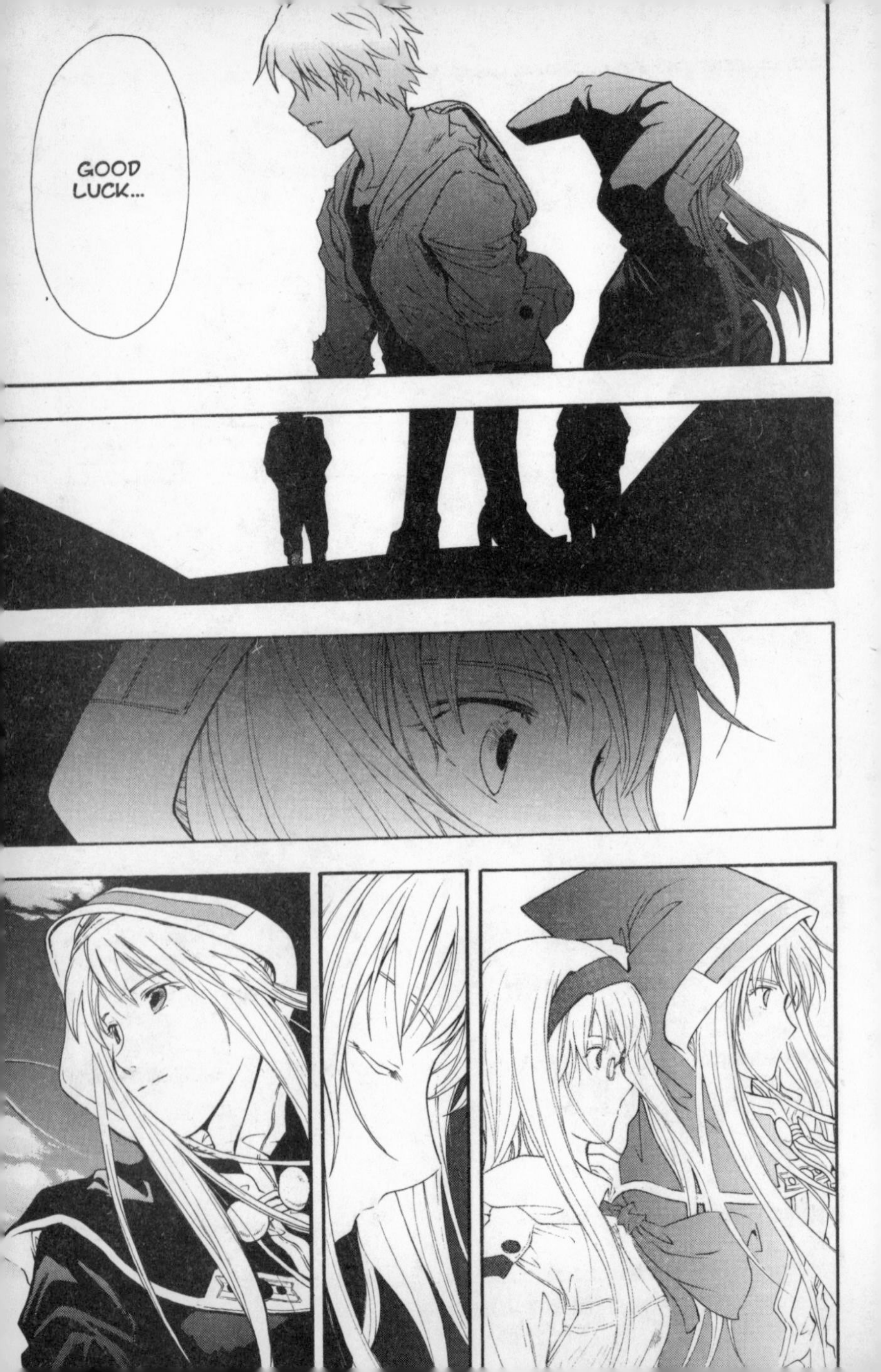
GOOD LUCK...

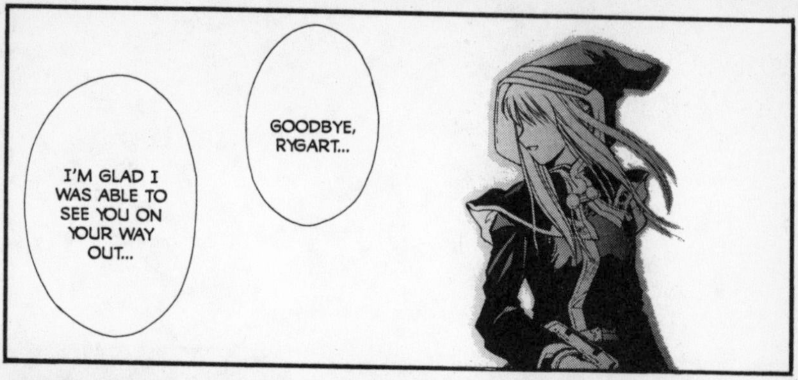
GOODBYE, RYGART...
I'M GLAD I WAS ABLE TO SEE YOU ON YOUR WAY OUT...
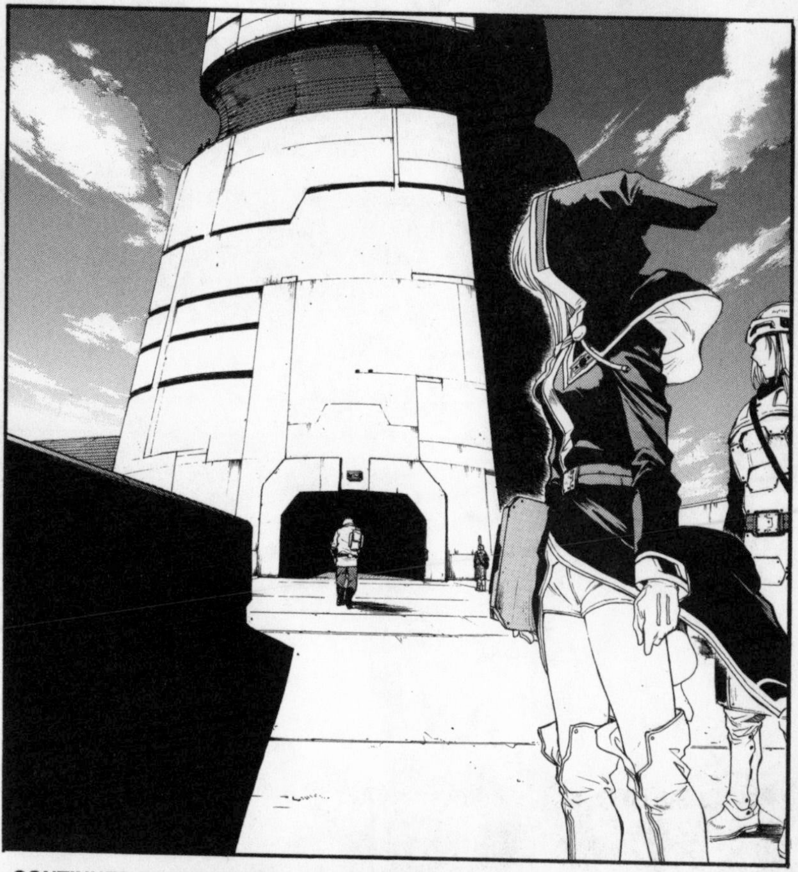
CONTINUED IN BROKEN BLADE VOLUME 3

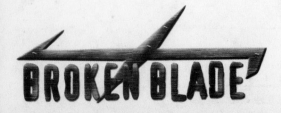
BROKEN BLADE

BROKEN BLADE

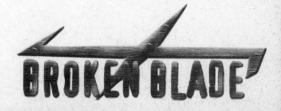

MAP OF THE CONTINENT OF CURZON

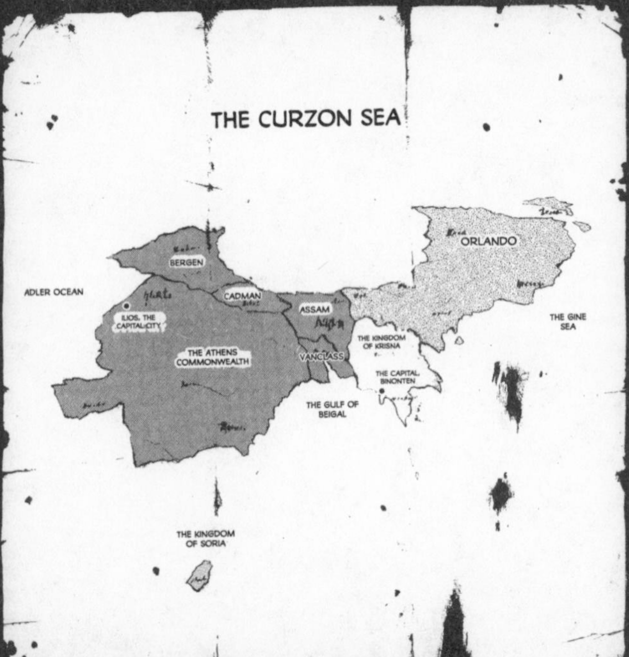
THE CURZON SEA
ORLANDO
BERGEN
ADLER OCEAN
CADMAN
ILIOS, THE CAPITAL CITY
ASSAM
THE GINE SEA
THE KINGDOM OF KRISNA
THE ATHENS COMMONWEALTH
VANCLASS
THE CAPITAL BINONTEN
THE GULF OF BEIGAL
THE KINGDOM OF SORIA

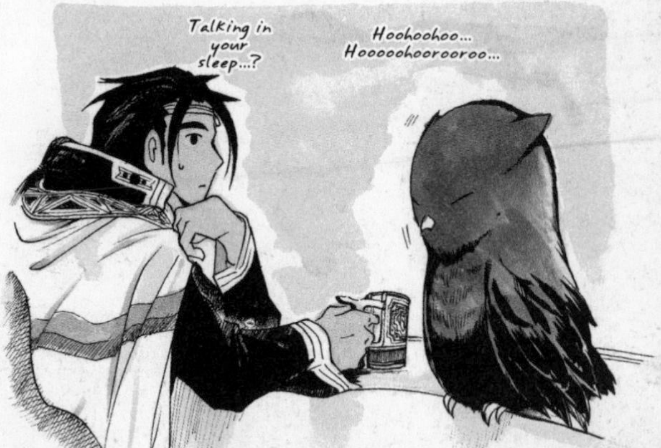
Hoohoohoo... Hoooohoorooroo...
Talking in your sleep...?

SIX YEARS AGO...

...784 CONTINENTAL ERA...

...AT THE ASSAM NATIONAL
MILITARY ACADEMY...

...A GIRL WAS BEING
OBSERVED.

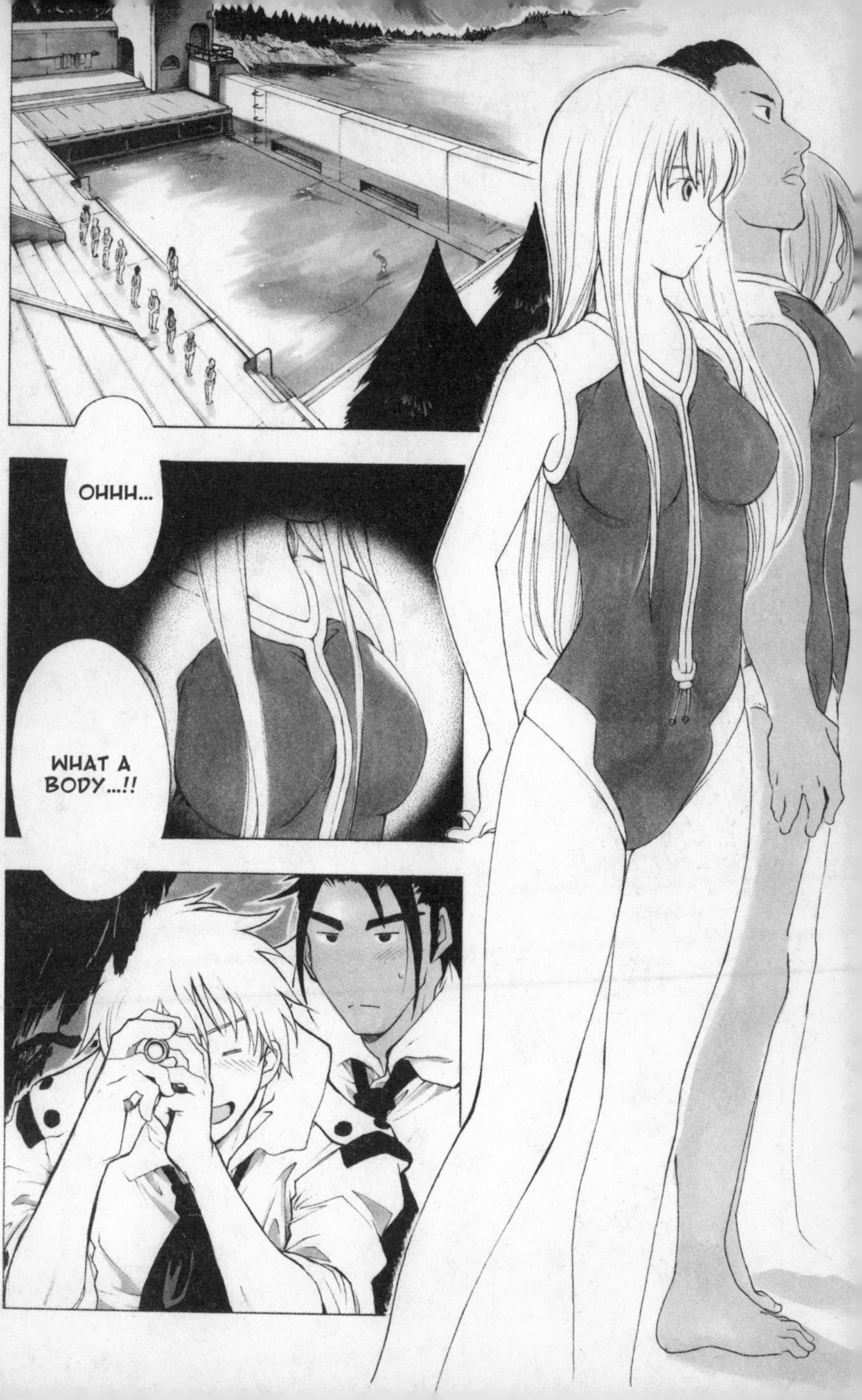
OHHH...
WHAT A BODY...!!

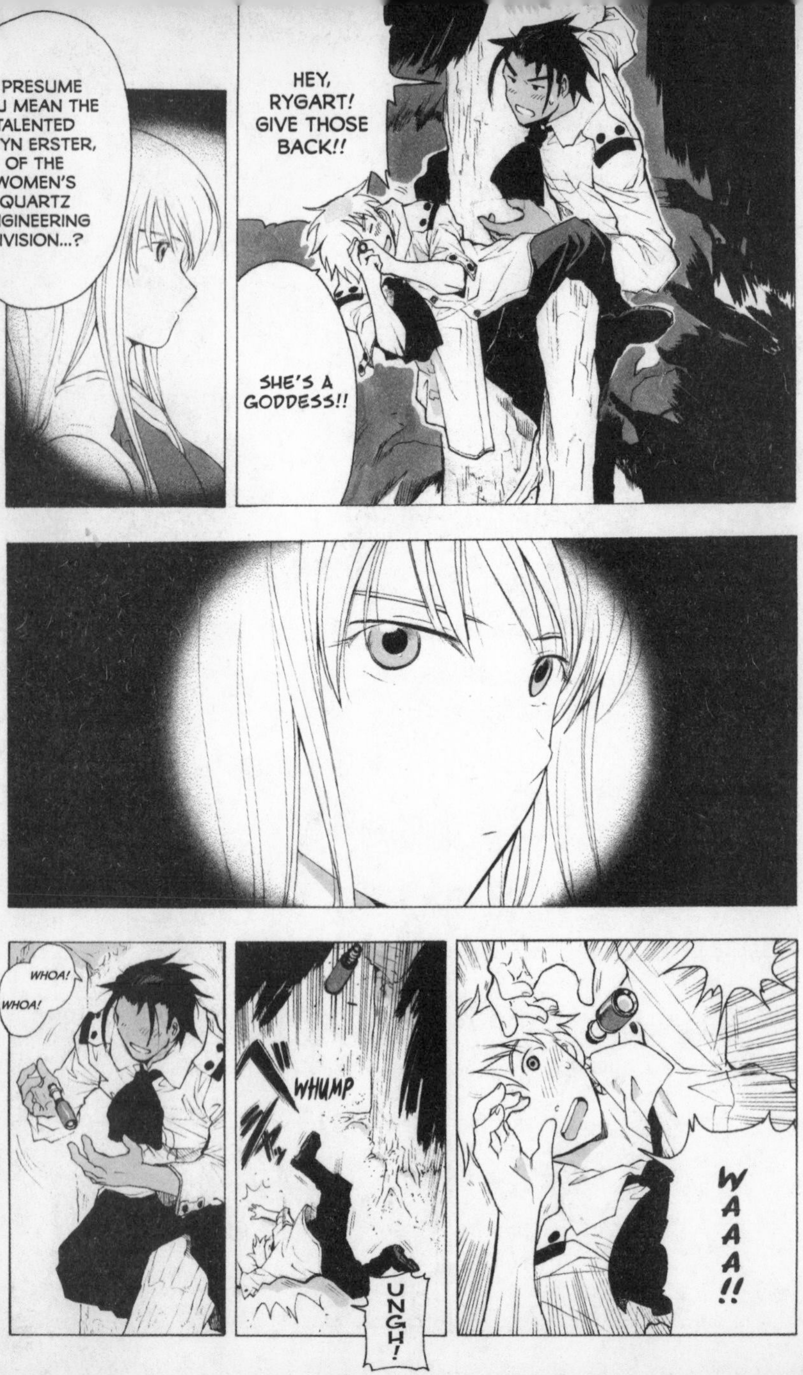
HEY, RYGART! GIVE THOSE BACK!!
SHE'S A GODDESS!!
I PRESUME YOU MEAN THE TALENTED SIGYN ERSTER, OF THE WOMEN'S QUARTZ ENGINEERING DIVISION...?
WAAAA!!
WHUMP
UNGH!
WHOA!
WHOA!

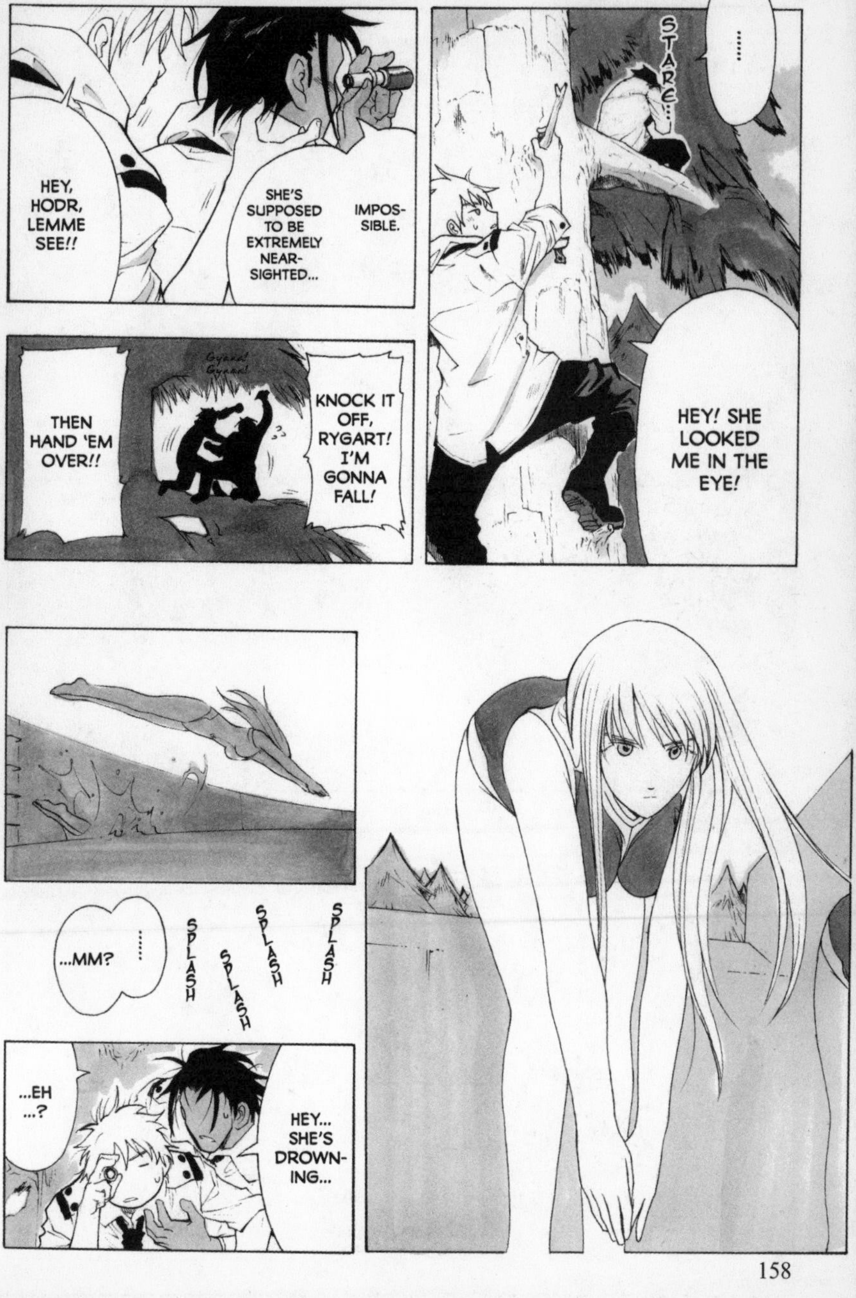
STARE...
......
HEY! SHE LOOKED ME IN THE EYE!
IMPOSSIBLE.
SHE'S SUPPOSED TO BE EXTREMELY NEAR-SIGHTED...
HEY, HODR, LEMME SEE!!
KNOCK IT OFF, RYGART! I'M GONNA FALL!
THEN HAND 'EM OVER!!
SPLASH
SPLASH
SPLASH
SPLASH
......
...MM?
HEY... SHE'S DROWNING...
...EH ...?

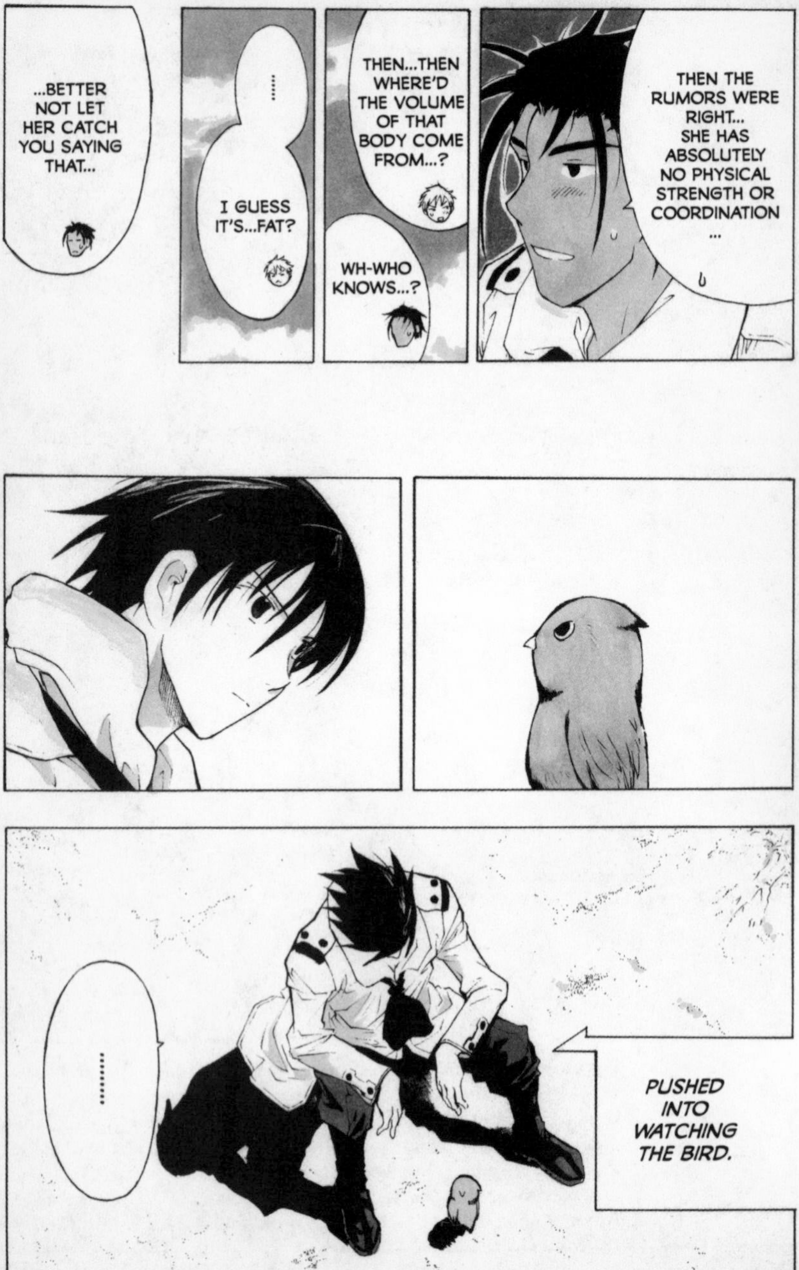
THEN THE RUMORS WERE RIGHT... SHE HAS ABSOLUTELY NO PHYSICAL STRENGTH OR COORDINATION ...
THEN...THEN WHERE'D THE VOLUME OF THAT BODY COME FROM...?
WH-WHO KNOWS...?
......
I GUESS IT'S...FAT?
...BETTER NOT LET HER CATCH YOU SAYING THAT...
PUSHED INTO WATCHING THE BIRD.
....

RYGART FACES ZESS IN A ONE-ON-ONE BATTLE!

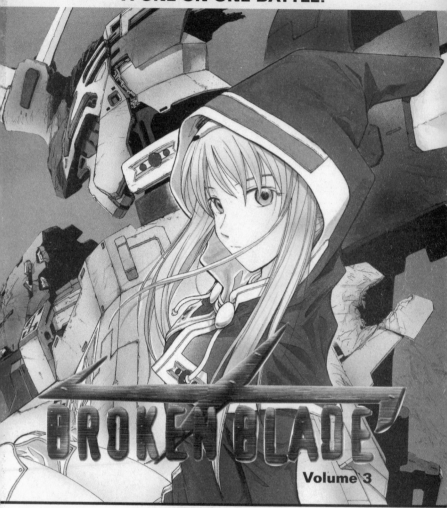

BROKEN BLADE

Volume 3

CMX

FLEX
COMIX

By Yunosuke Yoshinaga. Rygart deals with his guilt over the death of Dan, the Golem pilot. Later, he's officially sworn in as part of the Krisna army and his own Golem is outfitted with a new, external armor and given a new name. In the mountains outside of the royal city, Zess' unit sets up camp where they plot their next move. Cleo swears to exact revenge against the one responsible for Lee's death. But Rygart's going to have to take on his old friend Zess before Cleo gets her turn. On sale April, 2010.

BREAK BLADE Vol. 2 © 2007 Yunosuke Yoshinaga. All rights
reserved. First published in Japan in 2007 by Flex Comix Inc.,
Tokyo.

Broken Blade Volume 2, published by WildStorm Productions,
an imprint of DC Comics, 888 Prospect St. #240, La Jolla, CA
92037. English Translation © 2009 DC Comics. All Rights
Reserved. English translation rights arranged with FC Manga
Seisaku Fund and Flex Comix Inc. CMX is a trademark of DC
Comics. The stories, characters, and incidents mentioned in
this magazine are entirely fictional. Printed on recyclable
paper. WildStorm does not read or accept unsolicited
submissions of ideas, stories or artwork. Printed in Canada.

DC Comics, A Warner Bros. Entertainment Company.

This book is manufactured at a facility holding chain-of-
custody certification. This paper is made with sustainably
managed North American fiber.

Sheldon Drzka – Translation and Adaptation
MPS Ad Studio – Lettering
Larry Berry – Design
Sarah Farber – Assistant Editor
Jim Chadwick – Editor

ISBN: 978-1-4012-1883-6

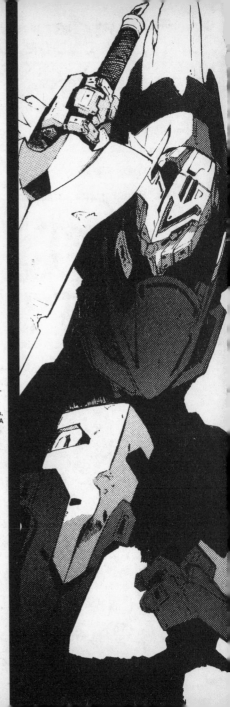

All the pages in this book were created—and are printed here—in Japanese RIGHT-to-LEFT format. No artwork has been reversed or altered, so you can read the stories the way the creators meant for them to be read.

RIGHT TO LEFT?!

Traditional Japanese manga starts at the upper right-hand corner, and moves right-to-left as it goes down the page. Follow this guide for an easy understanding.

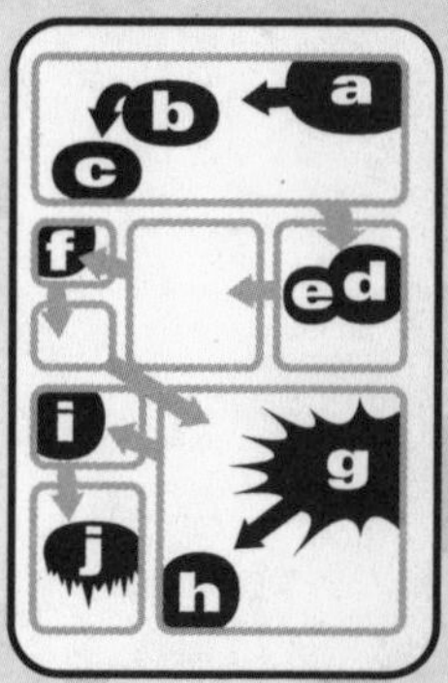
a
b
c
ed
f
g
h
i
j

For more information and sneak previews, visit cmxmanga.com. Call 1-888-COMIC BOOK for the nearest comics shop or head to your local book store.

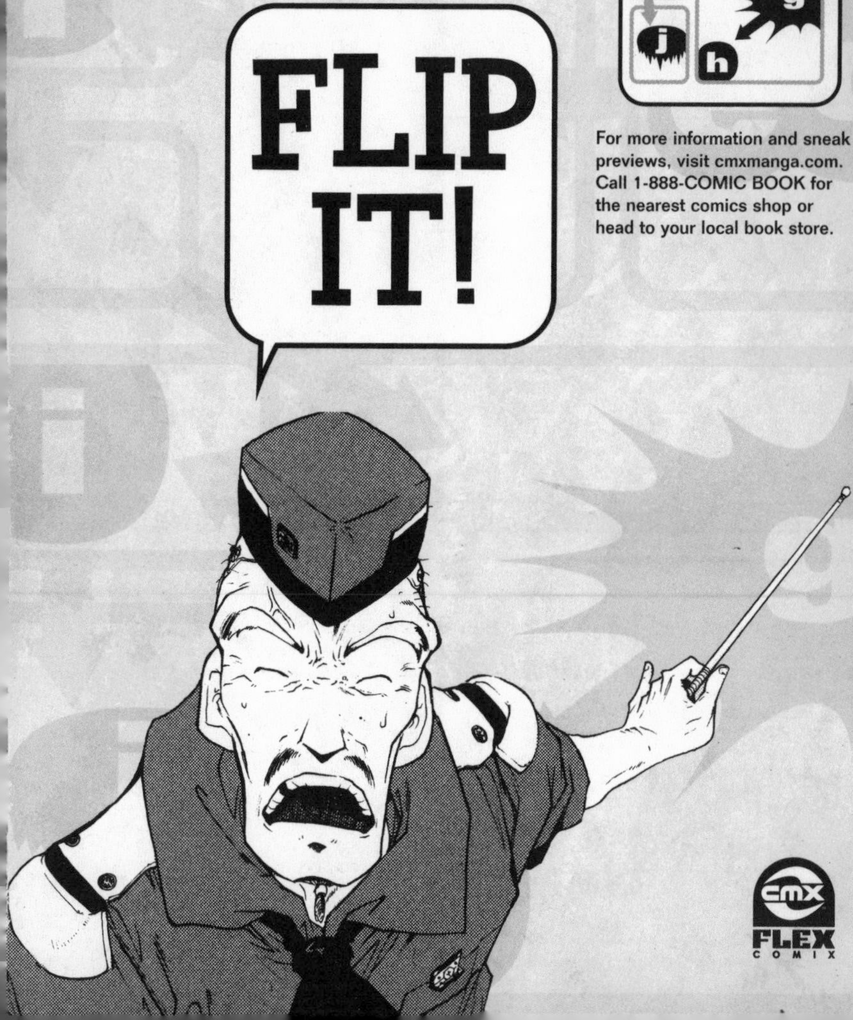
FLIP IT!